Women Playwrights
THE BEST PLAYS OF 1994

Women Playwrights:
THE BEST PLAYS OF 1994

edited by Marisa Smith

Contemporary Playwrights Series

SK
A Smith and Kraus Book

A Smith and Kraus Book
One Main Street PO Box 127 Lyme, NH 03768

Copyright © 1995 by Smith and Kraus, Inc.
All rights reserved
Cover and Text Design By Julia Hill
Manufactured in the United States of America
Cover Photos: Lynne Alvarez by A. Frank, Marlane Meyer by Wayne Shimabukuro,
Jacquelyn Reingold by John Abbott, Paula Vogel by Anne Sterling

First Edition: June 1995
10 9 8 7 6 5 4 3 2 1

Women Playwrights: The Best Plays of 1994
Contemporary Playwrights Series
ISSN 1067-327X
ISBN 1-880399-84-9

CONTENTS

Publisher's Note   vii
  by Marisa Smith

✳

OFF THE MAP   1
  by Joan Ackermann

THE REINCARNATION OF JAIMIE BROWN   51
  by Lynne Alvarez

MOE'S LUCKY SEVEN   117
  by Marlane Meyer

THE FAMILY OF MANN   167
  by Theresa Rebeck

GIRL GONE   233
  by Jacquelyn Reingold

HOT 'N' THROBBING   297
  by Paula Vogel

COME TO LEAVE   341
  by Allison Eve Zell

Marisa Smith has edited
Women Playwrights: The Best Plays of 1992,
Women Playwrights: The Best Plays of 1993,
Humana Festival '93: The Complete Plays,
Humana Festival '94: The Complete Plays,
EST Marathon '94: One-Act Plays,
EST Marathon '95: The Complete One-Act Plays,
and Showtime's Act One Festival '94: One-Act Plays.

PUBLISHER'S NOTE

Women Playwrights: The Best Plays of 1994 is the third volume in the Best Plays by Women Playwrights series initiated by Smith and Kraus in 1992.

Each year we consider plays, written by American women, that have premiered during that year's theatrical season. Submissions are made on a continuous basis by playwrights, agents, literary managers, and theatres.

Next year's book, *Women Playwrights: The Best Plays of 1995* will include plays that premiered between September 1, 1994 and August 31, 1995.

—*Marisa Smith*

Women Playwrights
THE BEST PLAYS OF 1994

OFF THE MAP
by Joan Ackermann

BIOGRAPHY

Joan Ackerman is a writer, actress, composer, and producer. In 1981, she co-founded Mixed Company, a year-round theatre which she continues to co-direct in Great Barrington, Massachusetts. Her plays that have premiered there include *Zara Spook and Other Lures*, *Bed and Breakfast*, *Rescuing Greenland*, *The Light of His Eye*, *Yonder Peasant*, *Off the Map*, and *Don't Ride the Clutch* which toured to the Edinburgh Theatre Festival Fringe in 1987. Actors Theatre of Louisville has produced *Zara Spook and Other Lures* as well as *Stanton''s Garage*, which was commissioned by the theatre. *Off the Map* was given a workshop reading at the Mark Taper Forum in Los Angeles. Ms. Ackerman's articles have appeared in *Time, the Atlantic, Esquire, GQ,* and several other magazines, including *Sports Illustrated* for whom she was a special contributor for six years.

AUTHOR'S NOTE

The first sentence of this play came into my head two summers ago when I was struggling to meet three deadlines for other projects. I couldn't ignore it; it was too loud, too clear, too self-possessed and intriguing. It took my brain by the hand and set me down typing. I was helplessly transported. Within an hour all the characters were there, fully formed, fully dressed, tickets in hand, waiting to get on the plane. That was it. The play still needs work and will undoubtedly get it, demanding thing that it is.

ORIGINAL PRODUCTION

OFF THE MAP was originally produced at Mixed Company under the direction of Robert Russell. The cast was as follows:

Adult Bo	Amy Judd
Bo	Anna Duhon/Vanessa Maroni
George	Mark Belcher/Jamey Schumacher
Charley	Buzz Gray
Arlene	Tamar Kotoske
William Gibbs	Andrew Hernon

CAST

ADULT BO, 35. Prim, conservative woman
BO, 11. Precocious, fiesty, sweet
ARLENE, 40. Earthy, sensual, maternal, wise
CHARLEY, 45. Inventive, normally energetic, high metabolism
GEORGE, 45. Big, heavy set, shy, loyal, a man of few words
WILLIAM, 28. Straight laced, restrained, intense

TIME

The present and early 1970s

SET

Off the map in Northern Mexico

OFF THE MAP

ACT ONE

A small bit of the front yard and homey inside of a cabin in northern New Mexico, creatively built out of logs, rocks, odd pieces. The kitchen area has a great wood table and chairs, old refrigerator, wood stove, a couch made out of wood and cushions, and a bathtub for winter use. Dried flowers and herbs hang from the ceiling. A screen door leads from the kitchen out to a side porch which should be like a clear open deck, a useful playing space.

SCENE ONE

ADULT BO: The summer my father was depressed, the face of our Lord Jesus Christ appeared on a tortilla at the Morning Glory cafe. Sophie, who saw the face emerge and fainted dead away, wanted to shellac it, put some sealer on to preserve it for all eternity. It was a wish of vanity for she'd hoped only to extend her new found notoriety. But time had its way and within the year the face was gone though something of its anguish lingered. It hung on a nail by the door at the Morning Glory and pilgrims came to bear witness. From the start, my father said it resembled not Jesus Christ but the devil; then later, Pinky Lee. My mother, a hellraiser and a cynic, never even went and looked. That was the summer a saint appeared on our doorstep, dazed and sore of foot, in a white shirt in the heat of high noon. Something of his anguish still lingers, hangs on a nail in my heart. I look to that summer for answers to great mysteries, of deep love. And loss.

(*Lights up on the cabin interior. Charley is sitting in his chair. Bo ties fishing flies at the table. George is standing awkwardly.*)

BO: Sit down, George.

GEORGE: I guess I'll be going.

BO: You said that twenty minutes ago.

(*Pause.*)

GEORGE: What are you tying?

BO: I'm still tying the same Yellow Sally, George. And if you ask me one more time, I'm liable to get vexed.

(*Pause.*)

GEORGE: Well. So long, Charley. Bo.

(*Charley nods, not looking at him, incapable of responding more. George doesn't move, keeps staring at Charley.*)

ADULT BO'S VOICE: It loomed like a dark cloud in our home, my father's depression. It was inescapable, like some fumigator's mist, filling our lungs. It came to be the focal point of our lives that summer, the geological formation around which everything else was defined. It grew in heft and weight, altering everything. George, my father's best friend and never any too swift, was undone by it. At a loss. Diminished. Ten feet away from the man he loved most, he may as well have been watching Charley on the far side of China in a sinking ship, going down.

(*George exits.*)

BO: Halleluja.

(*Bo looks at Charley who gets up and goes to the kitchen area to pour himself a glass of water. She moves over to the couch and settles in with a book as he sits back down. Arlene enters with a large stack of library books, the mail, and an old accordion.*)

ARLENE: Look what I found in the dump. I heard it moaning way down deep. Buried alive, isn't it a beauty? What have you two been up to? Planning a hold-up?

BO: George was here.

ARLENE: Oh yeah? How's George?

BO: Same.

ARLENE: That's the beauty of George; always reliably himself.

(*Arlene is tidying, moving about.*)

BO: Pardon me for saying it, but I think George is a little light in the loafers.

ARLENE: What does that mean?

BO: It means he's queer.

ARLENE: (*Studies her.*) Have you been outside at all today? Here, you got a package from Drake's, a brochure from an ocean liner, are you planning on taking a cruise, and a letter from American Express.

BO: (*Jumping up.*) At last.

ARLENE: What is it?

BO: It's an application for a card.

ARLENE: Mm. What are you going to do with your American Express card?

BO: Buy stuff. Buy a real house. With a lawn and an inbuilt sprinkler system. Buy a one-way ticket out of this hell hole.

ARLENE: Where would you go?

BO: Somewhere normal where I can be a girl scout.

ARLENE: You can be a girl scout right here. I'll take you, I told you.

BO: I can't be a girl scout. We don't have any money to buy a uniform.

ARLENE: I'll find you a used one.

BO: I don't want to be a used girl scout.

ARLENE: Ruth-Anne's daughter was a scout, I'll bet they kept her uniform.

BO: Don't you realize, if I wear Ruth-Anne's daughter's old used uniform, I'd be wearing Ruth-Anne's daughter's old used experience as a girl scout? I'd be as faded as that worn green cloth. I'd never earn any patches.

ARLENE: Bo, quit whining. (*To Charley.*) You got another card from your sister, Charley.

BO: I'll read it to you. (*Bo tears envelope while Arlene opens another letter.*) It's another get-well card, what do you wanna bet? I'll bet it is... I'll bet. Yup. It is. "Best Wishes for a Speedy Recovery." All of Greta's cards have hot-air balloons on them. That's Greta's idea of cheerful and uplifting—a multi-colored hot-air balloon.

ARLENE: We're getting audited.

BO: What does that mean?

ARLENE: Someone from the IRS is coming to review our tax forms. That's quite amusing.

BO: Why is that quite amusing?

ARLENE: Considering our annual income is less than five thousand dollars a year, it is.

Bo: I think if we had a television you wouldn't think it was so amusing. If we didn't live off the map. If we had a phone and plumbing like normal Americans. You might think it was pretty pathetic.

ARLENE: Bo, go weed the garden. You are woefully behind.

Bo: What if the bear is out there?

ARLENE: If the bear is out there, come back and tell me and I'll shoot him.

Bo: What if he attacks me first and I can't make it back to tell you?

ARLENE: No bear in his right mind would tangle with the likes of you.

(*Bo laces up her boots.*)

Bo: When my American Express card comes…

ARLENE: Yes?

Bo: I'm out of here.

(*Bo exits.*)

ARLENE: I saw Rifkin at the P.O. He asked after you. He's got some pigs he wants to trade us for wood. I got the Notebooks of Leonardo Da Vinci out again. Charley, do you think you could put the other muffler on? The old one is rusted to hell, I can't get the bolts off to save my life. (*Pause.*) If you feel like it.

(*Lights fade on them and up on Bo who is outside.*)

SCENE TWO

Bo is outside near Adult Bo. She is kneeling, maybe doing mystical motions with her hands.

Bo: Dear God, it's me again, Bo Groden the one stranded out in the middle of tarnation meaning nowhere. Word has it that the face of your lone and treasured son has appeared on a tortilla. I wonder if you could possibly send me some sign like that to give me hope that one day I will escape out of the desert into the real world. If you could just give me some sign, just really a very little sign, like maybe turning this stone a different color by three o'clock tomorrow afternoon. I'd appreciate it. Amen.

(*Lights fade on Bo and up on the deck.*)

Scene Three

On the deck Arlene is fixing the accordion, cleaning it, taping up the holes. George stands, looking on.

ARLENE: I read an article in the library today about how when you're depressed a real long time, when you just cry and cry, your body goes through a chemical change. Sometimes you need drugs to get out of it. I could try to get him some drugs, from the V.A. hospital down in Albuquerque. Think it'd be worth my driving down there, George? Most likely they'd want a prescription. Charley would never talk to a psychiatrist. Can't even get him in a dentist's chair, he yanked his own tooth out last week. The gum was all nasty, he grabbed a pair of pliers and pulled it out. I think the physical pain was a welcome relief, he came closer to cracking a smile than he has in four months would you put a piece of tape right there? I'm gonna need some drugs myself pretty soon. So. George, say something. I don't need two silent men on my hands.

GEORGE: I bought him some watercolors.

ARLENE: Watercolors? That's a good idea. Did you give them to him?

GEORGE: No.

ARLENE: You want me to? Tell him they're from you?

GEORGE: Don't tell him they're from me.

ARLENE: The problem is he's deeply ashamed on top of it all. And that does not help. *(Slaps herself.)* Damn, these horse flies are big enough to throw a saddle on. Would you take Bo fishing tomorrow? She's mad at the world.

(George nods.)

GEORGE: You have any paper?

ARLENE: Paper?

GEORGE: For him to watercolor on?

ARLENE: I'm sure we do. We've got rolls of wallpaper from the dump, he could fool around on the back.

(George nods. Pause.)

GEORGE: There wouldn't be glue back there?

ARLENE: Glue? I don't think so. George, would you mind going to a psychiatrist? To get a prescription so we could get him some drugs? I've got some names. What a face. George, what all you have done for that man—carried him near-to-dead down off a mountain, pulled him out from under a jeep in Korea, you're not up to lying on a couch, telling someone how much you hate your mother?

GEORGE: I love my mother.

ARLENE: Well, tell him how much you love your mother. Tell him you love your mother so much it's got you all depressed you need some drugs. I can't do it, wouldn't be the right dosage. Give it some thought, okay? (*Arlene looks up at the sky.*) He likes it better when it's overcast. He can't tolerate sunshine, he says. Can you imagine that? Charley Groden, Mr. Sunshine. I guess the bright light makes the shadows in him feel even darker.

(*Lights fade as Arlene takes the accordion and goes inside.*)

SCENE FOUR

Lights up on Adult Bo.

ADULT BO: I live in Salt Lake City now. I am blessed with a split level ranch with central vacuuming, air-conditioning, cable TV and a self-cleaning oven. I am executive secretary in a small investment firm and though the vice-president airily chirps in his foolish voice that when I type my fingers fairly tapdance on the keys, he has recently entrusted three major portfolios to my care.

(*Lights up on Bo and George who fish off the edge of the deck.*)

BO: George?

GEORGE: Mm?

BO: Bank accounts. How many numbers and how many letters are there in a bank account number?

GEORGE: I don't know.

BO: Well, you have a bank account, don't you? Do you have a check on you, you could look at? Maybe in your wallet?

GEORGE: Yeah, I do.

BO: What's your bank account number, just for example.

(*George takes out his wallet and looks at a check in it.*)

BO: GH62415380. Okay. (*Repeats, memorizing.*) GH62415380. GH62415380. Okay, and say, in a person's social security number?

I know there's three blanks, then two, then four. Is it all numbers or are there letters mixed in there? What, for instance, is your social security number?

GEORGE: I don't know.

BO: It's on your license. *(Pause.)* Here, give it to me. *(She reads his license.)* 034-38-8184. So it's just all numbers. Okay. GH62415380.

GEORGE: Why?

BO: Just wondering.

(Lights on them go to half and come up on Adult Bo.)

ADULT BO: The cabin where I grew up is four hundred miles south east of here in northern New Mexico and frankly that is not distance enough for me. Especially in the summer when my mind returns to that one summer twenty-four years ago my mother feared my father would take his life; returns and walks the landscape of my memories the way my father used to walk the dump, fingering piles and piles of junk, looking for something to salvage.

(Lights back up to full on Bo and George.)

GEORGE: Why?

BO: How was the psychiatrist?

GEORGE: She was a woman.

BO: Did she give you a prescription?

GEORGE: No.

BO: You didn't act depressed enough.

GEORGE: She wants to see me again next week.

BO: Really? Why? *(Pause.)* Why, George?

GEORGE: *(Embarrassed.)* I think she likes me.

(Lights fade.)

SCENE FIVE

Lights up on Arlene who enters the kitchen area. George exits with the fishing poles while Bo watches Arlene.

ARLENE: Charley? Charley? Charley! Charley, where are you? Charley! Oh Jesus Charley answer me where are you? Charley! *(Screaming.)* CHARLEY!!

(She goes out onto the deck, still shouting for him.)

Bo: Dad!

Arlene: CHARLEY!!

Bo: DAD! There he is.

(Charley enters from down front. Walks slowly up to Arlene. She tries to conceal a huge sigh of relief.)

Arlene: Charley, please do me this one favor. Please, if you go somewhere just let me know where you'll be? Okay?

(Charley puts his hand on her and nods. Heads into the house. She follows.)

Arlene: Where you going?

Charley: Bed.

Arlene: You want some company?

(He looks after her and shrugs, not knowing the answer. Turns and exits. She follows. Meanwhile Bo has picked up the stone to see if it's changed color. She goes into the house, takes a piece of paper and pen, sits down to write a letter.)

Bo: Dear Public Relations People, Thank you very much for the case of Hostess Twinkies. As you know I was quite dismayed to find some mold in the package which I had purchased at our local supermarket. Unfortunately, in the samples which you sent, one Twinkie contained what I can only describe as a rodent part. Internal organ or foot, I'm not sure. I wonder if you would send me some more and I will not mention this problem to my many friends. Thank you. Your concerned customer, Bo Groden.

(She folds the letter, puts it in an envelope and licks it. Gets into the bathtub and turns on a cassette player which plays Willie "The Lion" Smith's "Rites of Spring". She swings her legs to the music. Lights fade.)

Scene Six

It is night time. Charley is lying on the couch. Bo is lying in the bathtub with pillows in it, her legs hanging out over the edge. Arlene is reading to them by the light of a kerosene lamp, her voice compelling and serene.

Arlene: *(Reading.)* "One night, while we were in the tropics, I went out to the end of the flying-jib-boom upon some duty, and, having finished it, turned round, and lay over the boom for a long time, admiring the beauty of the sight before me. Being so far out from the deck, I could look at the ship as a separate vessel; and there rose up from the water, supported only by the small black hull, a pyramid of canvas, spreading out far beyond the hull, and towering up almost as it seemed in the indistinct night air, to the clouds."

BO: Excuse me but is there any stew left?

ARLENE: There is. I'll get you some. *(Arlene puts down the book. She goes to the stove and spoons a bowlful of stew.)* You want some more cornbread, too?

BO: No thank you.

ARLENE: Charley? Stew?

(He shakes his head. Arlene gives Bo the bowl.)

BO: Thanks.

ARLENE: You're welcome.

(Arlene goes back to her seat and the book and Bo eats the stew in the bathtub.)

(During the following, Adult Bo moves to the deck where she sits, her back leaning against the house, her legs stretched out in front of her. Gradually, lights fade on the others and moonlight comes up on her, listening.)

ARLENE: "The sea was as still as an inland lake; the light trade-wind was gently and steadily breathing from astern; the dark blue sky was studded with the tropical stars; there was no sound but the rippling of the water under the stem; and the sails were spread out, wide and high,—the two lower studding-sails stretching on each side far beyond the deck; the topmast studding-sails like wings to the topsails; the top-gallant studding-sails spreading fearlessly out above them; still higher, the two royal studding-sails, looking like two kites flying from the same string; and, highest of all, the little skysail, the apex of the pyramid, seeming actually to touch the stars, and to be out of reach of human hand. So quiet, too, was the sea, and so steady the breeze, that if these sails had been sculptured marble they could not have been more motionless. Not a ripple upon the surface of the canvas; not even a quivering of the extreme edges of the sail, so perfectly were they distended by the breeze."

(The moonlight rests on Adult Bo who has been drawn in in spite of herself.)

Scene Seven

Lights come up to full on Adult Bo.

ADULT BO: The afternoon William Gibbs arrived, my mother was weeding naked in the garden, dressed only in a Goodwill golf cap and my father's unlaced army boots. I realized even then as a young tender child, that it was that first blinding sight of her naked flesh that bonded William to us preternaturally, that set him on his fateful course with the Grodens. It was he who screamed. My mother's response was to grab a hoe and look down quick for snakes; then, seeing none, to ask him what his business was. Only when he kept his back to her and outlined his mission to the chicken house did it dawn on her to reach for Charley's coat off the scarecrow and cover herself. As I've already told you, she was a hell-raiser and a cynic. Shameless.

(Arlene enters from down front, from the garden, dressed only in a man's coat, golf cap and unlaced army boots. She is followed by William, a clean-cut young man dressed in a rumpled suit, hair combed down; highly flustered. He carries a briefcase.)

WILLIAM: I would have called to let you know I was coming but your phone number is unlisted.

ARLENE: We don't have a phone.

WILLIAM: No phone?

ARLENE: Would you like something cold to drink?

(They enter the cabin. He glances at his hand. Stares at her.)

WILLIAM: Fine. Thank you. Is Mr. Groden here?

ARLENE: Mr. Groden is here but he's not feeling very well. I think you're the first person wearing a suit who's come into our home.

WILLIAM: I'm sorry.

ARLENE: That's all right, don't apologize. I'm surprised you found us, all the way out here.

WILLIAM: It did take me a while. Four days, actually.

ARLENE: The IRS puts you up in a hotel, in town?

WILLIAM: Sometimes. Actually, I spent the last two nights in my car.

ARLENE: *(She studies him.)* Well, your suit looks very neat, considering.

WILLIAM: Thank you.

ARLENE: Where is your car?

WILLIAM: It's about two or three miles that way. *(Thinks.)* That way.

ARLENE: We'll give you a lift back. We never use the road; we just go cross-country. *(He continues staring at her.)* So.

WILLIAM: Ah, Mrs. Groden, have you been getting notices from us?

ARLENE: We have. We've gotten several.

WILLIAM: *(Nodding.)* Good.

ARLENE: *(Sitting him down.)* Now I can offer you some iced tea, but maybe you'd enjoy a glass of wild-chokecherry wine as well. I think you deserve it.

(Bo opens the door and enters. She sees William in his suit and exclaims:)

BO: Oh my God. Saved.

ARLENE: Saved? This is my daughter, Bo.

WILLIAM: Hello, Bo.

BO: How do you do. My full name is...Cecilia...

ARLENE: Cecilia?

BO: Cecilia-Amanda. I mean...Cecilia-Rose.

WILLIAM: Hello, Cecilia-Rose. I'm William Gibbs.

ARLENE: William Gibbs. *(Giving him iced tea and wine.)* Here you go.

BO: *(Embarrassed.)* Mom.

ARLENE: What?

BO: Don't you want to put some clothes on?

ARLENE: Clothes. Oh.

(Arlene exits. William, parched, quickly downs both glasses of liquid.)

BO: I like your tie. *(Pause.)* Yup. I like it.

WILLIAM: *(Awkwardly.)* What grade are you in, Cecilia-Rose?

BO: I'm home schooled. Have you been working for the IRS for long, Mr. Gibbs?

WILLIAM: As a matter of fact, I just recently made a career switch.

BO: Mm.

WILLIAM: I was a short order cook.

BO: *(Smiling.)* Sounds like you've been around.

(Pause.)

WILLIAM: Your father's not feeling well?

BO: He's depressed. I've been to New York City.

WILLIAM: Really?

BO: I was very small at the time. One, I believe. They have a good mass transit system, don't they? Would you like to stay for dinner?

WILLIAM: Dinner? Uh… no thank you. I'll need to be getting back. It's a long drive.

BO: I'll be leaving soon myself. I'm not going to be living here much longer.

WILLIAM: Oh, no?

BO: I'm just helping Arlene and Charley out.

WILLIAM: Ah.

BO: That's a very nice briefcase.

WILLIAM: Thank you.

BO: I like that briefcase. You could carry the word in that briefcase. I'll be ordering a briefcase very like that soon. What's wrong with your hand?

(Arlene enters. dressed in her own clothes.)

WILLIAM: My hand? *(Rolls back his sleeve. His arm is covered with welts.)*

ARLENE: Good Lord, look at your arm, you're covered with bites. You've been stung.

(She gets ice cubes out of the refrigerator and puts them in a bucket.)

ARLENE: Why didn't you say anything? We keep bees. For honey. I'm so sorry.

WILLIAM: Don't be sorry, I don't mind. *(Studying them.)* They really swell up, don't they? I've never been stung before.

ARLENE: No?

WILLIAM: *(Fascinated.)* A new experience.

ARLENE: Here, put your arm down in the ice, it'll numb the pain. You better take your ring off. Your finger's liable to swell up.

WILLIAM: All right.

(He takes off his ring and puts it on the table.)

BO: I'll guard it.

(She takes the ring and he puts his hand down in the bucket.)

ARLENE: Would you like something to eat? Some bread? Rice pudding? I could cook you up a steak. Bear.

WILLIAM: Oh no thank you. I'm fine. Mrs. Groden.

(Charley enters wearing only boxer shorts. Pours himself some water. William leaps up.)

ARLENE: This is my husband, Charley Groden. Charley, this is Mr. Gibbs. He's with the IRS.

WILLIAM: Pleased to meet you, sir.

(*William takes his hand out of the bucket to shake hands. Charley studies the bucket.*)

ARLENE: He's been stung, a lot. Maybe hornets. Not a very friendly greeting.

(*Charley shakes his hand. Exits.*)

ARLENE: We're pretty casual around here. You may have noticed.

BO AND ADULT BO: Very likely.

ARLENE: So, Mr. Gibbs, is there a problem with our tax returns?

WILLIAM: Only that you haven't filed for seven years.

ARLENE: Has it been that long?

WILLIAM: It has.

ARLENE: We used to file, we filed for years, but since we live on only five thousand dollars a year at some point it just seemed a waste of everybody's time.

WILLIAM: Ah. Well, they still like you to file, regardless. In fact, I'm afraid there's a penalty for not filing.

BO: Oh no. A penalty?

WILLIAM: Yes. Could I please have some more iced tea?

ARLENE: Certainly. (*Gets up to get it.*)

BO: Your arm is swelling up. I hope you're not allergic to bees. You could be in big trouble.

(*William looks at her, looks at his arm.*)

ARLENE: I keep a very detailed budget you're welcome to look at. We get three hundred thirty-three dollars a month veteran's compensation, my husband's a wounded Korean war vet, and we make about twelve hundred dollars a year selling crafts. That's what we use to pay the electricity bill, buy gas, Postum, margarine, anything else we need we can't grow or hunt for or find in the county dump.

WILLIAM: The dump?

ARLENE: Most of what you see came from the dump, every electrical item—the toaster, blender, coffeepot, clock, heaters. Charley, my husband, repaired them all. You'd be amazed what people throw away.

WILLIAM: Really.

ARLENE: We given away lots of bicycles and wagons to people less fortunate than us. Charley's philosophy is having a job is expensive. If you spend all your time working for someone else, you don't have time to learn to do things yourself. Would you like to stay for dinner, Mr. Gibbs?

WILLIAM: Uh…

BO: I already asked him.

ARLENE: We'd enjoy your company.

WILLIAM: Actually, I'm feeling a little bit… faint. I wonder, could… could I just lie down for a few minutes?

ARLENE: Lie down? Certainly. *(She helps him over to the couch and he lies down on it.)* Bo, get Mr. Gibbs a blanket.

BO: Cecilia-Rose.

ARLENE: I mean Cecilia-Rose.

(Bo gets a blanket out of a trunk. Arlene tries to take the blanket from her but Bo resists and covers him herself.)

BO: I'll do it.

(Lights fade.)

SCENE EIGHT

ADULT BO: Honey bees or hornets. It didn't matter which. One thing was certain: within fifteen minutes of entering the Groden's home, William Gibbs was flat on his back, sick with pain. At the time I thought it was the poison in my father's spirit that laid him low; I now know better. If you search long enough you will find that the blood of every human being with whom you come in contact has been tinctured with a common poison—a poison that is productive of error, that blinds the spiritual eye, that withers the love of the heart. The blood of it flows in the veins of every human being, everyone save a simple Jewish maiden, born free of this universal blight called original sin. William Gibbs had walked miles in the wilderness of a hot summer's day, the needle in the compass of his heart pointing to my mother's garden. In the high-noon heat, he might have thought the sight of her naked flesh was a mirage. It is no wonder he did not feel the bite of the honey bee as he stood at the edge of the garden and gaped at her breasts. I was less than ten feet away from him, crouched in the pumpkin patch, watching his eyes fixed on her, his hand that lifted to his open mouth as if taking in water.

(Candles light the table where George sits with Arlene; they drink homemade beer. Bo sits next to William who is sleeping on the couch. She watches him, almost asleep herself.)

ARLENE: I get so worried, George. The other day he took off and I didn't know where he was, I was sure something terrible happened. You don't think he'd do anything... self-destructive, do you?

GEORGE: I don't think he would.

ARLENE: I don't know. I don't know what to do. Charley's always the one who fixes everything. Maybe you should tell the psychiatrist the truth. Tell her you've got a friend who really needs some drugs.

GEORGE: All right.

ARLENE: How many times have you seen her now?

GEORGE: Three.

ARLENE: What do you talk about?

GEORGE: Talk about my childhood.

ARLENE: What about your childhood?

GEORGE: Things.

ARLENE: Oh. You like her? *(George nods.)* That's good. How many times does she expect you to come?

GEORGE: She hasn't said.

ARLENE: It must be costing you.

GEORGE: That's okay.

(*Pause.*)

ARLENE: It's a funny notion. Paying someone to listen to your childhood. *(Owl hoots.)* We've got stereo barred owls, one at each end of the valley. I wonder if animals ever get depressed. Wild animals in the woods. They must have moods. Maybe it's just a natural thing, maybe it serves a purpose, some cleansing process, we should relax and let it follow its course. I saw this coyote today, it was the wildest looking thing I've ever seen. You know how most coyotes you'll see are scraggly, sorry-looking, he was stunning, George, he really was fine. He had a clean handsome coat but it was the way he moved that took my breath away. Like... he wasn't of this world, like he was moving through another world superimposed on this one; some ethereal wild thing that would leave no signs, no tracks. I was in the garden, just happened to see him, he wasn't making a sound, stalking something. The way he moved. I felt... aroused. Something that wild. I think I would have come right there, standing, looking at him, if William Gibbs hadn't called out to me.

GEORGE: I've been thinking...

ARLENE: Yeah?

GEORGE: I might... ask her to marry me.

ARLENE: Marry you? George. Really?

GEORGE: She's a gentle person. Very thoughtful. *(He clears his throat.)* She cares.

ARLENE: You pay her to care. You know, George, you ought not to confuse romance with business. *(Pause.)* I know you're lonely these days. Bo and I'll keep you company. We need you, more than ever. *(Pause.)* Hm. Well, maybe something good will come out of all this.

(Lights down on them and up on Bo's face and Adult Bo.)

ADULT BO: If she only knew how her words settled into my mind, what confusion they stirred, her shameful response to that lowly beast. And to behave like that in front of, of all people, William Gibbs, God's messenger to me.

SCENE NINE

The light in the kitchen comes up to low as Charley enters. William is asleep. Charley gets the bottle of spring water and pours himself a glass. He goes over to William and shakes him. Shakes him again, waking him. William sits up abruptly. He is feverish, ill, cold.

WILLIAM: What? What is it?

CHARLEY: Thirsty?

WILLIAM: Huh?

CHARLEY: You want some water?

WILLIAM: Now? Not really. *(Lies back down again.)* Mr. Groden? *(Sits up.)* Okay. *(Charley pours him a glass, hands it to him.)* Thank you very much. Sir.

CHARLEY: You cold?

WILLIAM: Cold?

CHARLEY: I see you're sleeping with your clothes on, thought you might be cold. It's a hot night.

WILLIAM: Well. I don't have my pajamas. Here.

CHARLEY: Oh.

(Pause.)

WILLIAM: *(Making conversation.)* Good water.

CHARLEY: Mm. *(Pause.)* I never did have pajamas.

WILLIAM: No?

CHARLEY: Never did.

WILLIAM: I have always worn them.

CHARLEY: Is that right?

WILLIAM: I guess it's just a habit. There's no real need for them. I wouldn't start wearing them... if I didn't already. Wear them. *(Pause.)* Do you know what time it is?

CHARLEY: No. Late. *(Looks out the window.)* Then again, maybe it's early.

WILLIAM: I see you're up.

CHARLEY: Yeah.

WILLIAM: Couldn't sleep.

CHARLEY: How 'bout you?

WILLIAM: I could. I could sleep. I was as... *(Stops so as not to offend Charley for waking him).*
(Pause.)

CHARLEY: You're from Albuquerque?

WILLIAM: No, no I'm from Brookline. Outside of Boston. Massachusetts. I just moved to Albuquerque a month ago. This job for the IRS turned up, kind of a fluke, they hired me even though I'm not a CPA. They seemed quite desperate. *(Pause.)* I do have a law degree. This is a very strange state. They don't even require mandatory car insurance. Of course, that's probably good for you since you don't use money.
(Pause.)

CHARLEY: More water?

WILLIAM: Please. Thank you.
(Pause.)

CHARLEY: Excuse the crying.

WILLIAM: Certainly.

CHARLEY: I'm a damn crying machine. That's why I drink so much water. Won't have any fluids left in me. Have you ever been depressed?

WILLIAM: *(Thinks.)* I've never not been depressed.

CHARLEY: You've never not been depressed?

WILLIAM: Never. Not.
(Pause.)

CHARLEY: You've always been depressed?

WILLIAM: Yes, sir.

CHARLEY: First time for me. How can you stand it?

WILLIAM: I guess I'm used to it.

CHARLEY: It seems normal to you?

WILLIAM: Mm.

CHARLEY: I don't even remember how I got here. I can't... *(Shakes his head.)* Do you know what set it off?

WILLIAM: I think it started when I was six. I came home from school and my mother had hung herself.

CHARLEY: No.

WILLIAM: Yes.

CHARLEY: You found her, like that?

WILLIAM: Mm. In the front hall. It was awkward because I was carrying a large pyramid I'd made in school out of foam core, well it was like foam core, and I opened the door with my back and essentially walked backwards into her.

(Pause.)

CHARLEY: You put me to shame.

WILLIAM: No...

CHARLEY: Yeah, you do. A good reason like that.

(Pause.)

WILLIAM: Excuse me but I think I have a fever. I am cold. I'm freezing.

(Pause.)

CHARLEY: This is a terrible thing to say but, sometimes I think being dead would be easier.

WILLIAM: You will be dead very soon. Your life will be over in a heartbeat.

(Pause.)

CHARLEY: Is that...comforting?

WILLIAM: Uh...

(Bo enters. She is wearing a girl scout uniform, her best shoes, and her hair is neatly combed. She carries a cup full of pennies.)

BO: Good morning. *(They both stare at her.)* Mr. Gibbs. Would you mind if I tried out your briefcase?

WILLIAM: Tried it out? Okay.

(Bo picks up the briefcase and takes it out onto the deck. She puts down the cup and experiences the weight of the briefcase in her hand. Charley follows her out there as William curls up, shivering.)

CHARLEY: What are you doing? Bo?

BO: My name isn't Bo. It's Cecilia-Rose.

(He stares at her, as though he barely recognizes her. She puts down the briefcase and starts rolling her pennies into bank rolls.)

I'm rolling my pennies. *(Pause.)* A big multi-colored hot air balloon just went over the ridge. Today's balloon fest. You just missed it, dad. *(He stares at her. Sits down next to her. With huge effort he picks up a wrapper and puts a couple pennies in it.)* You have to count them. There's fifty pennies in each roll. *(He reaches for some more pennies and tips the cup. All the pennies fall onto the deck floor. He stares down, hopeless.)*

ADULT BO: I suppose I should have comforted him. At least thanked him for trying to help. Even then the irony was not lost on me, that he was incapable of holding on to money, especially mine with its powers to steal me away. All I could do was look at his hands which I had admired so many times, now stone still on his lap like two fine birds that had been shot. They had held me so many times, had swooped me up and hoisted me onto carts he'd made, tractors, horses, trees, places with a view, places only my father took me to. He stared at his hands, too, as though they weren't his own; they didn't belong to either of us anymore. With my pennies strewn around our feet, we sat there for a long time. Suddenly there was so much that was gone. Back then, I thought it was just me feeling that anguish of loss. But he must have felt it, too, perhaps more acutely. We were both losing my childhood. Maybe that's partly what had sent him on his downward spiral, losing himself. I should have… said something.

(Lights fade on all three of them.)

(Music to Willie "The Lion" Smith's "Rites of Spring".)

ACT TWO

SCENE ONE

Lights in the cabin are dim. William is lying down, eyes closed, holding on to Arlene's hand. Adult Bo is lit, speaking out front.

ADULT BO: Three days and nights William Gibbs cried out from another world, burning up with fever. Who can truly know the landscape of another's purgatory? Who could say what that lost pilgrim struggled for as he daily sweated through our entire albeit short supply of cotton sheets? The bible tells us "Judge not lest ye be judged", but was it perhaps the sight of my mother, standing naked in the garden, touching herself that he wrestled with so, that perilously overheated the molten core of his being? Perhaps the desire for honey that riled the poison from the honey bees coursing through him? She nursed him night and day, applying herbs and remedies concocted by her grandmother, a full blooded Hopi Indian. He would seize her hand and squeeze it so hard she could not hold her coffee mug with that hand for a week thereafter, could not turn the key in the ignition.

ARLENE: William. Let go. Ouch, oh God. William, let go of my hand.
(William lies still.)

ADULT BO: In point of fact, he never did let go. He never did let go of her.
(Lights up on Bo and George who are fishing off the deck.)

BO: You know what's really weird? When they send you a credit card and it's just in a plain envelope? You could so easily throw it away, not even know it was in there.

GEORGE: Who?

BO: I feel so bad for Mr. Gibbs. They completely stripped his car. We're going to the dump to get tires and everything.

CHARLEY: Who got a credit card?

BO: It's sitting there out in the desert like a corpse. Like vultures came and pecked out the eyeballs and everything. The radio, the seats.

GEORGE: Arlene got a credit card?

BO: How's your psychiatrist?

GEORGE: Okay.

BO: George, you've got to take me to the Morning Glory. There's a tortilla there on the wall I have to see. Maybe you could pick me up tomorrow after work.

GEORGE: Not tomorrow.

BO: Why not?

GEORGE: Not tomorrow.

BO: Why?

GEORGE: I'm busy.

BO: You're busy? Doing what? Well, some time this week you'll take me? (*George nods. Lights down on them and up on Arlene who faces the outhouse which can be partly seen or off-stage.*)

SCENE TWO

ARLENE: Oh God no. Charley! Not again, for Christ's sake. Charley! Come out of there! Come out! Now!! Enough! You can't spend another night in there! Charley! Look, you can lock yourself in the bedroom, you can lock yourself in the chicken house, the pig house, the barn, the car, no not the car and not the outhouse, come out of the outhouse now!! Where do you expect Bo and me to pee! We've got a sick boy in the house burning up with fever, a visitor, the least we should be able to offer him is a decent place to shit!! Now come out! You're being selfish, Charley, selfish, you're just sitting there, listening to me, just sitting there, being selfish and self-indulgent and self-pitying!! I God. (*She lies down, flat on her back, crosses her arms over her face. Lights come up just slightly on Bo who is sitting next to William. Bo looks outside toward Arlene, listening to her.*) (*Softer.*) Charley. I can't take this much more. Sweetheart. Humility, Charley; it keeps you from being humiliated. That's where the word humiliation comes from. Everybody gets depressed some time, why should you be above it. (*Sighs.*) I'll say this for you, when you take on a project, you give it your all. You've never done anything half-assed, and you're not doing it now. (*Pause.*) I've been thinking, maybe we should try to have another kid. We're getting kind of old for it, but... She can't stay a little girl forever, Charley. Just 'cause she's growing up doesn't mean we're losing her. (*She sits up, gets up, goes back into the cabin. Bo pretends she's asleep. Arlene comes out with a plate with some food*

on it and puts it down in front of the outhouse. Light on Bo fades.)
There's food out here. *(Pause.)* I'm sorry I yelled at you.
Sweetheart. *(Pause.)* Charley? *(Gets alarmed.)* Charley, say something.
CHARLEY: *(From inside.)* Thanks.
(She sighs, walks away.)

SCENE THREE

*Lights come up in the cabin on Bo on a chair next to William who
is sitting up in bed. Bo is holding a large knife in a sheath. His
focus is on wanting to see Arlene.*

BO: This is my survival knife. It's fourteen inches long. I use it to skin
squirrels. Squirrels are good, but there's not much meat on them.
WILLIAM: Where's your mother?
BO: In town. I brought you some copies of the Wall Street Journal.
They're a little out of date, three years old, but I thought you
might like to browse through them. Have you ever seen the
ocean?
WILLIAM: Yes.
BO: Which one, the Pacific or the Atlantic?
WILLIAM: The...
BO: *(Interrupting.)* Or the Indian or Arctic or Antarctic? Or the Red
Sea or the Mediterranean, Baltic, Central American, Irish, um...
there are some more that I could think of if I kept... thinking...
Bering, did I say Bering?
WILLIAM: No, you didn't. The Atlantic.
BO: Oh.
WILLIAM: You know a lot of oceans and seas.
BO: I know Latin. Did you like it?
WILLIAM: What?
BO: The Atlantic.
WILLIAM: Yes. I did like the Atlantic. Very much. I used to go to Cape
Cod when I was a little boy with my parents.
BO: I know Cape Cod. It's one of the New England states.
WILLIAM: I don't think Cape Cod is a state.
BO: It is. And you stood at the edge and waded in the water?

WILLIAM: Uh-huh. Will she be back soon, your mother?

BO: You kicked off your shoes and rolled up your trousers and stood at the very edge of the whole entire Atlantic Ocean? You look out and you keep looking and there keeps being water, very flat, and then more water and more water as far as you can see?

WILLIAM: Yes.

BO: And then what happens? At the end, when you see so far, at the very very very farthest point, how does it look?

WILLIAM: Well...the planet curves...

BO: *(Aghast.)* You see the curve of the planet?

WILLIAM: Well...you see the horizon, you see the sky touch down on the ocean...

BO: Oh my God. Mr. Gibbs, that's wonderful.

WILLIAM: You can see that here, in New Mexico. You see the sky out on the horizon, touching down on the desert. It's very much the same.

BO: I don't think it's the same. I don't think it's the same one bit. Did you know desert is another word for wasteland?

WILLIAM: What is your mother doing, in town?

BO: Stuff. We washed your shirt. I ironed your tie, would you like it?

WILLIAM: You ironed my tie?

BO: I had it on low setting. It's a polyester blend. *(She gets it, hands it to him.)* You want to put it on?

WILLIAM: Now? I don't think so.

BO: Go ahead. You'll feel better. *(William puts on his tie. Bo studies carefully how he does it.)* I see. Nice. I'm afraid we've got some bad news about your car. Did my mother tell you? They stripped it.

WILLIAM: Who stripped it?

BO: We don't know. Some guys. We just went to look at it yesterday. Don't worry we'll get you new parts for it. My mom's stopping at the dump on the way home. Do you have any paperwork you'd like me to help you with? I could write some letters for you, do some alphabetizing.

WILLIAM: So you think she'll be back soon?

SCENE FOUR

Lights come up down front on Charley who is walking toward the cabin. He stops and looks down at his foot. Bends over, unlaces a boot and shakes out a pebble. Laces up his boot and starts going. Stops. Turns around, goes back, unlaces his boot, puts the pebble back in, laces up the boot, goes inside.

SCENE FIVE

Lights come up on William who is pacing out on the deck, agitated. Arlene enters from down front carrying a used battery. Inside the cabin in the dark Bo is in the bathtub, writing a letter.

ARLENE: There's a junked Oldsmobile, Cutlass Supreme, same model as yours. Two years older but I'm sure we can get a lot of parts from it.

WILLIAM: Mrs. Groden...

ARLENE: You look much better. You've got some color in your face.

WILLIAM: Mrs. Groden I have to tell you...

ARLENE: Would you like to wash yourself? We have a shower, a waterfall in the river just above where the goats are penned. There's soap and shampoo in a dish on the ledge.

WILLIAM: I love you.

ARLENE: Oh. *(Smiles.)* That's nice.

WILLIAM: This is very serious, Mrs. Groden. I am in love with you. Deeply. So deeply.

ARLENE: Well...good.

WILLIAM: I appreciate your letting me tell you because there is a part of my brain that is eroded from how many times I have told you during the past I don't know how many days it seems like years I was delirious, over and over and over but, Mrs. Groden, I have to tell you the real you in front of me with my voice in my throat not the voice in my mind or my brain will explode will erupt like a volcano, a geyser, will splatter all over New Mexico.

ARLENE: Would you mind if I put this battery down? It's pretty heavy.

WILLIAM: The battery? Sure. Put it down. *(She puts down the battery.)* Thank you. *(Pause.)* When I first saw you, I don't know how many days ago it was... what day is today?

ARLENE: Tuesday.

WILLIAM: *(Thinks.)* Tuesday.

ARLENE: Should we sit down?

WILLIAM: No. The moment I saw you, Mrs. Groden, the very first instant, I knew my life as I had understood it was finished. I'd been up since sunrise, my second night in my car, in the desert, I was completely lost and I hadn't eaten for two days and what I had eaten had given me such terrible diarrhea I had nothing left in me. I must have walked ten miles in brand new penny loafers that didn't fit up and down arroyos, canyons, along the river, I finally found the road again. There was a turn to the left, to your house, I could see the house, but something in me made me turn to the right, made me walk off the road, walk quite a ways through heavy brush, to a clearing, to your garden. To you, standing there in all those vines, those vegetables, completely still, looking at something I don't know what. I saw you, and piñon trees behind, and the hill and up in the sky there was one cloud, right above you, one small cloud, not moving. Everything completely still, like a photograph, a huge flat picture so… beautiful, so pure, it was like a child's view, a child's view of life. And suddenly it all caved in on me, in my chest, flooding like a dam broke with all this sweetness and sadness and longing it was almost unbearable. It still is. Then later, in your house, holding your hand, I remembered being at this birthday party, children's birthday party, and my brother my older brother was acting out me discovering my mother, dead, my mother committed suicide, *but maybe she didn't,* and he was telling this story how I'd come home from school carrying a pyramid I'd made out of foam core and had opened the front door and walked in backwards and bumped into her, in the hall, she'd hung herself. But, now, I don't think it's true. I don't think it's a real memory, *my* memory. I think it's just a description I heard from my brother. I never remembered this before but I saw him with this party hat on walking backwards, pretending to hold this unwieldy object, turning around, making a goofy face. *I don't even think foam core existed back then, Mrs. Groden.* No one else in my family ever discussed my mother's death, how she died. My aunts who raised me. My father who moved to Salt Lake City with my brother. It was the only explanation I ever had. I always felt partly responsible, involved, being the one to find her. But now I don't think I did. I don't think I did. You know whenever I would tell people about finding her, I always sensed something on my head as I told the story and now I realize it was my brother's party hat. Don't you think that's amazing? It was like the cornerstone of my childhood, the event upon which I built everything else and now it's pulled out and everything has toppled, my past since then is just hanging, in space. It's like finding an error at the very beginning of a long proof of an algebra problem so the pages and pages of numbers after the error are worthless. *(Not displeased.)* Meaningless. The only concrete thing I can hold on to right now, Mrs. Groden, Mrs. Groden, the only thing I know to be true is my love for you.

ARLENE: *(Studying him.)* Mr. Gibbs.

WILLIAM: Yes.

ARLENE: New Mexico is a very powerful place. You've been living in a city all your life. Often when people first get here it's a little overwhelming. The boundaries disappear.

(Pause.)

WILLIAM: Uh...oh. Well, I do feel a little... displaced.

ARLENE: You're welcome to stay with us as long as you like. Till you get your bearings.

WILLIAM: Maybe just a couple more nights?

ARLENE: Sure.

WILLIAM: Thank you. Your husband won't mind?

ARLENE: Oh no, he won't mind.

WILLIAM: I can't hide my feelings.

ARLENE: I would hope not. We'll get this tax thing straightened out. I know it must be weighing on you.

(She starts to go in.)

WILLIAM: You know what else I remembered?

ARLENE: Maybe we should go in and sit down. Have a cold beer.

WILLIAM: After she died, after my mother died, I used to photograph my food. I had a Polaroid camera and I would take pictures of the food on my plate before I ate it, before it disappeared. I had albums filled with pictures of my food under my bed. No one could figure out why. I was too embarrassed to explain it. I thought it was obvious. Don't you think it's obvious?

(Arlene sympathetically touches him, nods.)

ARLENE: There're a couple of tires in the truck. Come help me carry them.

(*William exits with Arlene. Bo, who's been sunk down listening in the bathtub, gets up and goes outside, looks out after them, sits and reads a letter she's just written.*)

Bo: Dear Carlos Martinez, Greetings from the outside world. I'm sorry I haven't written to you in so long. Life has been busy, busy, did I say busy? Thanks for your letter. That's okay if you don't want to tell me what your crime was though if you murdered somebody it might feel good to get it off your chest. I enclose an article on birds I thought you might like since you don't get to see any in jail and you have wings tattooed on your arms. Did you know that the crafty ovenbird deposits its eggs in other bird's nests, then sneaks away so they'll raise them? And don't I know how that baby ovenbird feels when it wakes up in that foreign nest, Carlos, for I am a plain starling and my mother is an enchanting bluebird adored by one and all. But somewhere my true family waits for me, faithfully. So, Carlos. Gotta run. Take care. Your penpal, Bo Groden. P.S. Don't be surprised when a Nabisco company delivery man brings you some free samples. Just calmly thank him. Adios, amigo.
(*Lights down on her, up on George in the cabin.*)

SCENE SIX

Lights up. It's evening. In the cabin Charley is sitting in his chair and George is filling a glass with water. He puts it down on the middle of the table near the watercolor set and a roll of wallpaper, stretched out to be painted on. George puts a brush in the glass of water and sits down at the end of the table. Eyes Charley. Charley gets up, sees the glass of water, takes out the brush and drinks all the water. Puts the brush back in and sits down again. Wipes his mouth. Lights fade.

SCENE SEVEN

During the following, Bo sets the table with bowls of soup which Arlene dishes to her. Charley and William join them at the table.

ADULT BO: I live alone now. I have suffered my share of roommates, grown women who have nothing better to do than to weep at the body God has given them, to distort and color their features for whatever stray they land through the classifieds. Of course it fell on me to compose the personal ads. For a reasonable fee. I placed one myself to test the market and according to the editor received a record number of responses. I saw that as no great feat; you don't have to be Freud to figure the short range goals of that target group. I did brave a hot cocoa at a downtown Woolworth's with one no-account drifter who tucked his dandruff flecked comb in his sock and called himself a Christian. Ha! Of all the phone numbers I received, I kept only one. For a Mr. Henry Gibbs who also enclosed a signed photograph. I keep his number in my jewelry box, next to William Gibbs' high school ring. I haven't dated in years. I prefer the company of books on tape. I like living alone. I do. *(Clearly doesn't.)* I like it.

(It's day time. Arlene, Bo, William and Charley are seated, all eating soup except for Charley who occasionally wipes tears from his eyes. William is now dressed in an old flannel shirt of Charley's and jeans.)

ARLENE: Bread?

WILLIAM: Bread? Yes. Please. Certainly. Thank you.

ARLENE: Butter?

WILLIAM: No thank you. Actually, I would. On second thought. Please. Thank you. *(Butters his bread.)* Cecilia-Rose?

(No response.)

ARLENE: Bo?

BO: What?

WILLIAM: Would you like some butter?

BO: No, thanks.

WILLIAM: Mr. Groden?

(William passes the butter to Charley, then awkwardly aborts the move.)

ARLENE: There's a spoon by your bowl.

WILLIAM: I beg your pardon?

ARLENE: A spoon. For your soup. You're using your fork. *(Smiles.)* *(William smiles. Puts down his fork, picks up spoon.)* You don't happen to play the accordion, Mr. Gibbs, do you?

WILLIAM: The accordion? No.

ARLENE: Would you like to learn?

WILLIAM: The accordion?

ARLENE: We have one. It would be nice to hear some music.

WILLIAM: I'm afraid I'm not very musical. I'm sorry.

ARLENE: That's all right. You might try fooling around with it if you like.

BO: My dad plays every instrument. He used to anyway.

(Bo gets up from the table.)

ARLENE: Where are you going, sweetheart?

BO: Outside.

(Bo exits. Lights stay on William, Charley and Arlene, then fade.)

SCENE EIGHT

Outside, in front of the cabin, Bo is playing. Holding a stick with one hand to prod imaginary dogs, she directs a running circle of them to jump through a hula hoop she holds at various heights.

BO: Come on, up, up, up, Simba. Thata boy. Next... the very lovely Carl. Good boy, Carl. And now... Elaine, the pit bull from Spain. Come on, jump up, jump... oops... try again, come on, be brave, Elaine, you can do it, only you have super paws... perfecto! And now... Señor Chico himself... if he'll just get moving, come on boy, get cracking! Show some life! What's the story Señor Chico, we are waiting! Too depressed? Too depressed just sitting there with your tongue hanging out? But here comes Sandra and Phillipe and Oswaldo and Fernandez up, up! A cornucopia of talent. And now, a double helix, performed by my darling Renaldo, oh yes, with a triple side flip first... magnificent... how bold how daring... Señor Chico, you feel like getting up yet? No? And now, ohmyGod, the very lovely Carl is back in full form, yes, up, a record setting higher than imaginable Mt. Everest leap, the lovely Carl comes through. Not Señor Chico, he just sits there, droopy and poopy. Not prancing and dancing like Mr. Agenda. Mr. Agenda, folks, I give you the famous world traveler, the pedigree, I do agree, the star competitor of all universal time. Yes, up! Up! Up!

Scene Nine

Lights come up on Charley who is seated at the table, staring at a pill. Arlene and William sit with him. William is painting intently with the watercolors on the roll of wallpaper.

ARLENE: Just take it Charley.

CHARLEY: What is it?

ARLENE: It might make you feel better.

CHARLEY: It's a drug.

ARLENE: Yes.

CHARLEY: I don't like drugs.

ARLENE: I know. Just... please... try it. *(Charley studies it.)* It's been known to help people who are depressed. Sweetheart, you're in a chemically altered state. Chemicals might help you out of it.

(George and Bo enter from a trip to town. George sits and Bo goes to an opened package from Drake's in the kitchen.)

BO: What a bust. Burnt butter, that's all it is. Burnt fake butter on a tortilla, everybody's calling it the face of our Lord Jesus Christ. Jiminy Cricket. You wouldn't believe, the Morning Glory was packed. What a bunch of lulus. I mean, what is in those people's minds? Why would they think God would be interested in doing that, showing up in a frying pan looking up at Sophia doesn't even have one tooth in her head, never mind a thought in her brain? Don't they think he has better things to do and isn't it just a tad undignified. God deep fried? Who wants a Ring Ding? *(She passes them around.)* It's hanging on the wall by the door, people are actually praying to it. I can't believe it. I'm getting out of this state. I'm moving to Canada. Or Cape Cod. I'll send you all post-cards. *(Charley looks at her.)* What's going on?

ARLENE: This is the drug I told you about that William got for us.

BO: Take it, dad. Take it. What have you got to lose?

(He looks at her; looks at the pill.)

ARLENE: Look, Charley, we went to a lot of trouble getting you these. The least you can do is try them.

CHARLEY: I really don't care to.

ARLENE: William's taken them.

(*Charley looks at William who looks up at him. Charley looks at the pill.*)

BO: You better take it, dad, because we're going to sneak it into your food if you don't.

(*Charley suddenly puts the pill in his mouth and swallows it. Everyone stares at Charley. Pause. He looks around at everyone. Smiles a ridiculous tormented smile. William keeps painting. Lights fade.*)

SCENE TEN

ADULT BO: William Gibbs' first painting was twenty inches high and thirty-one feet wide, one foot shy of the perimeter of my room. The dimensions suited the subject, the ocean's horizon. He hung it so that when I lay on my bed, I could stare out fourteen miles to the horizon any way I looked. Encircled by water, I would turn and float on my back, arms outstretched, chin up, and feel in the small of my back the rounded curve of the planet, supporting me like a buoy, like faith. Though unsigned, the value of that painting is now recklessly high. Not just because of the "sheer volume of ocean and sky, the disturbing depths of emotion," as one lame-brained critic has put it, but because the art world deems it the only painting in William Gibbs' short but brilliant career that wasn't some view, some study of the garden. What those high-minded fools don't know is submerged in the water are some two dozen sketches of the garden, his first, of my mother, naked as the back of my hand. Those he sketched first in pencil, then, like a murderer burying the body, drowned in a wash of blue.

(*Lights come up. Bo is standing on a chair conducting a stirring piece by Handel. Arlene is seated, calculating figures, near William who still paints with the water color set on the same roll of wallpaper.*)

ARLENE: Okay, I've done it. You'll have to check these figures but I think including the penalties and all the interest we owe twelve hundred and sixty dollars.

WILLIAM: I'm so sorry.

ARLENE: Don't be sorry. It's not your fault.

WILLIAM: *(Studying her.)* You have flour on your face.

ARLENE: I've been baking bread.

(She wipes off the wrong side of her face. William reaches across and wipes her face with his hand.)

WILLIAM: *(Awkwardly.)* Now you have paint on your face. *(Goes to touch her again but can't quite.)*

(For the first time there is a moment of sexual tension between them. Flushed, she wipes her face.)

ARLENE: What are you painting?

BO: He's painting the curve. For me.

ARLENE: What curve?

BO: The curve of the planet. Where the ocean meets the sky.

ARLENE: Oh. *(William goes back to painting. Arlene looks at the painting. Looks closer.)* Is that a woman...? *(She recognizes herself. Bo stops conducting and looks over at them.)*

WILLIAM: You wouldn't happen to have any more paint, would you? I'm running out of blue.

ARLENE: We'll go into town later and get some. You can call your office. They must be expecting you. To come back?

WILLIAM: Oh, I'm not going back there.

ARLENE: No?

WILLIAM: No. I didn't come all the way out to New Mexico to work for the Internal Revenue Service.

ARLENE: What did you come out here for?

(William stares at her. Pause.)

WILLIAM: Uh...

(Bo has stepped down off the bed and abruptly turned off the music. She looks at the sketch of her mother which upsets her.)

ADULT BO: Five weeks William Gibbs spent painting thirty-one feet of the ocean's horizon. It was near about the fourth foot that it dawned on me that someone who I'd perceived as a link with the outside world had in fact been swallowed in the quicksand of mine.

BO: *(Angrily.)* He came out here for me. Mr. Gibbs?

WILLIAM: Yes?

BO: Where is your tie?

WILLIAM: My tie?

BO: What happened to it? And your briefcase. You shouldn't keep your brushes in your briefcase.

ARLENE: Bo...

BO: Well, he's going to get paint all over it, he's going to ruin it how can he show up at the office with paint all over his briefcase?

ARLENE: Bo...

BO: And what about daddy, how do you think he would feel?

ARLENE: About what?

BO: *(Gesturing at the painting.)* That.

WILLIAM: Where is my tie? I'll put it on.

(*Lights go to black.*)

SCENE ELEVEN

It is late night. The cabin is dark except for one lamp on the table where William is bent over, tie around his neck, sketching with a pencil on the roll of wallpaper to the right of several rolled feet of painted ocean and sky. Charley enters from outside and looks in at William; walks up behind him and looks over William's shoulder. William becomes aware of him and is startled. He nervously puts down his pencil and picks up the brush, continues painting. Charley sits next to him, blows his nose, leans forward and studies the penciled sketch on the unpainted part. William keeps painting. Charley studies the sketch intently. They don't look at each other. Lights fade.

SCENE TWELVE

Lights up on Adult Bo.

ADULT BO: Dear Ask Beth, I am an eleven and a half year old girl; healthy, outgoing. So far so good. My problem is this: my father is depressed. Not just quote blue unquote, but really, really, really depressed. He's been this was so long it feels like an eternity.
(*There is a loud rifle shot. Adult Bo looks toward the sound. Bo runs to the deck from inside, looks out, runs back inside.*)

My mother is afraid he's going to kill himself. I know he will not, he loves us too much, but it is really starting to get to me. He used to take me with him everywhere and I do mean everywhere with a capital E. He taught me how to hunt and carve and repair blenders and rebuild a VW engine and drive and do the jitterbug and more I could fill your column for a week. Beth, we haven't even been to the dump together to shoot bottles or get stuff in so long... I can't even remember! He has no desire to be with me. I'm afraid I may start to get depressed and have a life-long problem. Is it contagious? My last question is this: will he ever remember the good times? Any suggestions? Yours, too young to be depressed in New Mexico, land of enchantment.

ARLENE: *(Off-stage.)* Charley! Charley!

(William enters from down front. He staggers slightly. His arms and hands are covered with blood and there is blood smeared on his shirt. He goes to the deck and sits down on it, shaken.)

(After a little bit, Arlene, also with blood on her hands, enters from down front carrying a bloodied knife.)

ARLENE: Charley! Where'd he go? *(To William.)* Are you all right? *(William nods.)* Is that the first bear you've ever seen? *(William nods. Arlene chuckles.)* Well, you got quite a view, didn't you? You got a front row seat. He's been after our honey all summer. *(She reaches for a rag under the deck to wipe off her hands.)* He's destroyed a couple of our hives. *(Bo comes out. Arlene says to William:)* What were you doing back there, anyway? Looking to get stung again?

BO: Did you already gut him?

ARLENE: Yup. Where's Charley?

BO: He went for a walk.

(William starts to go.)

WILLIAM: I think I'll just... rinse off... in the river.

ARLENE: Good thinking.

(Bo starts to follow him.)

ARLENE: Bo.

BO: Yeah?

ARLENE: Let's do something special this afternoon. Just you and me.

BO: What?

ARLENE: Let's have a picnic.

BO: Where?

ARLENE: Where would you like?

Bo: In town.

ARLENE: Okay.

Bo: In the Wal-Mart parking lot.

ARLENE: Okay. Then we'll stop by the library, drop off some books, and... go to a movie.

Bo: A movie. Cool.

ARLENE: Come help me skin the bear. It'll just take twenty minutes. Then we'll pack a picnic and go. *(They start towards the front.)* Your letter's in yesterday's paper.

Bo: My letter? To Ask Beth? They printed it?

ARLENE: Yup.

Bo: Oh my God. It's published?

ARLENE: Yup.

Bo: Oh my God. That's a national column, that column is in papers all over the country.

ARLENE: Yup.

Bo: My letter is published all over the country. You have a copy?

ARLENE: I do. We'll read it together.

(They exit forward.)

Bo: My heart is pounding.

ARLENE: *(Concerned.)* So is mine.

(Lights fade on them and come up in the cabin.)

SCENE THIRTEEN

Lights up in the cabin. George is sitting down. He looks quite spiffed up in a western shirt, vest and a fancy bolo tie. Charley paces, uncomfortable, as if he's trying to crawl out of his skin.

CHARLEY: I'm going crazy, George. Crazy. It's these damn drugs. I feel like strangling something, I feel like going out in the yard and strangling the damn goat. I'm dangerous.

GEORGE: Sit down.

CHARLEY: I can't sit down. Look at me. Can I sit down? I just walked twenty miles. I ran up the ridge, out the highway, look at my legs, they're still going, look at them.

GEORGE: Have a beer.

CHARLEY: A beer. I can't have a beer. I'm not supposed to drink alcohol with these damn drugs, I'm apt to murder someone. Okay, I'll have a beer.

GEORGE: Maybe you better not.

CHARLEY: I'm having one. *(He takes some beers out of the fridge. Grabs a glass.)* I'm having five. I'm gonna drink till I pass out, I need some relief. *(He sits, pours beer into glass, takes a swig.)* I am pathetic. I'm so pathetic. *(He stands up.)* Wrestle with me, George.

GEORGE: Huh?

CHARLEY: Wrestle with me. C'mon. We'll go outside.

GEORGE: I don't wanna wrestle with you.

CHARLEY: Please

GEORGE: No.

CHARLEY: Why not?

GEORGE: 'Cause.

CHARLEY: 'Cause why.

GEORGE: I'm dressed up.

CHARLEY: Shit. That's why?

(George nods.)

GEORGE: I'm seeing someone.

CHARLEY: What?

GEORGE: I'm seeing someone.

(Charley takes this in, sits down. Keeps drinking, agitated. Charley suddenly takes his glass and throws the beer all over George's shirt. No response. Pours another glassful. Throws it at him. George lunges for him. In a flash George has Charley pinned down on the floor face first with his arm up behind him.)

CHARLEY: Thank you, George. Thank you so much. Ow. Thanks. Don't let me go, George. Don't let me go. *(Puts his head to the floor.)* *(George just holds him, pinned down. Lights fade.)*

SCENE FOURTEEN

It's very late at night. William is asleep on the couch. Charley enters with a lantern and stands by him, waiting for him to wake up. Eventually makes a noise.

WILLIAM: Hello, Mr. Groden. I'll join you.

(*Charley stands there with the lantern till William finally stirs and gets up. They go out on the deck and sit, leaning against the house.*)

CHARLEY: Sleepy?

WILLIAM: I am a little sleepy. I don't think I can do this every night.

(*Pause.*)

CHARLEY: Nice shirt.

WILLIAM: Thanks. It's yours.

CHARLEY: It's nice.

(*Pause.*)

WILLIAM: It's funny, when I put this shirt on it felt so good. So solid. It's like an anchor, this shirt. (*William reaches for an old telescope he is familiar with. Holds it in his lap.*) (*Pause.*) I don't know who I am.

CHARLEY: I don't either.

WILLIAM: Know who I am?

CHARLEY: You?

WILLIAM: You don't know who I am? Or who you are?

CHARLEY: No.

(*William nods. Pause.*)

WILLIAM: It's pretty amazing.

CHARLEY: Pretty pathetic.

WILLIAM: A person can live for twenty-eight years, and all of a sudden in one day, in one moment, they're undone. Like someone pulled a loose thread and all twenty-eight years just unravel. I have no past. I have lost my past.

CHARLEY: Maybe you're an artist.

WILLIAM: No, no, I'm just...painting. You know I really admire you, Mr. Groden. More than any man I've ever met. You don't have a penny in the bank, no life insurance, no credit. But your house is all paid for, you have four years worth of food stored away, three years worth of firewood, stockpiles of clothes. A beautiful wife, a great kid. Your life is yours. I think you're a genius. You didn't find this telescope in the dump, did you?

CHARLEY: It was my father's.

WILLIAM: It's a beauty.

CHARLEY: I give it to you. It's yours.

WILLIAM: I can't take it.

CHARLEY: It's yours.

WILLIAM: No, I can't.

CHARLEY: Yes. I'll get another one.

WILLIAM: Where?

CHARLEY: They're all over the place. Telescopes. They're everywhere.

WILLIAM: They are? *(Charley nods.)* Well. Thank you. Very much. Thank you. *(Pause.)* Mr. Groden. *(Struggles to tell him.)* You know what I told you about my mother, about me finding her hanging in the front hall?

CHARLEY: Yeah.

WILLIAM: It's not true.

CHARLEY: It's not true?

WILLIAM: No. I don't know how she died. But I wasn't... involved.

CHARLEY: Oh.

(Pause.)

WILLIAM: My mother would never have done that. What woman would do that? Be there, like that, knowing her son would be the first one home, would walk in. By himself. Her little boy. Just a little kid. My mother wouldn't do that. She was *(Starting to cry.)* nice... she was a nice person she...

CHARLEY: 't's all right. *(He reaches for Kleenex box, drops it, passes it to him.)* Kleenex?

ADULT BO: Through my window, in my room above the deck, the warm night air carried the sound of my father dropping the complimentary box of tissues from the Kleenex company as he passed them over to William Gibbs, passing as it were between athletes a baton on a relay team. For as the valve opened in William Gibbs—he who could not feel the sting of the honey bee, who had not shed a tear in twenty years—releasing a torrent of tears, it seems that same valve continued turning in my father all the way to the off position, shutting off that steady leak that had streaked his face and our lives for more than half a year. In comforting others do we comfort ourselves. Christ redeemed us. But we save ourselves through the application to our own souls of His grace and merits which were won on Calvary's heights. The tears of William Gibbs flowed into the estuary of my father's despair like a tide that rolls in and gently prods the stranded boat up off the shoals to set it free.

Lights up in the cabin. Arlene is in the kitchen, frosting a cake. Bo, who has been helping, steps back from her, upset.

BO: No!

ARLENE: What?

BO: He can't move!

ARLENE: Bo…

BO: No!!

ARLENE: What's the matter?

BO: He can't move! I don't want him to move!

ARLENE: Sweetheart…

  (*Charley enters.*)

CHARLEY: What's the matter?

ARLENE: I'm not sure. I think she's upset because of George. I just told her…

BO: He should be here right now! He's half an hour late!

ARLENE: Sweetheart, he's on his honeymoon.

BO: But it's daddy's birthday!

ARLENE: Well, when he comes back, he'll come over.

BO: Not if he moves to Albuquerque!

ARLENE: Of course he will. He'll come up. He'll visit.

BO: I don't want him to visit! I want him to be here! I want him here! Now! He's never not been at daddy's birthday!

ARLENE: Bo…I'm stunned. You've never shown that much affection for him. You're always making fun of George.

BO: He's my godfather!

ARLENE: Yes, he is your godfather and he'll always be your godfather.

BO: Not if he lives in Albuquerque! I don't want him to move! I don't want him to move! He'll be so far away! (*She falls down on her knees, crying.*) George. George.

ARLENE: Sweetheart, come here. Come here. (*She gathers Bo up and takes her to a chair, sits, holding her, comforting her.*) Sweetheart, I'm really surprised you're so upset.

BO: George… I want George…

ARLENE: We should be happy for him. He's making a new family for himself.

BO: We're his family.

ARLENE: Yes, we are. And we'll always be his family.

Bo: *(Crying.)* He comes to dinner practically every night now he won't. he won't come.

Arlene: He won't come as much but he will come. My love. We're not losing him. He hasn't died. He's healthy, he's on his way to Las Vegas right now with Consuela, he's very very happy.

Bo: He's supposed to be here. It's daddy's birthday.

Arlene: *(Stroking her hair.)* Sweetheart. I think he'd be very touched to see you so upset.

Bo: He won't even take me fishing any more.

Arlene: We'll take you fishing. So many other people in your life will take you fishing.

Bo: Nobody fishes like George.

Arlene: George will take you fishing again. With his new bride.

Bo: *(Screaming.)* She can't even speak English!

Arlene: She can speak a little. You can teach her.

Bo: No!

Arlene: *(Hugging her.)* Sweetheart. I'm sorry you feel so bad. I guess this came as kind of a shock to us all. I think what happened is George really liked talking to that psychiatrist. I don't think he'd ever held as sustained a conversation with a woman before. Don't you think that's what might have put him in the mood to look for someone?

Bo: He talks to you.

Arlene: I'm married. Daddy can talk to me whenever he likes. Now George has someone.

Bo: He can't talk to her. He doesn't know Spanish.

Arlene: He's learning it. You know, sometimes change feels like loss, like you're losing something and it's sad but change is just a way of clearing a space for something new. Sometimes you have to be really clever to see what that new thing is but it's almost always there. Life is full of changes, Bo, that's what's so interesting about it. The better you are at letting go of things, the freer your hands will be to catch something new.

Bo: George is really gonna freak out in Las Vegas. He's not going to know how to act.

Arlene: He'll do fine. Remember when Harry Dean Stanton died we talked about the stars, about how after a star has died you still see the light from the star, and Harry Dean Stanton was still a light in our lives, even though he was gone, and you said...

Bo: I don't need to hear this. Harry Dean Stanton was just a goat!

ARLENE: ...bear with me, I need to remember it. I'm a little sad today. I found the coyote in the woods this afternoon. You said, and I thought it was a lovely thought, that there were all those stars up there that you couldn't even see yet, all those new sources of light, new possibilities yet to come.

BO: George was my best friend. He would do anything I told him to.

ARLENE: It's very nice of you to feel so much for him, Bo, it's very sweet.

BO: He's the only one who knows what I got dad for his birthday.

ARLENE: What did you get him?

BO: A boat.

ARLENE: A boat. That's nice.

BO: I know. It's not gonna get here for a couple of weeks, dad. I cut out the picture and pasted it in your birthday card. It's on the table.

(*Charley gets the card and opens it.*)

ARLENE: That's a lovely idea.

BO: It sleeps two, we can all take turns.

ARLENE: It sleeps two? How big is this boat?

BO: Pretty big.

ARLENE: What's it made of?

BO: Stuff. Boat stuff. I ordered it from a magazine. It's a West Wight Potter. It's fifteen foot, has amazing stability and it's easy to sail.

ARLENE: You ordered a boat from a magazine?

BO: Yeah.

ARLENE: Really?

BO: Yeah.

ARLENE: I think they'll probably want some kind of payment.

BO: I charged it to my American Express Card.

ARLENE: Bo. (*Studies her.*) You got an American Express Card?

BO: Yeah. It came in the mail.

ARLENE: I never saw it.

BO: I know. They disguise the envelope. I almost threw it away.

ARLENE: You ordered a boat from a magazine?

BO: The only problem is it doesn't come with sails. But I thought we could make some. I thought it would give you something to do, dad. I thought it might help cheer you up.

CHARLEY: This is a beautiful boat.

ARLENE: Where is this boat right now?

BO: On some highway I guess. It's coming from California.

ARLENE: Could I ask how much it costs?

BO: It's a present, mom.

CHARLEY: It sleeps two?

BO: Maybe we can all squeeze in, or I'll just sleep on shore.

CHARLEY: I wonder if it would take a spinnaker.

ARLENE: That last letter you got from them. That was a bill?

CHARLEY: You got me a boat for my birthday.

BO: Yup. Happy Birthday, dad.

CHARLEY: Thanks.

BO: You're welcome.

(*Lights fade.*)

SCENE SIXTEEN

Adult Bo is sitting in the rocking chair on the deck. Lights come up on her.

ADULT BO: We lost George that summer. He and Consuela settled in Mexico, in Ojo Caliente where he was informed he'd been elected mayor without knowing he was on the ballot. I missed him terribly. The truth is I've never been very good at loss. This, I'm beginning to suspect, may have prevented certain personal areas of my life from... developing. I get lonely. I met Mr. Henry Gibbs at his brother's funeral seventeen years ago. Like all the other men at the service and in the entire country it seems, he was more bent on meeting my mother than me, having seen her naked in at least one of the close to three hundred paintings hanging throughout the southwest. Mr. Henry Gibbs asked if there was any possession of his brother's I wanted. I said I wanted the twenty-three albums of pictures of his meals he had kept under his bed as a child. I have kept them now for seventeen years. I have studied each picture a hundred times, each mound of mashed potato, each pork chop, orange and roll. For my birthday, I purchased one of his paintings, a portrait of me, a detailed study of the pumpkin patch below the garden. Even the artist himself did not know that I am there crouched beneath the leaves watching him watching my mother watching the coyote watching his prey watching its certain death. One constellation, six stars, three now out, we each have a different picture of the same fateful moment etched in the scrapbooks of our minds. The first time I laid eyes on William Gibbs.

(*Bo and Charley are sitting closely together at the table, studying figures on paper. Arlene is in the kitchen, cooking, more serious than she usually is. Charley is still not quite himself but on his way.*)

CHARLEY: Nice graph.

BO: Each chicken has its own column. Here it shows how many milligrams they get.

CHARLEY: I think we need another rooster for this experiment.

BO: Why?

CHARLEY: We have six hens, only two roosters. And we need more behavior categories. All we have is sleepy and aggressive.

BO: How else is a drugged chicken going to act?

CHARLEY: There's more categories.

BO: Like what?

CHARLEY: Happy. Disoriented.

BO: Dad, all chickens are disoriented. Anyway, we're almost out of drugs.

CHARLEY: We should get some more. This is interesting.

ARLENE: I don't think you should be feeding those drugs to the chickens. It's unkind.

CHARLEY: You fed them to me.

ARLENE: Bo, would you take this sandwich out to William? He's painting in the bus.

BO: I know. He's working on my painting. (*Bo gets the sandwich and exits. Charley watches Arlene in the kitchen.*)

ARLENE: I covered the tomatoes. I think there's going to be a frost tonight. Summer's over.

(*She chops vegetables on a cutting board. Charley watches her.*)

CHARLEY: What did you do to your hair?

ARLENE: My hair? Nothing.

CHARLEY: It looks different.

ARLENE: No it doesn't.

(*She keeps working. Upset.*)

CHARLEY: I asked him to do a painting of you. In the garden. You don't mind? (*She shakes her head.*) I'm going to make him some oil paints. I was reading in Da Vinci's notebooks. To make azure blue put cornflowers and then wild poppies. Amber is the latex of the cypress tree. You only have one boot on.

ARLENE: Mm. I took the other one off. *(He stares at her foot.)* Charley, how are we going to deal with this? We owe the government twelve hundred and sixty dollars and we owe American Express four thousand, seven hundred and seventy-six dollars. What are we going to do?

CHARLEY: Would you come here?

ARLENE: Huh?

CHARLEY: Would you come over here. Please?

ARLENE: What? *(Arlene, holding on to a bunch of carrots with greens, goes over to Charley. They look at each other.)* What?

CHARLEY: Put your foot up here.

ARLENE: Charley...

CHARLEY: Put it here.

(She puts her bare foot up on the chair. He takes hold of it, studies it as if it's the first time he's ever seen it. He slowly studies her calf, her knee, running his hand up her leg.)

ARLENE: *(Softly.)* Charley.

(She folds over him, her head on his head, as he slowly kisses her leg. Lights fade. They exit.)

SCENE SEVENTEEN

Lights up on William and Bo who are fishing off the deck. William holds the pole between his knees while he sketches with a pencil in a sketchpad. He wears a tie with a flannel shirt, scruffy, hair uncombed. Bo holds the pole between her knees while she reads a letter she's written.

BO: Dear George, I miss you. Today is Monday and Dad and I are going to the dump to get material to make a spinnaker. He thinks the boat will need one. Mom is in town at a softball game because Angel Rodriguez got too pregnant so mom is the catcher in the play-offs. All the women on the team wear blue fingernail polish. I still miss you very, very did I say very? much. There's a hole in the day here without you. Do you like your new job?

How's Consuela? Tell her again thanks for the t-shirt from Las Vegas. It's a little small so we're going to sew it into the spinnaker. Do you know what a spinnaker is? It's really a big sail that looks like a hot air balloon in the front bow of the boat. Oh. Dad says thanks for the watercolors. They really did the trick. So, that's it for Monday. I'll write tomorrow. Don't be surprised if a Nabisco delivery man pulls up with one of your many wedding presents from me. Your faithful goddaughter forever, Bo Groden. (*William looks at her, smiles, and kisses the top of her head. Resumes sketching. Bo smiles up at him, leans against him, puts her arms around him and keeps them there till she moves.*)

Scene Eighteen

ADULT BO: The funeral was in Santa Fe where William Gibbs' show at the Hungry Coyote Gallery received rave reviews in the New York Times that same day. They featured him on their Sunday magazine cover, his hair, thank the Lord washed, in a pony tail down to his waist. My thirty-one foot long painting of the ocean's horizon sold in that show for two hundred fifteen thousand dollars. When we sold it the fall my father was no longer so depressed to a wily art collector by name John Garlick, it fetched nine thousand dollars, enough to pay off the government, American Express and fit me with a set of braces. I have of late been pondering that painting. It has struck me to view the ocean as the past, the sky as the future, and the present as that thin precarious line where both meet, precarious because as we stand there it curves under foot, ever changing. Today I am 35 and more philosophical for it. At 35, my sky should be as big as my ocean, should hold a fair share of stars yet unseen. I'd forgotten my mother's words. About the stars. Change feeling like loss. (*Pause.*) William Gibbs died at 35, the same age his mother died, of the same rare disease. The summer my father was depressed William Gibbs thought he had lost his past, but it turned out his past had kept tight reins on him.

(*Arlene, Charley, William, George and Bo enter and take seats. Bo gets comfortably settled in the cushions in the bathtub, hanging one leg out the side. Arlene picks up "Two Years Before the Mast" and holds it as if she's been reading to them all.)*

ADULT BO: I plan to throw out those cherished albums of food, the journals of his youth. I have come to realize that although food is perishable the past is not. The notion of letting go of the past is a ridiculous one because the past will never let go of you. This revelation actually comes as some comfort to me.

(She keeps rocking as inside Arlene reads.)

ARLENE: "Every day the sun rose higher in the horizon, and the nights grew shorter; and at coming on deck each morning there was a sensible change in the temperature. The ice, too, began to melt from off the rigging and spars, and, except a little which remained in the tops and round the hounds of the lower masts, was soon gone. As we left the gale behind us, the reefs were shaken out of the topsails, and sail made as fast as she could bear it; and every time all hands were sent to the halyards a song was called for, and we hoisted away with a will. *(For the first time, Adult Bo enters the cabin, slowly walks behind her mother and rests her hand on Arlene's shoulders.)* Sail after sail was added, as we drew into fine weather; and in one week after leaving Cape Horn, the long top-gallant-masts were got up, top-gallant and royal yards crossed, and the ship restored to her fair proportions. The Southern Cross and the Magellan Clouds settled lower and lower in the horizon; and so great was our change of latitude that each succeeding night we sank some constellation in the south,…

ARLENE AND ADULT BO: …and raised another in the northern horizon."

(Lights have been fading. Music to Smith's "Rites of Spring" comes up.)

END OF PLAY

THE REINCARNATION OF JAIMIE BROWN
by Lynne Alvarez

In memory of Peter Jay Sharp:
Thank you

BIOGRAPHY

Lynne Alvarez arrived in New York in 1978 planning to be a hot shot poet. On a whim, she accompanied a friend to a gathering of Hispanic writers at the Puerto Rican Travelling Theatre. At 31, she had never had a thought of writing a play, but was now hooked. Lynne wrote two plays under the auspices of Miriam Colon and the Puerto Rican Travelling Theatre: *Graciela*, which was presented at the Puerto Rican Travelling Theatre and *Guitarron*, which earned Lynne an NEA Fellowship and premiered in 1984 at *St. Clements Theatre* in New York.

Lynne was a member of New Dramatists for seven years where she wrote *Hidden Parts* (1981) which won the Kesselring Award in 1983. She also wrote *The Wonderful Tower of Humbert Lavoigent* (1983), which won two awards: The Le Compte De Nouey Award in 1984 and an FDG/CBS Award for Best Play and later, Best Production at Capital Repertory Company in Albany, New York in 1984/85. In 1984, the Actors Theatre of Louisville commissioned a one-act play which became the full-length play, *Thin Air; Tales from a Revolution*. *Thin Air* premiered at the San Diego Repertory Company in 1987 and won a Drama League Award and a Rockefeller Fellowship in 1988. Lynne won a second NEA Fellowship in 1989/90.

Lynne has also done commissioned translations and adaptations: *The Damsel and the Gorilla* or *The Red Madonna* by Fernando Arraval for INTAR in 1988; Tirso de Molina's *Don Juan of Seville* for Classic Stage Company (CSC) and an adaptation of Boccaccio's *Decameron* called *Tales From The Time of the Plague* for CSC as well. Lynne's adaptation of the children's story, *Rikki Tikki Tavi,* and a musical based on *The Pied Piper of Hamlin* called *RATS*, had their premier at the Repertory Theater of St. Louis in 1991 and 1992.

Most recently Lynne has been the recipient of a New York Foundation grant in 1994 and has created two plays for ACT's Young Conservatory including *Jaimie Brown* and *Eddie Mundo Edmundo*. She is the author of two books of poetry and her plays have been widely published and anthologized. Her most current play, *The Absence of Miracles and the Rise of the Middle Class* is a murder mystery about class war in New York City.

AUTHOR'S NOTE

The truth is, I wrote *The Reincarnation of Jaimie Brown* for the pure fun of it. I was taking a breather from an unbroken line of serious plays such as *Thin Air* and *The Absence of Miracles and the Rise of the Middle Class* and decided to try my hand at comedy. Of course I'd never written a comedy before, so you'll find that *Jaimie Brown* does deal with suicide, various kinds of sexuality, reincarnation, hair loss, and so on. But I was delighted to have a chance to be a relatively free spirit—at least on paper.

I've always been fascinated by the interplay of character and destiny, fate and free will—especially in a country which bristles at the mention of fate and views the concept of destiny as a ludicrous delusion. Yes, there is desultory agreement that one can be genetically "fated" to have brown hair, to be thin, gay, subject to heart attacks or sudden attacks of creativity. But for the most part we Americans feel that if it exists, we can tamper with it. In any event, I saw no reason to cease exploring this theme because I was writing a comedy. I could also indulge a writer's prerogative to include any damn thing he or she wants by using references to people I love, or art I admire—*i.e.* dragging in a poem of Richard Wilbur's, some favorite astrological arguments, references to jazz, rock n' roll, and some very early, very earnest poems of my own.

What's more, I could grind any number of axes under the guise of comedy including: intolerance, the difficulty of finding an apartment in Manhattan, money and art, personal property and taste, flowers, champagne, youth and old age.

What could be better?

ORIGINAL PRODUCTION

THE REINCARNATION OF JAIMIE BROWN was first presented through the New Plays Program at American Conservatory Theater (Carey Perloff, Artistic Director), San Francisco, California. It was directed by Craig Slaight; costumes by Allie Floor; lighting by Kelly Roberson; music composed by Lois Cantor, and Richard Taybe was the assistant director. The cast was as follows:

Jaimie Brown . . . . Stephanie Potts
Jimmy. . . . . Mike Merola

David Baldwin	Ryan Kennedy
San Bot Lhu (Sammy)	Sarah Hayon
Hudan Bot Lhu (Hughie)	Uri Horowitz
Tina, Marie, Joyce	Christianne Hauber
Boris	Brad Clark
Wilson Meredith	Jack Sharrar

THE REINCARNATION OF JAIMIE BROWN by Lynne Alvarez. © 1994 by Lynne Alvarez. All rights reserved. Published by permission of the playwright. All inquiries concerning rights should be addressed to Joyce Ketay, The Joyce Ketay Agency, 334 West 89th St., New York, NY 10024. For caution note please refer to copyright page.

CAST

In order of Appearance:

JAIMIE BROWN, 19. Street Poet.

JIMMY (JAMES HOBARTH III), 19., Juggler, or other street performer. (Educated at Princeton)

DAVID BALDWIN, 23. Singer, composer.

SAN BOT LHU (SAMMY), Any age, all ages, expert in reincarnation. Played by a woman, but appears as a man until the end.

HUDAN BOT LHU (HUGHIE), As above, but a man, dressed identically to Sammy. Always speaks in questions.

MARIE, 20s. Brooklyn, intermittent girlfriend of David's.

JOYCE, 20s. Wilson's onetime date.

BORIS (The Butler), 20s-30s. Strapping, handsome, blond Russian.

TINA, 40s. The Polish maid. Boris' wife.

WILSON MEREDITH, Late 60s. Tycoon, literal, but cultured.

All bits and crowd scenes should be played by cast members who are not in the immediate scene. No effort should be made to hide this fact. The same actress plays Tina, Marie and Joyce.

SET

All action takes place in the present at:

Port Authority Bus Terminal in New York City

Jaimie's Apartment

Wilson's Estate

The Beach

Kennedy Airport

THE REINCARNATION OF JAIMIE BROWN

ACT ONE

Jaimie Brown enters in black. She carries a paper cup of coffee and wears a derby. She has obviously just awakened. Port Authority Bus Terminal takes shape around her. People wander by, pillars come down (obviously made of cardboard). They descend unevenly. One lands on a passerby who yelps and is extracted by two other people. Jaimie dodges one.

JAIME: Construction in New York's a bitch. (*She passes a donut stand, hands the vendor a sheet of paper and grabs a donut. He starts to protest.*) Don't sweat it, man—in a couple years that'll be worth a fortune. I sign all my copies. A small investment now could set you up for life, you know what I mean? (*People pass, she tries to sell them a poem.*) You want a poem, Miss...uh you there, Miss, how about a poem? Thanks a lot. And you sir...a poem, an adventure—
(*The man stops and looks her up and down lasciviously. Opens his raincoat and flashes Jaimie. Jaimie confronts him. As she walks forward, he walks back until at some point he turns and flees.*)
not that kind of adventure, man, but thanks for sharing.
I bet you and I are thinking alot of the same things right now.
I'm out here selling poetry, but you're walking around naked under that raincoat with the same question burning between

your...ah...ears.

"What's happened to poetry in America?"

Am I right?

I mean when was the last time a poem

rattled your bones?

Well here I am to remedy that.

Cast off, blast off

I'm the new wave poetry slave

I know what you're thinking — you have to study Elizabethan English to read poetry; you have to buy an arcane insane esoteric totally prosaic literary magazine available in only one bookstore on 47th street twice a year — am I correct?

Or you feel to hear a good poem you have to kneel at the knees of some MMP—Major Male Poet preferably facing his crotch.

Now tell me if that isn't true? Sad isn't it?

Well I say, no way

I give you your poetry straight

no rap, no rock, bee bop or hip hop

So how about five dollars, man?

You can afford it. Think of what you must save on clothes.

(*The Flasher turns and runs.*)

Yes, yes, yes

I'm the new wave poetry slave

the last living purist in America—

(*David walks by with an instrument case. She looks him over.*)

Well maybe I'm not all that pure,

Hey you—superdude.

Yeah you. What's up? (*She follows him.*)

You want a poem? A touch of culture, a touch of class

Love'em and leave'em right?

I have something just for you...

A road poem, a heartbreak poem, lonesome sexy blues.

DAVID: Are you trying to pick my pocket?

JAIME: Dude, those jeans are so tight

no one could pick your pocket without a surgical instrument.

Looks good though. Don't get me wrong.

Now, how about a poem?

I'm in a difficult profession here.

I'm a major if undiscovered poet

reduced to selling original works of art on the street.

I have hundreds of poems ready made—for all occasions,

every mood, theory, relationship and philosophy of life.

Only two dollars. Five dollars will get you

an original, custom–composed on the spot, stirring, moving unique

work of art and for only one dollar—and this is an introductory

offer. I can write you a limerick as effective as a quick kick in the butt.

What do you say?

DAVID: Sorry, kid.

JAIME: Signed. Dated, limited copy.

Think of it as an investment.

Or if you like, you can pass it off as your own.

You take the credit, I'll take the cash.

No problem.

DAVID: You're broke. *(He hands her a dollar.)*

JAIME: Totally.

But this isn't charity.

You get your limerick.

Now—who's this for? Sweetheart, mother, boss. The judge that let you off the hook, what?

DAVID: A girlfriend.

JAIME: Figures.

Her name?

DAVID: Marie.

JAIME: Catholic, round collars, flat shoes.

DAVID: Not quite.

JAIME: Okay. Forget it.

Marie…Marie…

Romantic, raucous, rancorous or vindictive?

I have a great vocabulary.

What mood do you want? I'm talking tone here.

DAVID: Romantic.

JAIME: Dirty or clean?

DAVID: Jesus.

JAIME: Okay, clean. Got it.

Where's she from?

DAVID: I have to meet her bus, all right?

JAIME: If I were making a suit, I'd take your measurements correct?

DAVID: She's from Arkansas.

JAIME: Nobody's from Arkansas...

Okay, Arkansas, the dude wants a rhyme for
Arkansas...

Arkansas *(She's writing.)*

I like a challenge.

All right.

DAVID: Shoot.

JAIME: I'll read it for free, but it's 50 cents if you want a copy.

DAVID: *(Hands her 2 quarters.)* Go buy an airplane.

How long've you been doing this?

JAIME: Eight months. *(Reads)*

There's a sweet young thing
named Marie...

DAVID: Must be tough.

JAIME: No problem. *(Starts to read again.)*

There's a sweet young thing named Marie
Who I'm just dying to see...

DAVID: Have you ever thought of taking on a regular job?

JAIME: What are you talking about? I could get a steady job any day,
but I believe you are what you do, okay?

If I'm waitressing and waiting to be a poet—then I'm a waitress
waiting to be a poet. Simple, I cut the waiting.

Now let me read the damn thing, so I can get on with this.

There's a sweet young thing
named Marie.

Who I'm just dying to see
She's got what it takes
So I don't need no brakes
Cause Marie's just dying to "blank" me.

DAVID: Blank?

JAIME: As in fill in the blank...

I don't know you. So I couldn't tell how strong to make it...
so what do you want...hug, kiss, fuck?

Fill it in.

DAVID: You didn't use Arkansas.

JAIME: What do you want for a dollar?

(Announcements of arrivals and departures.)

DAVID: Here's five kid.

    Keep the wolf away from the door.

JAIME: I got to give you a poem then. A real one. *(She finds one.)*

    I personalize them.

    What's your name?

DAVID: David.

JAIME: Hi. I'm Jaimie Brown.

DAVID: Gotta go.

JAIME: Right.

    You're a musician, right?

    Guitar?

DAVID: Synthesizer. *(He exits.)*

JAIME: Musicians are cool.

    (A mugging is going on.)

    There must be a better way to make a living.

    (Jimmy walks by, also in black. Pale, thin. He carries a small bag. Stops nearby, opens his bag. Starts juggling. He puts a hat on the floor. The muggers come by. Stare and then throw him some money. The muggee comes by and takes it out angrily. Sammy comes in wearing a suit, tie, etc. Watches Jimmy and throws in a coin. Jaimie starts her routine.)

JAIME: Okay, all right.

    Poems for sale.

    Poetry

    the real thing

    right from me.

    Choose the topic, choose the tone

    Buy a poem

    that's all your own.

    No rap, no haiku.

    (Sammy watches standing close, peering.)

    Look buster, if you don't want a poem, move on.

    Okay?

SAMMY: You have a mole on your face.

JAIME: Mole! What mole? That's a beauty mark.

    Get lost.

SAMMY: Are you an orphan?

JAIME: Look. I'm not a runaway. Okay? Or a crook, or a hooker.

    There's no poster out on me no photo on a milk carton, got it?

SAMMY: I'd like a poem.

JAIME: Two dollars ready made and five bucks made to order.

SAMMY: What do you have already made up?

JAIME: I have hundreds of poems.

    I mean I have everything—suicide to seashells.

    I have lots of love poems. People usually want love poems.

    Do you have any idea what you want?

SAMMY: What kind of love poems do you have?

JAIME: Let's see. Ecstatic, dramatic, trivial, passionate…

SAMMY: No other kind of love?

JAIME: Right. Weird.

    I should have known. Look.

    I deal with heterosexual love.

    If you want me to work it around a little

    I'll have to charge you.

SAMMY: I see. No love of God, love of mankind, nature, beauty, truth, a rose and so on?

JAIME: Oh.

SAMMY: Yes?

JAIME: How about me writing you one on the spot.

SAMMY: Fine.

JAIME: Five dollars though.

SAMMY: Fine.

JAIME: You choose the topic, but I write what I want. And if it goes over 10 lines, there's an additional fee plus 50 cents for giving you a written copy.

SAMMY: Fine.

JAIME: So. You want one on love, right?

SAMMY: No.

JAIME: Okay.

    What then?

SAMMY: *(Meaningfully.)* The number one.

JAIME: The number one.

    As in one, two, three, four, five…?

SAMMY: Yes.

    The number one.

    (Jimmy has stopped juggling and has come to watch.)

JAIME: Half up front.

    Don't wander off. This'll take a minute.

    (Sammy hands her the money. Jaimie scribbles, Jimmy juggles.)

JAIME: Okay. *(To Jimmy)*

That beats it friend. Leave. I can't concentrate. Got it?

(Jimmy shrugs and walks away still juggling.)

Look, I have your poem Mr...

SAMMY: San Bot Lhu.

JAIME: Yeah. I personalize my work here. I put a dedication "to" and your name.

Now San Bot what?

SAMMY: Sammy, put Sammy.

JAIME: Great. *(Writes it in.)*

This is heavy. But I write what comes out, okay?

You ready?

SAMMY: *(Crosses his arms.)* Sure thing.

JAIME: *(Reads)* To Sammy

One bears witness

disguised as the enemy

among us.

The burning stake

the bloody pike is his

the mother covering her

child's eyes.

One watches and remembers

One is the tower and the well.

the woman rocking in the street,

One is the empty house, the empty pocket,

the glass about to be filled.

(A moment of silence.)

SAMMY: You don't look like you'd write a poem like that.

(Takes the poem.)

JIMMY: Appearances are deceiving.

JAIME: What do you know?!

JIMMY: You're not a bad poet.

SAMMY: Are you here every day?

JAIME: When the sun's out I'm in Central Park. Rain, snow, frost, hail—I'm here.

SAMMY: I see. *(Sammy exits.)*

JIMMY: Are you all right?

JAIME: I'm fine. Why?

JIMMY: That poem was pretty depressing.

JAIME: Sue me.

I've had a lousy life.

Don't just stand there. This isn't a freak show.

You make me nervous.

JIMMY: What?

JAIME: It's a big planet. Feel free to explore it.

JIMMY: We'd do better if we stuck together.

JAIME: No way.

JIMMY: *(Juggling.)* Who'd cross the street to buy a poem?

Really.

But juggling has high visibility.

(Juggles high.)

Get it?

Juggling draws a crowd.

Bingo. They see me, hear you,

their hand's already in their pocket,

voila.

JAIME: It won't work now.

Business is lousy.

JIMMY: So we'll go somewhere else.

JAIME: This place has always been lucky for me.

Just the last couple of days have been rotten.

JIMMY: Last couple of days?

JAIME: Yeah, the pits.

JIMMY: Mercury retrograde.

JAIME: Mercury retrograde. What's that? Metal pollution?

JIMMY: My dear, my dear...

Metal pollution.

You're a poet...think of the planets—Venus, Mercury;

think Romeo and Juliet; think starcrossed;

think getting into the bathtub and the phone rings:

think sending a letter and forgetting the zip code;

think bounced checks, stalled cars, accidents, strikes

misunderstandings—that's mercury retrograde.

Mercury rules communications. When it goes retrograde—

miscommunications—thus people lose things or fight.

JAIME: Shit. That bad?

JIMMY: The only good attribute of Mercury retrograde is...

Finding lost objects and people from the past.

Mercury retrograde brings them back.

JAIME: So how long do I have to look forward to everyone fighting and striking and whatever—

JIMMY: It goes direct in three weeks. At noon I believe.

JAIME: Three weeks. No money for three weeks?!

JIMMY: Two hats are fuller than one.

James Hobarth III. Jimmy to you.

And?

JAIME: Jaimie Brown, here.

JIMMY: Jimmy and Jaimie…unfortunate.

But then, it could be quite vaudeville.

Jimmy and Jaimie.

Okay, try Jaimie and Jimmy…

(*Sammy returns dragging Hughie. They are dressed exactly alike.*)

Dear Heart, speaking of duos…

HUGHIE: This is her?

SAMMY: Ask her for a poem.

HUGHIE: Will you write me a poem? (*He holds out money.*)

Is this enough?

SAMMY: Look at the mole.

(*Hughie peers at Jimmy.*)

JIMMY: (*Touches his face, he has a bandage on his cheek.*)

How did you know I had a mole?

I cut it off shaving.

SAMMY: Not him.

Her mole.

(*Hughie peers.*)

JAIME: Beauty mark, man.

HUGHIE: Are you an orphan?

JAIME: (*To Jimmy*) Can you believe this?

(*To Hughie*) Look, tell me what kind of poem you want.

(*Sammy and Hughie strike identical poses, identically dressed.*)

(*Jaimie looks at them.*)

No. No.

Let me guess.

You want a poem about the number two, right?

HUGHIE: How does she know that?

SAMMY: What did I tell you!

JAIME: Just give me a minute.

JIMMY: I can do a routine about the number two. (*He juggles two balls.)* And number three. *(He juggles three balls.)* Number four. *(He juggles four.)* Should I go higher?

SAMMY: Yes. Yes.

JIMMY: Watch. *(He juggles the four balls very high.)*

JAIME: All right you guys,
you dude…

SAMMY: She wants your name.

HUGHIE: Why?

SAMMY: This is Hudan Bot Lhu.
Call him Hughie.

JAIME: To Hughie…
Here we go.
Two is always hungry,
the doublebarrelled shotgun
propped against his chin
the knock on the door
the stillness of night
Two is the black horse and rider
the streak of horizon
Nose to nose and belly to belly
Two is always hungry
and in mortal danger.

HUGHIE: *(Excitedly)* Did you hear?

SAMMY: Yes!
The shotgun!

HUGHIE: How about the "knock on the door?"

SAMMY: The stillness of night!
The suicide
That's just how it was.
Amazing.

HUGHIE: You wrote this?

JAIME: No I dreamed it.
Two fifty plus twenty five cents.

SAMMY: *(Hands her the money.)* We need your birthdate.

HUGHIE: When were you born?

JAIME: Off limits.
Sorry guys.

SAMMY: We are experts in reincarnation!
We need information.

JIMMY: Reincarnation—a perfect Mercury retrograde activity. Finding lost people!

SAMMY: I assure you we are legitimate.

HUGHIE: Are there not wine connoisseurs who from the mere taste and appearance of a wine, can tell you the site of its vineyard and the year of its origin?

Are there not antiquarians who by a mere glance at an object, can name the time, place and individual maker?

SAMMY: And we, given certain details, can tell what your last incarnation was. We have clients.

We are searching for someone in particular now.

JIMMY: Give them your birthdate.

What can it hurt?

JAIME: February 25, 1976...

JIMMY: I was born on February 25th!

HUGHIE: And where were you born?

JAIME: On a farm in Missouri.

JIMMY: He needs the city.

JAIME: How do you know?

JIMMY: This is very exciting.

JAIME: I was born near Jefferson City.

JIMMY: What time?

HUGHIE: What time?

JAIME: How would I know?

SAMMY: *(Whips out cellular phone.)* Call your mother and ask.

JAIME: She's dead.

Sammy and HUGHIE: Ahhhhhhhhhh.

HUGHIE: Are you an orphan?

JIMMY: Go ahead. Admit it.

I'm an orphan. No big deal.

JAIME: Okay. All right.

I'm an orphan.

(To Jimmy) What is this, a club?

(To Hughie) So how can I tell you what time I was born?

HUGHIE: Were you born in the morning?

JAIME: How would I...

Wait—My mom always said I was born an early riser...

(Sammy elbows Hughie.)

SAMMY: This has been very interesting. Thank you.

HUGHIE: What's your name?

JAIME: Jaimie.

SAMMY: Jaimie. James.

HUGHIE: You see?

JAIME: So who was I?

SAMMY: We'll be in touch.

(*They exit.*)

JAIME: You can have this place. It' s too weird.

JIMMY: We've seen the hand of God.

We've just seen fate at work.

JAIME: We?

JIMMY: Now I know why we hit it off.

We're both Pisces.

Giving, sensual, sensitive.

JAIME: Are you hitting on me?

JIMMY: No. (*He turns abruptly and juggles away.*)

JAIME: Sensitive is right. (*Goes after him.*)

So what's your problem?

JIMMY: I need a place to stay.

JAIME: Hey, I only have one room, no running water.

JIMMY: No problem. It's warm out.

Point me to a park bench.

I'm cool.

JAIME: You're crazy.

Where are you from?

JIMMY: Boston.

JAIME: In New York, you can't just sleep anywhere.

JIMMY: Don't worry about it. It's not your problem.

JAIME: Yeah. Sorry.

(*David walks by, arguing with a girl in a tight, short leather skirt, with tank top and spiked red hair. She has a heavy Brooklyn accent.*)

DAVID: I'm here, aren't I.

MARIE: So what? I'm supposed to be ecstatic?

I wake up and you left a note pinned to my chest.

You call that romantic?

DAVID: I knew if I said anything, we'd argue.

MARIE: And whaddaya call this?! (*She slaps him hard and walks off.*)

JIMMY: Typical.

Mercury retrograde.

Never leave a note.

66　✻　LYNNE ALVAREZ

JAIME: *(To David)* Class act.

You always pick them like that?

DAVID: I like women who are hard to handle.

If they're too easy, I get bored.

JAIME: I guess she doesn't bore you, then. She seems like a three–ring circus.

DAVID: Actually, she's pretty predictable. She'll call me tonight between six and seven.

JAIME: So that's Arkansas.

DAVID: Via Brooklyn. *(Hands her back the limerick.)*

I didn't have a chance to give her this.

JAIME: Sorry. No refunds.

DAVID: Store credit?

JAIME: Read it to her when she calls.

DAVID: What if I'm not home?

> *(Jaimie shrugs.)*

What if I'm out with you, darling?

JIMMY: He's hitting on you.

JAIME: *(To Jimmy)* Mind your own business.

(To David) You're not going out with me.

DAVID: I like feisty women.

JAIME: You didn't ask me out.

DAVID: Will you go out with me?

JAIME: I don't know.

What would we do? Hang out?

DAVID: Sure. Go to the park, drink wine, listen to music.

JAIME: Your treat?

DAVID: Why not?

JAIME: Okay.

(To Jimmy) I'm going to take your advice. Why fight the stars, right? The joint's yours.

JIMMY: Thanks.

DAVID: Do you have everything?

JAIME: Yeah.

Just a sec.

(Goes to Jimmy) Look. You can't stay in my room. I need my privacy. But you can stay in the hall.

The lady I take care of lives right across, but she won't mind.

Here's the address. *(She writes it out for him.)*

Ring the bell. I can see you from the window. Second floor, left front, there's tomato plants on the fire escape—and don't pick any!

I'm pretty sure you're safe, but I sleep with a knife, got it? So, keep out of trouble

(She exits with David.)

JIMMY: I knew it.

Pisces are a soft touch.

(Wilson's Estate. Paneled room with many windows looking out over grounds. Sunlight. Wilson is listening to Gregorian chants. His girl of the moment, Joyce, in a two–piece thong bikini, with a bright luxurious scarf knotted as a skirt, jewelry. She's bored. Boris the Butler in white slacks and pale pink polo shirt is serving drinks. Boris is stoic, Joyce flirts outrageously when she thinks Wilson isn't looking.)

WILSON: Joyce—this music is magic, it's time travel, it's immortality, don't you think?

JOYCE: Divine.

WILSON: These Gregorian chants date from the 8th century. I can smell the damp ancient stone, the incense; I can see the brown–robed tonsured monks. Primitive. Extraordinary.

The eighth century experienced now in the twentieth!

Boris, Dewars please.

(He holds out his glass. Boris rushes over and fills it.)

JOYCE: *(Stretches so Boris notices. Wilson admires her too.)*

Mmmmmmmmmmmmmmmmmmmmmmmmmmmmmmm.

WILSON: Do you know what they call these?

JOYCE: Sure. Gregory chants just like you said.

WILSON: Antiphonal psalmody. Plain chants. So many names. It reminds me of my son. He was a monk you know. The only way I can understand his calling is to listen to this music, ascetic grave. This music has given me hope through its own immortality. It expresses the possibility that my son is also immortal. Somewhere I believe his spark of life has been transferred to a new and startling soul—

just the way a song lives on by being passed from mouth to mouth down through the ages. My son too, lives on, reincarnated—and I will find him if it's at all possible.

Do you think it is, Joyce? Possible?

JOYCE: *(Runs her hands over Boris' thighs.)* Anything's possible. That's my motto.

My mother said those were my father's first words when he saw me as a baby.

What do you think he meant?

WILSON: Joyce dear—I'm a very rich man and I can afford to have the best—and the way I determine the best—is through a series of tests and you my dear...

JOYCE: Yes. Tell me.

WILSON: Have failed. *(He takes her glass.)*

The only reason I keep a butler who looks like a porno star is to separate the wheat from the chaff. There's a helicopter waiting for you on the lawn.

(Joyce gets up to leave.)

JOYCE: Wilson...

WILSON: Now. Now. Let's not spoil a perfectly superfluous weekend with attempts at insight.

A lovely weekend, Joyce.

(He kisses her cheek. She exits. He savors his drink.)

BORIS: Sirrr...

WILSON: No need to apologize.

I'm a capitalist. I believe in competition.

You can bring in the boys now.

(Boris exits and returns with Sammy and Hughie.)

WILSON: *(Without turning. Facing the ocean.)* Did you know that if you stay near the ocean and in the proximity of young women, you never get old?

Passion—the elixir of youth!

HUGHIE: *(Very interested.)* Really?!

(Sammy elbows him.)

WILSON: Would you care for anything after your travels?

Champagne, perhaps?

HUGHIE: *(Delightedly)* Champagne?

(Sammy elbows him.)

Do you have something to eat?

WILSON: Of course, of course.

Bring some carrots.

SAMMY: We're starving.

WILSON: And some celery.

Would you like that with salt or plain?

HUGHIE: Salt?

SAMMY: Plain.

WILSON: And turn down the music as you leave. *(To Sammy and Hughie)*

Isn't it extraordinary?

SAMMY: Extraordinary.

WILSON: So gentlemen.

What do you have for me?

SAMMY: We have three candidates. All born within three years of your son's death. All orphans, discovered at the same latitude 40 North and longitude 73 West within a radius of 66 miles from his death.

HUGHIE: Don't you think it should be from his birth?

SAMMY: We've discussed this.

HUGHIE: Have we?

SAMMY: Yes. But we don't agree.

WILSON: I thought you were experts.

SAMMY: We always disagree over beginnings. But we never disagree at the end.

HUGHIE: Didn't we guarantee, no results, no payment?

WILSON: Yes you did.

No results, no payment.

HUGHIE: And weren't our references impeccable?

WILSON: You wouldn't be here otherwise.

SAMMY: The Dalai Lama himself and the Maharajah of Jaipur.

HUGHIE: Didn't we also get a prelate from the Orthodox Church?

SAMMY: No.

HUGHIE: Prince Charles?

SAMMY: Enough.

WILSON: Enough.

HUGHIE: *(Stage whisper.)* Could I have a mint julep?

(Sammy elbows him.)

WILSON: You two are my last hope of locating my son's reincarnation. I've already used psychics and numerologists and astrologers, white magic, black magic and psychotherapy. I've behaved like a dotty bereaved eccentric of the worst kind.

Yet I know, I sense that I can find my boy. I can find him.

But if I can't, if you two who are deemed the best in your field cannot find him, I'll accept defeat as gracefully as I can. I'm prepared to will my entire estate to a series of worthy causes—although to see my life's blood in the hands of lawyers and trustees is almost more than I can bear to imagine…

HUGHIE: *(Trying to be sociable. Holding a drink, slightly tipsy.)* Really?

WILSON: Does he always ask questions?

SAMMY: That's how he talks.

He distrusts reality. *(To Hughie, cueing a set speech.)*
Hughie?

HUGHIE: Why aren't questions enough?

Why do people insist on answers
if all answers fall short of reality?
Don't people see that questions are a journey?
Why must people insist we end the quest with finality?

BORIS: Another mint julep?

(Hughie takes it and smiles.)

SAMMY: Our candidates, sir.

WILSON: Yes.

SAMMY: Each candidate had a quality that was extremely pertinent to
your son's life and character.

HUGHIE: Aren't there three?

SAMMY: Three. Yes three. The number of full expression; Number one
became a successful stockbroker at 15.

HUGHIE: Didn't your son take his vows as a novitiate at 15?

WILSON: Yes.

HUGHIE: How could an adolescent take a vow of silence?

SAMMY: Number two specializes in illumination of sacred texts in gold
leaf. He also adores skeet shooting.

HUGHIE: Like your son?

WILSON: Yes.

HUGHIE: What about the girl?

WILSON: A girl?

Discount that one.

SAMMY: Unlikely perhaps, but your son did like men.

WILSON: Yes, he was a homosexual.

SAMMY: This girl likes men. She is also unusually attuned to mystical
poetry.

WILSON: My son would never come back as a woman.

SAMMY: We think that this was his first incarnation as a man and therefore...

HUGHIE: We?

SAMMY: And therefore it was something of a shock to find himself a
man and he left before his incarnation was completed...

HUGHIE: Wouldn't it be far more logical to conclude that his next incarnation would be as a woman and therefore he was preparing himself...?

SAMMY: In any event, finding himself in a man's body proved extremely agitating to him and before he could fully learn this life's lesson—what it is like to be a man who loves men—he...

WILSON: Propped a shotgun against his temple and pulled the trigger.

SAMMY: Yes.

HUGHIE: Perhaps we should look for someone suicidal?

(*Sammy elbows him and Hughie doubles over.*)

WILSON: Your conjectures don't interest me.

I want results.

No results, no money.

We have agreed on the criteria...

SAMMY: Yes.

The size of the cranium, slant of the ears, the mole, the nails with no half moons, coincidence of preferences, identification of your son's favorite ring, walking stick and mare.

HUGHIE: Mayor? Was he political?

SAMMY: (*To Hughie*) Mare. Mare. A horse.

(*To Wilson*) Moreover the person must be a Pisces, the ruling sign of your son's fourth house, the house of endings...

HUGHIE: Wouldn't you think...?

(*Sammy covers Hughie's mouth.*)

WILSON: I'm very anxious to see these people.

I'm actually nervous, can you believe it?

There are many strange and wonderful things in the world and yet...

How will I know—without a doubt—that this person is my son reincarnated? I can't imagine what proof could possibly convince me absolutely that I have found my son.

SAMMY: First,

discard the idea of proof.

Proof refers only to causality; results produced by an observable and logical sequence of classified and isolated phenomena.

The only thing proof gives you is objective correlation; statistical proof.

So discard proof.

Accept—coincidence.

Coincidence is more than chance.

Coincidence is the interdependence of all events in a single moment in time. Synchronicity!

And we, who are trained in this field, will find for you the one detail in the moment of coincidence that reveals the absolute truth.

When you find the absolute truth—there is no doubt.

I promise you. It will be a true revelation.

WILSON: Shall we toast the truth?

(*They hold their glasses aloft.*)

To revelations.

HUGHIE: Revelations?

SAMMY: Revelations.

(*They wait. Wilson is lost in thought.*)

WILSON: My poor son died for passion,

while passion gives me something to live for. (*He exits.*)

HUGHIE: (*Takes more champagne from Boris' tray.*) Another toast?

SAMMY: To what?

HUGHIE: Passion? (*He toasts and drinks by himself.*)

SAMMY: You drink too much.

HUGHIE: (*Toasts by himself again.*) Isn't the body the tavern of the living spirit?

SAMMY: Temple.

The body is the temple of the living spirit.

HUGHIE: Ahhhhhhhhh.

(*Later that evening, the street. Jaimie and David returning from the park. A couple of bums are lying around as parts of Jaimie's small room are being assembled. They grumble and are pushed aside. One bum grabs a bag from the other. Bum One yells "Help". Police come. Bum Two yells "Stop, Thief" and points ahead of himself. Police run off. Bum Two saunters across stage.*)

JAIME: This neighborhood is the pits.

They always ask if it's affordable. No one asks

if it's livable. (*The apartment or rather room is assembled. Jaimie points to different corners.*)

No bathroom. But McDonald's is two doors down and

they're open all night.

DAVID: Starving artist, eh?

JAIME: Yeah.

I find it therapeutic to refer to different corners

of the same room as the living room, dining room, kitchen...

DAVID: Bedroom.

JAIME: Yeah. It's the bedroom. So?

DAVID: Nothing. *(Pointing to a poster.)*
Who's that?

JAIME: Rimbaud. The French poet.

DAVID: Didn't Sly Stallone do him? *(Imitates Rambo with a machine gun.)*

JAIME: You're thinking of Rambo you jerk—

DAVID: I know honey. I know.

JAIME: Well I like him. He did his best work by 21, quit to run guns and leave graffiti on the pyramids.
Great poets die young you know. I'm going to die when I'm 27, maybe 28 tops.

DAVID: Really?

JAIME: And this is...

DAVID: Let me guess.

JAIME: Shut up.

DAVID: My psychic energy, my spiritual guide tell meee...Bob Dylan.
Greatest rock poet ever born...

JAIME: And a great outlaw. I love outlaws.

DAVID: *(Checking out her windows.)* You must. These windows are an open invitation to any outlaw who happens by. Put some bars on the windows—eh. Then you can chose which outlaws come into this pad.

JAIME: How sweet. You want to protect me.

DAVID: Do you bring just anyone up here?

JAIME: Do you go up to just anyone's pad—dude?

DAVID: You seem pretty sure I'm not going to jump you or anything.

JAIME: You seem cool. I'm a good judge of character.

DAVID: So was Jesus and Judas nailed him.

JAIME: Right.

DAVID: That was a joke.

JAIME: I know. It was good. Smart.

DAVID: Hey. What's up?

JAIME: Nothing. I'm great.

DAVID: We were having a great time and now you're like...

JAIME: Like what?

DAVID: Down, beat. I don't know.
Shall I leave?

JAIME: No.

DAVID: Fine.

(*They stand awkwardly.*)

JAIME: I'm nervous.

DAVID: What's the matter?

JAIME: I like you.

DAVID: (*Moving closer.*) Great!

JAIME: I mean really.

And now that I got you up here. I don't know what to do.

DAVID: What do you usually do?

JAIME: Usually? Are you nuts?

With all the disease–ridden, murderers, punks, pimps and per-verts out there—do you think I'd be stupid enough to bring any-one to my room? Let alone have them know where I live?

DAVID: So I'm the first?

(*He moves away from her. Jaimie nods.*)

JAIME: Don't sweat it. I've been deflowered.

Cowboys.

DAVID: Cowboys?

JAIME: (*Hooks her fingers in her jeans.*) Walllll ma'am, been real nice, but I gotta be movin' on.

Cowboys!

How about you?

DAVID: Me?

JAIME: Are you in love now?

DAVID: Let's just say I'm a cowboy, ma'am.

Better steer clear of me.

JAIME: Really?

DAVID: The only thing I know how to do is play music.

JAIME: So play.

DAVID: Right. (*Takes out his keyboard.*) Just happen to have my little keyboard.

JAIME: What kind of stuff do you play?

DAVID: Sorta post–punk, semi–funk, hillbilly–hardcore with a bluesy edge.

JAIME: Oh.

DAVID: (*Setting up.*) I have a new song.

JAIME: Groovy.

DAVID: Groovy? What's this sixties shit?

JAIME: I'm a purist. I'm trying to preserve classic language. Play.

DAVID: It doesn't have a title yet. (*He plays.*) So...what do you think?

JAIME: I think you're the real thing.

DAVID: Thanks.

JAIME: It's in your blood, isn't it?

DAVID: Yeah I guess. My dad was a jazz drummer. You know the kind in bars, plays, smokes pot with his friends—what people in jazz do.

Didn't really know him too well.

JAIME: My mom was into country. She was an Elvis freak.

We're pretty different.

DAVID: Very. *(He goes to kiss her.)*

JAIME: Do you believe in love at first sight?

DAVID: You're going to spoil this, aren't you?

JAIME: I thought that was romantic.

DAVID: Romantic? Love?

Love's a responsibility.

Now sex—that's romantic.

JAIME: I don't just go around saying that, you know.

DAVID: Why did you just say it now?

JAIME: Cause that's what I was feeling.

Cause I thought you'd dig it.

I've never been in love before.

DAVID: And you're not afraid to tell me this?

JAIME: Well shit, yeah!

DAVID: Jaimie, you're too open. You got to protect yourself. Look, I don't have a lot of experience with heart-on-the-sleeve kind of people. Maybe I should leave.

JAIME: Maybe you shouldn't take it so hard.

Maybe I was just trying to nail you against the wall to see what you'd do—rip your skin off a little before I decide whether to put salt or ice cream on you.

Do you want to leave?

DAVID: No.

JAIME: I could read you some of my stuff?

DAVID: No love poems.

JAIME: Right.

This one's great.

I based it on a man I overheard downstairs... *(Reads)*

"I just like to see'em fall, slow
like in the movies,
drops of blood spread,
sailing through the air

as if they don't belong nowhere
and land, spla—a—at, like rain
on the river..."
DAVID: Uh...no. I don't think so.
JAIME: That's just how he said it.
DAVID: I believe you.
JAIME: You said no love poems.
DAVID: You need a sense of humor.
JAIME: I thought that was kind of funny. "Spla—a—a—at, like rain on
a river."
DAVID: But you're talking about blood, sweetheart,
What's this?
JAIME: Don't read it now.
DAVID: I don't like women who tell me what to do. (*He opens it and
reads.*)
"When you are old"
When did you write this?
JAIME: In the park.
Look...
DAVID: When you are old
And mysterious to me,
a dim figure on a
fragile horizon,
Think back
Across the years,
That on one summer night
we broke out of ugliness
and fled
Two conspirators
with bottles full of
Wine and joyous music
on the radio
and remember,
if
you
can
That it was right and
fine and sometimes
More, and we left

Pain.
That interminable fire,
only scorching
Our heels."
(*Silence*)

JAIME: It's not funny.

DAVID: No. (*He kisses her.*)

(*They move to the bed. A pale face appears at one of the windows. It's Jimmy. He taps on the window. David and Jaimie spring apart.*)

JIMMY: Hey you guys. (*Taps*)

JAIME: Just tell me, (*Covers her face with her hands.*)
Does he have a gun?

DAVID: It's the guy from the terminal...the little guy that juggles.
Should I let him in?

JAIME: Oh God.
Mercury retrograde.

DAVID: What?

JAIME: Bad timing.
Crossed stars.
Romeo and Juliet.
Never mind.
Let him in.
(*Jimmy comes in through the window.*)

JIMMY: I guess you guys didn't hear me throwing pennies at the window.

DAVID: Guess not.

JIMMY: (*Looks at them, half undressed.*) I'm sorry.

JAIME: Yeah. (*Starts dressing.*)
You want some wine?

JIMMY: I could use it.

JAIME: You have to drink it from the bottle...

DAVID: The bathroom's down the street.
At McDonald's.
Look. I better be on my way.

JIMMY: Don't leave on my account,
I'm really sorry.
I'm just not good on the streets.
I was juggling along the way...
attracted quite a crowd...only I looked up and

noticed quite a few were sexual deviants and psychopaths.
Not that I'm prejudiced.
It's live and let live with me, but I don't think we
shared that philosophy so I...uh...ran.
But I'll be out of here in a moment.
Just let me catch my breath.
Oh God, I can't believe I did this.

JAIME: David?

DAVID: I have a gig at eleven anyway.
I'm a disk jockey
Strangers in the Night on Staten Island.
Power pop and yuppie rock.
Best sound goin' round
etcetera, etcetera.

JAIME: He's really an artist—he writes songs.

DAVID: *(Gives her a light kiss on the cheek.)* It was sweet.
See you around.
Ciao good buddy.

JAIME: *(Following him to the door.)* Can I see you again?
Maybe I can come down to the club.

DAVID: I don't like women who pursue me. *(He leaves.)*
Be in touch, babe.
(Jaimie stands at the door. Her back to Jimmy.)

JIMMY: Perfect timing.
James Hobarth III does it every time.

JAIME: You probably did me a favor.
You just don't have a one night stand with someone you love.

JIMMY: Bad omen.

JAIME: What?

JIMMY: Wrong place. Wrong time.

JAIME: I thought we were just experiencing Mercury retrograde.

JIMMY: We are...it is but...
How can I have a fabulous new beginning under Mercury
retrograde?
It does not bode well.
Here I was ready to strip my life to its barest essentials; to live
without a past, without a dime.
Yes. I was going to be self–reliant, complete unto myself and
what happens? I freak!
One look at that park—the black trees, the moonless night, the

quiet pierced by occasional screams—

I couldn't hack it.

JAIME: Don't be so hard on yourself. A person doesn't sleep on a bench in a city where mugging's considered a rite of passage. You did the right thing.

Have some more wine and sit down.

JIMMY: Then I stumble over here and fuck things up.

JAIME: Just shut up and relax.

JIMMY: I'm not good on the streets.

I need a home.

It's okay if I sleep here?

JAIME: You're not going to rob or rape me, are you?

JIMMY: No really, I never...

JAIME: I'm joking.

Cool it.

It's fine.

I could use the company tonight.

You okay?

JIMMY: Yeah.

(Jaimie gets into bed.)

JAIME: *(Sighing)* I'm messed up.

Do you have an aspirin?

I have a monumental headache.

JIMMY: Cheap wine?

JAIME: Cheap date.

JIMMY: You know I bet you and I are a lot alike.

We need someone to love.

But we keep choosing crazy people, idiots, sociopaths,

the lame, the maimed, the married, right?

JAIME: Right.

JIMMY: If I make one more bad choice. it's over.

I swear. Plug pulled.

Lights out.

JAIME: Things'll get better I'm sure.

JIMMY: It's not a sure thing at all.

(Tragically) I have Venus in Pisces.

JAIME: Oh, I see.

JIMMY: You don't.

If Venus is what you want

And Pisces is the sign of the martyr

That means I want to be a martyr. God!

Oh well, Good night.

(Next day. Wilson's Estate. We hear the helicopter taking off.)

JAIME: So is white slavery a possibility?

Will I wake up in Saudi Arabia in a duffel bag?

JIMMY: I doubt it.

JAIME: Man. I could live like this.

A helicopter, a pool,

the ocean.

I mean there's less bugs on this lawn than there
are in my apartment.

JIMMY: I must say, being airlifted is quite an experience.

JAIME: So is being paged at Port Authority. The only other place I've
had my name called in public was at the dentist.

Can you believe it?

It's enough to make you believe in reincarnation.

*(Boris walks in with a tray of champagne. Jimmy gives him an
appreciative look which Boris returns discreetly.)*

JIMMY: *(Checks his watch.)* It's ten o'clock and that's champagne.

JAIME: Shit. What a life.

BORIS: Would you care for a mimosa?

JIMMY: *(Looking at the label.)* Krug Brut '76…not bad…
terrific, actually.

I'd rather not spoil it with orange juice.

BORIS: Excellent decision.

JIMMY: Thank you.

BORIS: Do you know wines?

JIMMY: A little.

BORIS: I could sneak you a little "Taitinger Blanc de Blanc."

JIMMY: Fantastic.

BORIS: I know you'd appreciate it.

And you Miss?

JAIME: It's questionable whether I should drink given the
circumstances. Oh what the hell.

Sure give me a glass.

(Boris serves her and winks to Jimmy as he leaves.)

JAIME: So you appreciate good wine, eh?

JIMMY: Another life, dear

A previous life.

JAIME: Yeah, a life where you're fluent in astrology and wines.

JIMMY: Princeton '96...

> Educated to ponder the universe and such questions as —
> If the subways in New York are air conditioned, but no one has ever felt air conditioning, is the subway really air conditioned? But not to worry. I'm just folks.
> I was summarily disinherited when I was fifteen.
> My father caught me...let's say, he loathed my lifestyles.
> Then he died and we were never able to patch it up properly...
> Oh well... *(He sips his champagne.)*

BORIS: *(Enters)* They'd like to see you now, Miss.

JAIME: If I turn out to be this man's son, all this will be mine, right?

JIMMY: Right.

JAIME: Groovy. *(She exits.)*

BORIS: We have 500 species of the rhododendron.

JIMMY: Lead the way!

BORIS: We have skeet shooting if you like.

JIMMY: *(As they leave.)* You're Scandinavian, aren't you? I'd say Danish.

> The Danes have eyes the color of blueberries.
> *(They exit.)*
> *(A half hour later. Enter Wilson, Sammy, Hughie, and Jaimie, single file.)*

SAMMY: Her ears are the right size.

HUGHIE: And did you see—she was missing part of the right lobe too?

JAIME: A dog bit me. I told you.

SAMMY: And she has the mole.

JAIME: Beauty mark.

SAMMY: Nails with no moon showing; she identified the cane, the photograph of his mother and his worry beads.

> *(Jaimie wanders around the room as they talk. Flipping open books; opening boxes, etc.)*

WILSON: And she's one in three chosen from the entire world's population as the probable reincarnation of my son. Hmmmmm.

SAMMY: You haven't seen the others.

HUGHIE: Do you think you should be looking through Mr. Wilson's things?

WILSON: No. No let her. I want to see what she picks out.

JAIME: Oh wow, you have Richard Wilbur. Great poet. *(She thumbs through the book.)*

WILSON: Yes. He was my son's favorite.

> Do you know him?

JAIME: Oh yeah. He wrote the single greatest poem I ever read!

WILSON: My son was an avid reader.

JAIME: Oh I don't read much—it clouds your mind, but I do know Richard Wilbur.

WILSON: Is there a poem you'd like to show me?

JAIME: Are you kidding? *(She shows him.)*

WILSON: "Love Calls Us To The Things Of This World"
   Oh my... *(He takes out his handkerchief.)*

HUGHIE: What is it?

SAMMY: What is it?

JAIME: What is it?

WILSON: There's something here I tell you. There's something definitely here.

HUGHIE: Yes?

SAMMY: Yes?

JAIME: Yes?

WILSON: This was my son's favorite poem. His very favorite. My God!
   'Bring them down from their ruddy gallows
   Let there be clean linen for the backs of thieves;
   Let lovers go fresh and sweet to be undone
   And the heaviest nuns walk in a pure floating
   Of dark habits
   keeping their difficult balance'
   (He turns away.)
   Excuse me.

JAIME: Wow.
   I'm sorry.

WILSON: No, no dear. You've brought my son to me. I felt him nearby today.
   Gentlemen. I'm convinced she's the one.

HUGHIE: But the others?

SAMMY: I agree. You must see the others.

HUGHIE: Emotions might be clouding your judgment, don't you think?

SAMMY: I agree.
   We must always offset emotional mysticism with mental balance.

WILSON: No. I tell you—intuitively, and by all the rules of your game—she is the reincarnation of my son. The percentages of correct answers are astronomical. I believe it was one hundred percent. Not one wrong guess, not one wrong move and now this...this... *(Holding up the book.)*

HUGHIE: Would you like a drink?

SAMMY: Hughie!

WILSON: You see? I have both intuitive and statistical proof, congratulations gentlemen.

I'm ecstatic.

Boris! Boris!

Of course there will be a longer period of examination, but I feel it.

I feel it just as you two said. A revelation.

Boris! Boris!

(*Tina comes out.*)

TINA: (*She is Polish.*) You called sir?

WILSON: Where is your husband?

TINA: I don't really know. I believe he's showing someone the grounds, sir.

WILSON: Never mind. Bring me my checkbook. It's on top of my desk. (*To Sammy and Hughie*) You've earned your fee.

SAMMY: No!

HUGHIE: (*To Sammy*) Are we refusing it?

SAMMY: Yes!

This is incomplete. We do not do incomplete work.

WILSON: I'll make out the check and you can do with it what you will.

SAMMY: It's not that we're so certain the girl is not your son.

We're just not sure she is.

JAIME: (*Haltingly*) I have to tell you all something...

WILSON: Yes?

HUGHIE: Yes?

SAMMY: Yes?

JAIME: I don't feel like a man.

And I don't remember consciously anything about this place.

SAMMY: You wouldn't necessarily remember.

You share a soul with the old James. The soul is the unit of evolution.

The soul is old. But the personality is brand new and the personality is the unit of incarnation. So you wouldn't necessarily remember anything.

HUGHIE: Do you think that's quite true?

SAMMY: Of course that's what I think. I said it, didn't I?

HUGHIE: Not a trace of past lives? Not a preference carried over? Not a talent? Not an interest? What about the cane? The ring? The poem?

SAMMY: All right, a trace. There's a trace of previous lives.

WILSON: Why don't you wait for me in the library, gentlemen. I want some time alone with Jaimie.

(*Sammy elbows Hughie. They exit.*)

(*To Jaimie*) So, what do you make of all this, my dear?

JAIME: Mercury retrograde.

WILSON: I beg your pardon.

JAIME: This could be a terrible mistake.

WILSON: Not so terrible.

Why don't we agree to give this a little time.

JAIME: All right.

WILSON: Three weeks?

JAIME: I guess.

WILSON: Anyone I should notify? Anyone you want to call?

JAIME: There's one dude...but no. Let him stew. It'll be good for his ego.

WILSON: Fine. Tina will show you to your room.

JAIME: What do I have to do?

WILSON: Be a poet, I imagine.

JAIME: I am one.

WILSON: Yes I know. So was my son.

JAIME: This is really spooky.

WILSON: It is eerie isn't it?

JAIME: It's too much. I can't see myself living here.

WILSON: Oh I see. You have a prejudice against money.

So did my son.

He couldn't imagine himself here either.

He went into a monastery.

JAIME: I'm different. I could never be a monk...I mean a nun. Whatever. I believe in sex.

WILSON: So did my son.

He was a Franciscan—of course.

Truly mystic. A fatal paradox.

He was a passionate boy who took a vow of chastity; a sensual person who lived in poverty; a romantic who engaged in affair after affair each sadder and more desperate than the last. He always chose someone inappropriate—a drunk or a married man. He was a homosexual who never made his peace—except with a double barreled rifle at the end.

JAIME: I'm sorry.

WILSON: I loved him very, very much.

JAIME: I'm sorry.

WILSON: So—where were we?

Three weeks.

Give it a chance.

Immerse yourself.

Try an external approach to inner development.

Try the clothes, the food, the freedom, the richness

the color, sound, the perfume.

Let yourself awaken to the possibilities.

This is not preposterous.

Look at yoga—by adopting certain outer physical postures

a resonant chord can be struck in the inner soul.

JAIME: I'll do it.

WILSON: Just relax, let this experience wash over you—

money isn't evil, you know.

Lord, how many times did I say this to my son.

Money is time, space, loveliness—I can take money

and create a garden full of flowers and color and streams

and moss...I can take money and have musicians play

day and night, or have composers write music,

or architects build dream houses for the poor.

I can take money and change the direction of rivers,

or cure the sick...money is godlike in the right hands

It can even help poets...

That's why this money, this wealth I've

somehow impossibly accumulated, must end up in the right

hands.

So stay. If you can't believe. Don't disbelieve.

And we'll see.

I feel this inexplicable tenderness towards you.

JAIME: Your son could've come back as a woman. Then he wouldn't be so torn up about loving men.

WILSON: You'll stay then? Wonderful. Go upstairs and see if Tina's around.

JAIME: I think your son had Venus in Pisces. (*She exits.*)

(*Hughie and Sammy march in very determined. Tina follows with the checkbook.*)

HUGHIE: Would you please listen to us for a moment?

SAMMY: Yes.

We want to talk to you alone.

(*Sammy pulls Wilson aside.*)

We feel what you're doing is wrong.

We feel quite strongly about it.

WILSON: Do you agree, Hughie?

SAMMY: We agree.

We always agree about conclusions.

We won't take the check.

HUGHIE: How could we risk our reputation?

How could we betray our gods and our talent?

How could we permit you to mistake passion for perspective?

WILSON: You needn't worry. I'm not about to hand over my fortune to a charming little street poet—no matter how charming.

If in three weeks Jaimie has doubts, and I have reservations—I'll call off the search and create a foundation.

HUGHIE: Why three weeks?

SAMMY: Three is the number of full expression;

WILSON: Because that's sufficient.

Now I must find Boris. We have some excellent recordings of the Tango, Gardel himself, 1928, Paris.

The tango of course—it's a Latin American dance in duple metre—much like the habanera. *(He exits.)*

HUGHIE: What about the other candidates?

(*Tina enters. Boris and Jimmy are outside. Jimmy is shooting at geese. We can't hear him fire.*)

TINA: Oh, there's Boris.

(*She taps on the window and waves. Boris waves back. She exits*)

HUGHIE: Are you positive the girl's not the one?

SAMMY: I'm as convinced as you are.

We can't let him do this.

We must find the right person and bring him back here.

HUGHIE: And if we can't?

SAMMY: Fate.

This person is doomed to repeat his mistakes over and over and over until he is ready to redeem the qualities that destroyed him in his previous life.

HUGHIE: Does that mean, perhaps…?

SAMMY: Suicide.

HUGHIE: Ahhhhhhhhhh.

(*He puts his arm around Sammy's shoulders in comradely fashion. Behind the glass doors, in full view, Boris gently takes the rifle from Jimmy, leans it against one of the glass doors and embraces him passionately.*)

END OF ACT ONE

ACT TWO

Three weeks later. Jaimie's room. Also we see part of the street outside. Inside Jimmy has his juggling paraphernalia around. Jimmy is stripped to the waist, wearing sweat pants and juggling first three and then four balls. Rock music. In the street, David is walking. There is also another couple; the woman with a fur boa. A dummy falls at their feet. The Woman: "Quick Charles, up here. I do believe we've finally found a vacant apartment." She yanks him off stage. David steps over the dummy. He goes to the window over the fire escape and taps loudly on it, but Jimmy can't hear. He taps harder and shouts. Jimmy is startled and makes a big show of almost dropping all the balls, but then recovers. David indicates Jimmy should open the window. Jimmy still juggling, manages after several attempts to turn the radio down with one hand.

JIMMY: *(Yelling)* It's open!
　　Just lift it. It's open.
DAVID: *(Climbs in.)* Well what do you know. Jimmy the juggler.
　　How's tricks?
JIMMY: Wonderful. I'm in love.
DAVID: I see. Congratulations.
JIMMY: I highly recommend it.
DAVID: Is...ah...Jaimie around?
JIMMY: Oh no, no, no, no, no.
DAVID: Don't worry, I'm here for a signature, not a seduction.
JIMMY: She's not here. She's living with a millionaire.

DAVID: Hold on. I thought you were in love?

JIMMY: Oh, you thought Jaimie and I...? No.

She's hit an incredible streak of luck.

For that matter so have I.

We have a truly karmic connection. Both Pisces.

Born on the same day.

She has a mansion. I have this apartment.

She's got Daddy Bigbucks and I—have a brand new friend.

DAVID: What's she doing with this millionaire?

JIMMY: I don't know—what time is it? Just kidding.

DAVID: Let's go find out what she's up to.

I assume you know where she is.

JIMMY: My my, aren't we headstrong.

What's the hurry?

DAVID: Here's your hat. Let's go.

JIMMY: I don't need a hat.

Actually I don't wear it any longer. It weakens my hair follicles.

Does it look like I'm losing my hair?

I'm only nineteen, but the brush looks full...

DAVID: You look great.

JIMMY: *(Puts on a shirt—rather Hawaiian.)* I'm wearing colors now.

I always wore black.

But I feel like a prism these days.

Light passes right through me...ah love...

Are you sure my hair doesn't look thinner? I can see the scalp.

DAVID: Is Jaimie in love too?

Seeing as you have such a karmic connection.

JIMMY: If I'm in love, she's in love.

DAVID: Are you ready?

JIMMY: Wait!

DAVID: Why?

JIMMY: Sorry.

DAVID: What?

JIMMY: Today's out of the question.

Momentous decisions are pending.

She can't be interrupted. No. No. Impossible.

I'll tell her you called.

DAVID: I have to see her now.

JIMMY: Now? After you waited three weeks, it has to be now, right this minute no matter whom you inconvenience or—destroy?

DAVID: Right.

JIMMY: Well you're no Pisces!

DAVID: Not on your life.

JIMMY: Don't tell me, don't tell me. Let me guess... *(Walks around him.)*

Reddish tinge, brash, headstrong. Headstrong.

You're an Aries, right?

Aries rules the head.

You're headstrong.

Brash, romantic...

If you want fireworks, take an Aries. Romeo was probably an Aries.

DAVID: So does that get me your recommendation?

JIMMY: No. Aries are romantic—but have no follow through.

Give me a Taurus. Steady. Built.

I'm in love with a Taurus.

I have the most beautiful, sweet, exotic big blond Russian Taurus you ever laid eyes on.

Silver white hair, blue eyes, skin like a rosebud

And best of all—silent.

One of those one–word Taurus wonders like Gary Cooper—the original "Yuuup" man.

There was a Taurus.

They're so terrific. Like stoked fire

Always burning and just stir them up a little...

But oh, I do go on...

DAVID: Where do we have to go to find this millionaire?

JIMMY: So do you love her?

DAVID: I like her.

JIMMY: "Like"... "like"...how paltry.

I don't even remember "like".

I've never been in love like this before.

It's a three ring circus with four clowns

and my head going 'round like a four ball shower. *(He does a four ball shower and tosses the balls into a canvas case.)*

DAVID: This has got nothing to do with love.

We co–wrote a song together.

A major label is making interested noises.

I want to talk to her about rights and money.

JIMMY: Not love?

DAVID: Definitely not love.

JIMMY: Look, I know you're an Aries and it's hard, but think of someone besides yourself.

DAVID: Fuck you.

JIMMY: I shouldn't complicate things for her. Certainly not for "like". Now if you had been in love with her...

DAVID: I can say the word if that's what you want.

JIMMY: I'd do quite a lot for love.

I understand passion, but business *(He shrugs.)*

I mean this fellow is cultured, civilized, rich...

DAVID: And old. All that goes with old.

JIMMY: Seasoned.

Well I won't take you.

You'll queer the deal.

DAVID: I'm sure I'd have no effect on her.

She's probably deeply in love with this man.

Didn't you say you two were so cosmically attuned that if you're in love, her heart's going pitter pat as well?

JIMMY: Actually, I know for a fact she's in love.

DAVID: Good for her.

JIMMY: Well, it may not be. But she has a mentor.

Poets need mentors.

Us jugglers, on the other hand,

we're independent—there's the street, the circus, bar mitzvahs—n'est-ce pas?

But a poet?

What can a poor poet do?

You don't have a lot to offer her.

DAVID: I have a voice that can kill a cow at a hundred yards.

I have talent, management ability...

JIMMY: And money?

DAVID: I don't buy into a billboard mentality—money equals happiness—buy this, buy that, own it all and you'll turn into a cougar, jump on top of a billboard, screw the girl in the black velvet dress and ride off into the sunset. However, if this deal goes through, they may offer me quite a bit of money.

JIMMY: But it won't help you. Sorry.

DAVID: *(Pushes Jimmy against the sill. He drops his juggling balls.)* Looking to get your balls busted, buster?

Let's go.

JIMMY: All right. All right.

I respond to passion as well as the next man. In fact I was going there anyway.

Mercury goes direct today at noon.

All this will be straightened out.

No more Mercury retrograde.

Thank God. *(He gets his things.)*

I'm waiting until five past noon myself and then,

I'll ask my Taurus to live with me.

We'll walk by the ocean, hold hands, kiss, caress, embrace…

My God,

And I thought I'd die young, poor and

alone.

There's hope I tell you.

There's always hope.

Well follow me, what can you do with an Aries?

(David exits first.)

Typical Aries—always has to lead even if he doesn't know where he's going! *(He exits.)*

(Later that same morning. Jaimie's bedroom on the second floor. A canopied bed. A desk piled with papers. A full length mirror and a large glass door opening onto a balcony. We only see sky beyond billowy curtains. Hints of luxury. Tina the maid enters with a stack of lingerie. She steps out onto the balcony for a moment and catches sight of someone.)

TINA: There you are you tomcat, you rooster.

I know you have a lover, you lovesick bull, you peacock,

I won't put up with this. I tell you…

JAIME: *(Enters wearing jeans, a tee shirt, a flamboyant headdress.)* What is it, Tina?

TINA: I will not put up with this! *(She puts the lingerie on the bed and preens in front of the mirror.)* I don't have to.

My father was a calvary officer in the Polish army and my uncle was a prelate in the Catholic Church.

I didn't have to settle for a Russian serf, a vulgar bulgar, a peasant always in heat!

JAIME: A love spat, right?

TINA: A love spat! I'll kill him.

No. I'll kill her!

The laundress found a note in his pocket.
signed your "adoring, worshipful servant," imagine!
In his trousers
And after all I've done.
I left my family, my country, my training for him.
I was trained as a ladies maid. A fine ladies' maid. No one else
could fold lingerie or arrange drawers the way I could.
My ladies never had a pleat out of place,
a button missing,
a spot on their lace—
and although I was always slimmer, taller,
more naturally elegant—
all of my ladies went out feeling like a million bucks.
And now?
Cotton underwear for Miss Bluejeans.
What's more—
I answer doors, announce guests, set the table—all to cover for...
(*She shoves the note under Jaimie's nose and quickly withdraws it
and reads.*)
You see, here's the note.
Can you believe...
"Never have I been so in love, so enthralled, so overwhelmed.
We'll meet on the beach at noon there is so much to say..."
Can you believe?
Well, she'll believe.
I'm going to confront her, this woman, this girl.
I'll tell her to her face that Boris is mine, married
in the Church in front of all the saints. I bet Boris the Bull did not
tell her that!
I betcha!
She'll see. And let her "overwhelm" herself someplace else!
Your lingerie is clean. (*She stalks out.*)
(*Jaimie is in a good mood. She sits at a table and puts her hair up.
Tries it different ways. Then she puts on makeup. She is wrapped
in a towel. She turns the radio up. There is a soft knock on the
door. Another knock. Wilson lets himself in carrying a stack of
books.*)

WILSON: Jaimie...
JAIME: Oh Wilson, I'm not ready yet.

WILSON: I'll stay here and wait. May I?

JAIME: Sure. *(She turns the music down.)*

Hope you don't mind rock.

WILSON: No as a matter of fact I was reading about rock and roll. Did you know it's a commercial amalgam of the styles of American White country music and Black rhythm and blues?

JAIME: *(Putting on some huge sapphire earrings.)* Yeah. *(She looks at herself. Takes another sip of champagne.)* Wow! Not bad.

WILSON: Yes. And Rhythm and Blues is particularly interesting. Did you know that the 12-bar melodic and harmonic pattern and the three line stanzas are now common to much of the popular music of recent decades?

JAIME: Yeah. *(Wrapping a long piece of black silk around her until it forms a slinky dress with one strap.)* I'm almost ready Wilson.

WILSON: I think the idea about these get togethers to share interests is a splendid idea.

I wish I had been able to do this with my son—originally that is.

JAIME: *(Steps out.)* Ta Da!

What do you think?

Pretty hot, right?

Watch out Vogue—here I come.

I feel like a peacock.

WILSON: You look like a bird of paradise.

JAIME: These earrings are devastating.

WILSON: They belonged to the last Raj of Sinukhan who presented them to my mother who was a very beautiful woman.

She'd be pleased to see them on you. She wanted them to go to a daughter if I had one, or to my son's wife if he married.

JAIME: Wilson. I can't keep these.

WILSON: We'll see.

JAIME: You're not treating me like a son.

WILSON: Like a daughter.

I can't ignore the fact that you've come back to me as a girl. You look absolutely beautiful.

JAIME: *(Changing the subject.)* So our topic for today is...

WILSON: Oh yes—our topic of conversation for today.

JAIME: *(Taking the books.)* Emily Dickinson, Elizabeth Bishop, Ann Sexton—Women poets.

WILSON: Like you—blessed by the Greek literary goddesses Calliope, Erato and Euterpe no doubt.

JAIME: No doubt.

WILSON: You make me want to show off.

JAIME: All women poets, eh?

WILSON: I wanted to do something of special interest to you.

JAIME: So because I'm a woman I'm interested in women poets?

WILSON: I suppose that is a bit simplistic isn't it?

Well, I'm only a businessman puttering around in the arts.

JAIME: You're very kind, Wilson.

WILSON: Kind? Kind? I meant to be exciting.

Well—in any event you really should read more. You have a fine untutored mind.

JAIME: I like being untutored.

Every time I write, I'm an explorer.

WILSON: But you need heroes.

JAIME: My friends are my heroes.

WILSON: How gallant.

JAIME: You're my friend. My gallant friend.

I'm going to miss you.

WILSON: You know, Jaimie—I was thinking.

JAIME: Yes.

WILSON: Although the three weeks are up at noon, I really think we should prolong this experiment. We both have doubts still and I see no reason why you can't stay a few more weeks. You should be here to see the ocean in the Fall—it would inspire you. It's grainy and tempestuous. I've found I can learn all the seasons through the ocean's lens. You see—it even inspires me to wax poetic—'ocean's lens'—not bad. Just think what it would do for you.

JAIME: I don't know what to say.

I love it here. This is so decadent.

I grew up in the Midwest.

I shouldn't feel this way.

WILSON: Do you really think it's harmful for an artist to have money? Do you think you'd be the first? What about Baudelaire or James Merrill or Tolstoy? Do you think Bob Dylan's starving in a garrett or Baryshnikov is without a sinecure? Please—you sound like my son.

JAIME: Wilson...

(*David appears on the balcony and sees the embrace. He stays hidden. David enters.*)

WILSON: (*As he exits*) Think about it. We'll discuss this at lunch. Today the three weeks are up in any event and we should discuss the future. I'll see you at noon then. Wear what you have on now.

(*He kisses her cheek and embraces her tightly.*)

There's a reason we've been brought together. Can't you feel it?

Fate is at work here, Divine Providence.

We should explore it together.

DAVID: Some outlaw.

JAIME: What?

DAVID: You look like you belong in a harem.

Have you fucked him yet?

JAIME: David? What are you doing here?

DAVID: Ditto.

JAIME: How did you find me?

DAVID: Cosmic intervention.

Stand up. Let me take a look at you. (*Whistles*)

JAIME: Get out of here.

He'll hear you.

DAVID: Have you fucked him yet?

JAIME: You're really a limited person, you know that.

DAVID: Yes. How boring. I relate to life through my cock. They all say that. (*He languishes on the bed.*) But what's a poor boy to do?

JAIME: Did anyone see you come up?

DAVID: Not to worry.

All my years of seeing married women have paid off.

JAIME: What the hell do you want now?

DAVID: Now?

You sound hurt. Did I wait too long? Of course I haunted Port Authority in my off hours.

I climbed your firescape on several occasions.

You don't seem to have a phone or a fax—or a brain in your head. How was I to know you'd been reincarnated during the last three weeks?!

(*He goes to kiss her. She moves away.*)

Well, I just dropped in to say 'Howdy, Ma'am'.

JAIME: David...

DAVID: Not to worry little lady—I'm here to complete your streak of luck. I have good news. I'm frontman in a new band, Harm's Way.

JAIME: So glad you dropped by to tell me.

DAVID: And our first hit single will be none other than "Conspirators".

JAIME: Great.

DAVID: You should be happier than that. It's going to make you rich— although I see you're quite comfortable already. And here I thought you were a waif shivering in the woods.

JAIME: Hold on a minute. I don't get it.

Why should this song make me rich?

DAVID: It's our song. The song we wrote.

JAIME: What "we" is this?

DAVID: As in you and I—we.

JAIME: What are you talking about?

DAVID: I took that poem you gave me. Did a little editing. Now it's a rock song.

JAIME: Are you kidding?

DAVID: Cut a demo with some of the guys at the club; sent it to Pacific Records. They loved it. Soooo we're gettin' a contract. All you have to do is sign on the dotted line.

JAIME: I didn't say you could use it.

DAVID: You gave it to me.

JAIME: It was private. Special. I wrote that poem just for you.

DAVID: And I wrote this song—just for you.

JAIME: Yeah, you and the guys had a good laugh, I bet.

DAVID: Will you at least listen to it for chrissakes?

(*He plays the demo tape.*)

We are...we are...we are
conspirators
against the past
armed with bottles full of wine
lost for time
with joyous music blast-ing
on the radio
so did you know
we are conspirators
we are, we are
conspirators
breaking out of ugliness and
fleeing
just you and me
conspirators.
We take what life deals

take back what it steals
we love and leave
pain—that interminable fire
only scorching our heels.
We are conspirators...we are...we are...
conspirators.
(*Pause*)

JAIME: I didn't hear from you for a long time.

DAVID: You disappeared. What was I supposed to do—consult an astrologer to find you? At least, can I have your signature?

JAIME: No.

DAVID: Why?

Revenge?

JAIME: It's not revenge.

DAVID: Look. I won't fuck with your karma, if that's what you're afraid of.

I'll just copyright this song and send you some checks.

You love my ass. You won't pass this up.

JAIME: Drop dead.

DAVID: I didn't need to come here to find you. I could've cashed in all by myself.

JAIME: I would have found out and sued your ass.

DAVID: So sue me. (*He holds her.*)

Call the cops.

You're really gorgeous, you know.

JAIME: You dig sapphires and silk.

DAVID: I dig skin like silk and eyes of brilliant blue.

Jaimie—come on tour with us. We could write other songs.

I won't pressure you. If you want you can be one of the boys.

JAIME: One of the boys with extra holes, right? Don't come on to me because you want to use my lyrics.

DAVID: Fine. Forget the come-on. Sign this, you'll have real financial independence. You won't have to lay around with an old geezer and eat bonbons.

JAIME: You're so stupid.

I've been working.

DAVID: Good. Let's see what you've been up to. (*He grabs some papers off her desk. He reads.*)

"Black ivy in a wasteland of debris..."

Hmmmm not quite...

Let's see. *(He reads.)*
"Her dreams are made of plasterboard and paste."
That's hearty.
Oh, yeah, here,
How about
"The faulty skein of sky and road has strung me out from place
to place"
Glad to see you're so happy here.

JAIME: I always write sad stuff.

DAVID: You write sad stuff because you're sad and have sad things to
say. Not much has changed here. On paper.

JAIME: I haven't digested this experience yet.

DAVID: Right.
Besides which,
you're his son.

JAIME: Jimmy told you.

DAVID: Son.

JAIME: Yeah. But we're going to talk more about it. Today in fact.

DAVID: Well there's nothing to talk about...it's perfectly obvious you're
this guy's...this guy's...I can't say it, honest-to-God—

JAIME: Son.

DAVID: Whore.

JAIME: *(Slaps him hard.)* You asshole.

DAVID: I thought you were different than anyone else I'd met.
Free, open, out to conquer the world.
But I see I was wrong. You talk a good game
but all you're looking for is shelter, safety, a harbor in the storm.
That's great if you're protecting babies—but not if you want to be
out there—being an artist. Sorry.
You've lost your nerve.
(Tina knocks.)

TINA: Lunch, Miss.

DAVID: *(Falsetto. Imitating her.)* Are you coming, dear?

JAIME: *(To Tina)* I'm coming.

DAVID: I'll be at Kennedy Airport. My flight leaves at five thirty-six for
L.A.

JAIME: What? You snap your fingers and I jump? No way!
*(Grabs the paper from David. Signs it and thrusts it into his
hands.)*
Here. Buy yourself another girlfriend!

And don't put my name on the song. We never met.
(*She starts to leave. David stops her.*)

DAVID: Now we know what love at first sight means, don't we!

It sure ain't love at second sight!

JAIME: You shit! (*She exits.*)

DAVID: Ditto my love. Ditto.

(*He exits from the balcony. Empty room. Curtains billow. An exaggeratedly long dining table half set. Noon. Sammy and Hughie sit side by side. Boris and Tina come in and out arranging the table setting. Everything Boris puts down Tina rearranges.*)

BORIS: Stop! Enough!

You think I am uncompetent.

TINA: Incompetent!

BORIS: (*Checks his watch.*) Ten before noon. I must go for a walk.

TINA: No!

BORIS: You do luncheons.

TINA: Don't go.

BORIS: I'm tired of your not founded jealousies.

TINA: Unfounded.

It's not unfounded!

I am not a fool.

BORIS: You are the only woman I ever love. I swear. I promise.

Boris is many things, a sportsman, a wanderer, a great lover but never a liar. You are the only woman I love. (*Checks his watch again.*) I must go.

TINA: Those are your last words?

BORIS: Yes.

TINA: Fine.

I will be right back. (*She flounces off.*)

BORIS: Where are you going?

TINA: Ahh, my big Russian bloodhound.

Don't worry so much. I only go to little ladies room.

(*She exits. Boris storms out and then returns. Throughout, Boris continues setting table and waiting impatiently.*)

SAMMY: I'm glad we don't fight.

(*Hughie says nothing.*)

We talk things over.

For instance, there is the matter of failing Mr. Meredith.

HUGHIE: Have we failed?

SAMMY: We've failed.

The girl is not the right person...

HUGHIE: Ahhhhhhh.

SAMMY: You're no help. We've failed. Where are your suggestions?

HUGHIE: Where are your suggestions?

SAMMY: We've found the person.

We always find the person. But we haven't identified him!

HUGHIE: Or her?

SAMMY: We have the big picture.

Orphans, Pisces, mid-town Manhattan, August.

Eighth house of legacies in a water sign.

HUGHIE: Wasn't it the fifth house of hidden karma

in a fire sign?

SAMMY: No! Well, maybe…But that's not it.

There is something we've overlooked.

HUGHIE: Do you really think we've failed?

SAMMY: We've failed.

It's the beginning of the end.

HUGHIE: Of what?

SAMMY: Of us, you nincompoop.

We don't work well together, we've run out of rope, out of ideas, out of steam.

HUGHIE: Are you kidding me?

SAMMY: I need someone decisive, energetic,

Someone who can come up with answers, make statements, take the bull by the horns.

HUGHIE: Do you mean that?

SAMMY: Tell me something!

HUGHIE: What?

SAMMY: Something. Anything.

BORIS: *(Worriedly)* Tina! Tina!

HUGHIE: What do you want from me?

SAMMY: Decisions. Action.

HUGHIE: Don't you know by now what I'm like?

Do you know what you're asking?

SAMMY: Yes.

HUGHIE: Sure?

SAMMY: Yes.

I'm asking for…

HUGHIE: What?

SAMMY: My needs are different.

We're facing a crisis. I need someone who confronts reality. I need someone different.

HUGHIE: Haven't we always worked well together?

SAMMY: Until now.

HUGHIE: Why throw out a perfectly good partnership?

SAMMY: Is that all you can say?

HUGHIE: Do you want me to leave?

SAMMY: Do you want to leave?

Answer. Yes or no. Do you want to leave?

HUGHIE: *(Crestfallen)* Why are you doing this?

Can't you see you're making me miserable?

Aren't you miserable too? Don't you have any feelings?

What's wrong with you?

SAMMY: That's it?

All right.

I can't stand it.

Leave. Go. Get.

HUGHIE: Do you really mean it?

SAMMY: Fight for what you want, you fool!

Can't you say anything?

HUGHIE: *(Leaving sadly)* What's there to say?

(Hughie exits. Sammy slumps in his seat. Jaimie enters.)

JAIME: Hi guys...guy...what's wrong?

SAMMY: Nothing.

JAIME: Okay.

Nothing's wrong with me either. *(She sits primly.)*

BORIS: *(Enters)* Have you seen Tina?

JAIME: No.

BORIS: She went to the little girls room. But

now she's late...

This is special lunch for you and Mr. Meredith.

Big decisions. Big deal. BIG deal. Believe me.

He wants everything special. And if there's no service, Tina and I both be fired. For sure. NO doubt. Kaput!

JAIME: Sammy?

SAMMY: I don't know anything about this. I'm no mindreader.

JAIME: I see. Well. Don't count on Tina being on time.

(She sits. Boris stands. Sammy sits.)

Nice day.

BORIS: Yes.

No.

Miserable day.

People suffer.

SAMMY: Yes.

People suffer.

BORIS: Why do you say Tina is late?

JAIME: I didn't say she'd be late.

BORIS: You know something. Tell me.

It's your friend who will suffer.

Your friend? *(He does juggling action.)*

JAIME: Jimmy?

It's about Jimmy?

Oh no.

BORIS: Tina is a strong lady, a very strong lady. Jimmy is tender, too tender. He will be upset, destroyed.

Do you know what I mean?

JAIME: Yeah, sure I got it.

You creep.

BORIS: Is Tina on the beach?

JAIME: She found a note.

BORIS: My God.

JAIME: The laundress.

BORIS: My God.

JAIME: I take it, Jimmy doesn't know about Tina.

BORIS: My God. *(He exits.)*

JAIME: My God. *(She exits after leaving her high heels on the table.)*

(Sammy sits dejectedly. Wilson enters. Pressed starched white shirt, blue and white striped pants, blue blazer. Perfumed, pomaded. Excellent.)

WILSON: I see I'm early.

SAMMY: You might enjoy a walk along the beach.

WILSON: I'll just wait.

Thank you...Hughie?

SAMMY: Sammy.

WILSON: Would you care for a drink?

SAMMY: No. Thank you.

(They wait.)

WILSON: Yes. Well.

Did you know the scale most typical of Chinese music is the pentatonic scale?

SAMMY: I see.

WILSON: You are Chinese?

SAMMY: No.

WILSON: I see.

Well, I'll tell Boris.

He'll find some books on it.

Boris?

Tina? *(He waits.)*

How strange.

SAMMY: My highly developed intuition tells me

you would gain great insight into your present circumstances if you went for a walk along the beach.

WILSON: *(Picks up Jaimie's high heels.)* Why? Has something happened on the beach?

SAMMY: It will.

(Wilson exits. Sammy sits.)

(Along the beach. We hear water and gulls. Jimmy is sitting on a dune, pant legs rolled up, bright sweater knotted around his shoulders. Picnic basket by his side. Peaceful. Tina awkwardly making her way carrying a rifle. Two tourists obviously from Manhattan by their dress, with some minor adjustments to the beach such as jacket slung over one arm, or carrying shoes. Perhaps they are a large woman and a small man. Woman speaks as they make their way across the stage: Woman: "You call this a beach? You call these waves? You call this is a vacation? Where have you been all your life?" Continues as they walk offstage. The Man meekly behind Woman: "You call these birds? You call this a stroll along the shore? You call this fun? You call this romance? You call this..." We hear a thud. The man returns alone. Tips his hat at Tina, who has now reached Jimmy, and exits.)

TINA: Excuse me. Do you have the time?

JIMMY: Yes. Certainly.

It's almost noon.

TINA: Good.

JIMMY: Aren't you from the house over there?

TINA: Mr. Meredith's. Yes.

I'm the maid.

JIMMY: I thought so.

TINA: You're a friend of Boris's and the young lady.

I've seen you.

JIMMY: Yes.

Hello.

TINA: Listen. I am looking for a young lady. Have you seen her?

JIMMY: No one's come by, but what's she look like? I'll keep an eye out for her.

TINA: No, that's all right.

Can I wait with you?

JIMMY: Sure.

Want a sandwich. Chips? A coke?

TINA: No. I have lost my appetite. Believe me!

JIMMY: You're upset.

TINA: So sensitive. Such a nice young man.

Too bad about your hair.

JIMMY: My hair?

TINA: A nice young man like you. But women don't mind baldness in a man. Mature women don't, that is.

JIMMY: Thanks. That's good to know.

TINA: But yes. I'm upset.

Love is so sad.

JIMMY: You've had a fight with your lover?

TINA: My husband.

We always fight.

I love him and he loves me. But we always fight.

He's unfaithful.

JIMMY: You know how men are.

TINA: Yes.

I would make him jealous too.

JIMMY: Why don't you?

TINA: Too tired. *(She sighs.)*

I am ruining your picnic.

JIMMY: No. I'm waiting for someone.

TINA: A lover. Lucky you.

Boris and I were lovers once. My wild Russian bear, my love.

He is a bit younger than I am, twelve years or so...

JIMMY: Boris?

TINA: Boris. Your friend. My husband. The butler over there...

I cannot stand to have him running around so...

It makes me sad, so sad.

JIMMY: Boris.

TINA: Yes.

Do you have a tissue?

JIMMY: I. No.

Boris.

TINA: You are surprised.

I know.

He does not give the appearance of being married.

JIMMY: I have a napkin.

TINA: *(She wipes her eyes and nose.)* But he loves me. In his way. He
loves me so much.

He lets me know what he is doing. *(She holds out the note.)*
(Jimmy takes it and gives it back, dazed.)

JIMMY: He gave this to you?

TINA: Yes.

We share everything.

He is loyal, but not faithful.

It is my cross to bear.

JIMMY: Yes.

TINA: No. I make you sad.

I'm sorry.

This girl has stood him up!

Hah!

JIMMY: It happens.

TINA: I say, Hah! on you my Soviet stallion.

Hah!

I leave you waiting for your lover.

And I give you advice, be firm, but quick too.

You're young, but you're losing your looks.

Even men need their looks. I'm glad I have a full head of hair,
not one grey strand. I really don't look so much older than my
Boris, do I?

JIMMY: No.

TINA: That comes from having a stallion for a husband.

My Russian stallion.

Well, you look like a sad boy, but I wish you luck. *(She exits.)*

JIMMY: *(Jimmy picks up gun to tell her she's forgotten it, but changes his
mind.)* I really must do something about my life.

I really must

I can barely breathe, all of a sudden…

The sky, the ocean, the wind is catching my breath...

He didn't even come.

Perhaps he sent her.

Jim you idiot, you stupid idiot. Be a man. Do something.

(*He takes up the gun.*)

Why don't you shoot something

Some poor dumb gull. (*He sights something and follows it.*)

Some poor dumb, dumb (*He lowers the gun sits down, holds it between his knees. He props the barrel against his forehead.*) creature.

(*Jaimie comes running up the beach.*)

JAIME: Oh, Jimmy, stop!

JIMMY: Get away from me.

JAIME: Jimmy, please.

Put that gun away.

Nothing can be that bad.

JIMMY: Does the whole fucking world know?

What a laugh!

Everything I thought was beautiful and private

is a public joke.

JAIME: Hey dude, come on.

JIMMY: Dude?!

JAIME: Yeah, 70's, "dude." You're a major dude. You can work it out.

Man to man.

Talk to the guy, will you?

JIMMY: (*Gets up.*) Don't follow me.

JAIME: (*Follows him.*) This is no time to tune out. I mean you just turned a corner and ran smack into the love of your life. Who knows what'll happen next.

JIMMY: Just say I can't stand the suspense, all right?

JAIME: This is a minute in your life. It'll pass. Let it pass.

JIMMY: It won't pass. This minute resembles too many others.

I told you I either get them sick. Maimed or married. I'm stuck.

Next time around, things'll be different.

Now turn away for Christ's sakes. (*He kneels.*)

God's in his heaven and all's right with the world. (*He points the rifle at his temple and closes his eyes.*)

(*Boris lumbers up, quite out of breath.*)

BORIS: Jim, stop.

(*Jimmy freezes but keeps the gun in place.*)

JIMMY: Please.

BORIS: Tina talks with you. I know.

She exaggerates.

JIMMY: Exaggerates! How the hell do you exaggerate being married.

BORIS: Things are mixed up.

You don't understand.

We can talk.

You told me. Mercury is straight now. It's noon.

Everything be all right.

JIMMY: Mercury is what?

JAIME: Retrograde?

JIMMY: Not anymore. It's direct.

You're right. Mercury is direct.

That's why I came here.

BORIS: So now we get things straight. You know. We talk.

JIMMY: *(Opens his eyes.)* How could you give Tina my note?

BORIS: What note?

JIMMY: The note where I said I loved you.

BORIS: Ay...yayayayay

In my pocket. The laundress found it. *(He walks over and gets Jimmy up. Takes away the gun gently.)*

It was a mix up.

Come on. We can talk. Boris is a big man, full of feelings, but not smart.

JIMMY: I don't know, Boris.

BORIS: Boris is dumb. I love you. I love Tina and everyone is mad.

How can love produce madness?

JAIME: That's the question of the century.

BORIS: *(Puts his arm around Jimmy.)* You see?

You explain it to me.

(They walk down the beach. Hughie comes running up.)

HUGHIE: Where is everyone?

JAIME: Walking down the beach into the sunset, Hughie.

HUGHIE: And your friend...?

JAIME: Jimmy?

HUGHIE: And Jimmy...is with...?

JAIME: Boris.

HUGHIE: He's with Boris? With a man? A man with another man?!

Delightful, no?

And this, Jimmy, is short for James?

JAIME: You got it.

HUGHIE: Ahhhhhh.

Don't you think that's perfect? *(He trots after them.)*

(Wilson comes up, perfectly groomed.)

WILSON: Jaimie, Jaimie dear. Wait a moment.

I've had an epiphany.

JAIME: Wilson, I have to talk to you.

WILSON: I know dear.

Oh I'm glad.

I thought you were leaving me.

Here—sit with me.

(They sit.)

The waves are pounding. How perfect. *(He presses her hand to his heart.)* I must tell you, Jaimie. I've made a mistake.

JAIME: Yes, I know.

WILSON: You're not my son.

JAIME: I know.

WILSON: Strangely I feel my son is near.

I feel his passionate presence. That sensitivity. But not in you. However, all those feelings I've had for you are real. Those stirrings. That tremendous excitement and tenderness.

It all became clear when you kissed me.

I tell you. When I saw you, it was love at first sight.

JAIME: Love at first sight!

WILSON: You believe in love at first sight too?

JAIME: Yes. Yes, I do.

WILSON: I knew it! What poet could resist it!

And this life, this opulence, this sumptuousness hasn't put you off completely, has it?

JAIME: No, but Wilson...

WILSON: There's hope...like a delicate bud...Oh forgive me—I sound like a greeting card.

JAIME: Wilson...

WILSON: And I haven't told you how magnificent you look. You can change so—wrapped in a bit of silk and those sapphires—you look so mysterious, a quiet fire...how's that? Less like a card. I think. My son would have been proud. He never knew me like this, you see.

JAIME: Wilson.

WILSON: Yes?

JAIME: This is all wrong.

WILSON: Oh I know it's doomed, but who cares. You don't have to
love me. I love you enough for both of us now. I feel like a
giant. I could straddle continents and oceans and lift mountain
ranges and polar caps for you.

Yes. Yes and I'm so much older. I'll die soon and you'll be rich.

If I can't find my son, I want you to have the money.

JAIME: I've got to be real careful here.

I can't take what's not mine.

It would make me weak.

What would my life be if I were saved before I've ever been in
danger?

WILSON: You're right. You're right. Whatever you want.

No money. No things.

I understand that too.

You see, that's part of my epiphany.

How lovely.

I understand finally. The curse of things.

All these years in love with the beauty and power of money

the supreme luxury of it all.

But now, because of you

I understand the greatest luxury may be freedom

from the clutter of possessions, their care, the fear of their loss.

I understand my son. At last.

Because of you.

He was wise, not foolish.

He wanted to be free and let his spirit soar

and now that's what I want as well.

Jaimie—you've given me a new life; nothing short of rebirth.

And you'll be my perfect companion.

JAIME: Wilson.

WILSON: I bore you. I terrify you. I disgust you.

JAIME: I love someone else.

WILSON: Oh.

JAIME: I'm sorry.

WILSON: Don't. Don't. *(He takes out a handkerchief.)*

JAIME: It was love at first sight.

(Hughie comes back nearly dancing.)

HUGHIE: And Sammy?

WILSON: We're talking.

HUGHIE: Do you have a moment?

WILSON: Not now. *(He turns to Jaimie.)*

It is good-bye then.

JAIME: Yes.

WILSON: I see.

JAIME: I'm terribly sorry Wilson—that I wasn't your son and that I can't share your passion.

WILSON: Passion! Who wants passion!

I can see why it runs young people ragged.

JAIME: I would have missed a whole world if I hadn't met you. *(She kisses him.)*

WILSON: It's strange.

HUGHIE AND JAIME: *(Simultaneously)* What?

WILSON: I feel closer to my son than I ever have—although the search has failed and you're leaving me.

HUGHIE: Do you have a moment?

WILSON: Not now.

(To Jaimie) How will you get home?

JAIME: Your helicopter?

WILSON: Of course.

JAIME: Groovy.

(Wilson hugs her and then turns his back.)

Good luck Hughie. *(She exits.)*

WILSON: Stupid girl. *(He wipes his eyes.)*

Just delightful.

HUGHIE: Ahhhhhhhhh.

WILSON: What are you "ahhhhhing" about?

HUGHIE: Don't you see?

WILSON: See what?

HUGHIE: You have your wishes, don't you?

WILSON: Wishes? What are you babbling about?

The bottom has just dropped out of my world.

HUGHIE: Don't you feel young? Didn't you say young women make you feel young?

Didn't you say passion makes you feel young? Didn't you want passion?

WILSON: She doesn't feel passionate about me, you fool.

She walked away, didn't she? You saw it.

Passion. How can you babble on about me getting any sort of

wish about passion when I'm the one who... *(Looks at Hughie.)*
Yes, I'm the one who feels passion.
Ahhhhhh.

HUGHIE: And you wanted to find your son?

WILSON: Please.

(Boris and Jimmy approach arm and arm.)

HUGHIE: And who's that?

WILSON: Boris?

No.

That young man?

HUGHIE: Can you guess his name?

WILSON: James?

James.

Ahhhhhh.

(Lights dim.)

(Kennedy Airport. The next day. Flights being announced. People walking to and fro. Jaimie looking for David. A tour guide with some extremely foreign people huddled in a group walks by giving instructions. Tour guide: "When you get to New York, never establish eye contact with anyone. Babies are technically okay, but follow your instincts." David walks by with Marie. She is dressed for tropical weather and wears sunglasses. Jaimie approaches.)

JAIME: *(She comes up behind Marie.)* Hey you.

Beat it.

MARIE: I can't believe it.

Are you talking to me?

Hey David, get a load of this!

DAVID: Jaimie!

JAIME: Howdy, good-lookin'. Jus' thought I'd stop by and give my fondest regards.

DAVID: Jaimie.

MARIE: You know this broad?

Great.

Terrific.

JAIME: Either of you have a quarter?

MARIE: *(Digs through her purse.)* Here. Call the zoo and tell them you escaped.

JAIME: Thanks...

Listen. I have the perfect limerick for you guys.

Half price. A real deal.

Are you prepared?

"There was a young dude name of David

Who liked all his women stark naked."

MARIE: This is offensive.

JAIME: "Who liked all his women stark naked.

When one of them balked

He got up and walked

And lost out on the best damn thing he ever had

in his whole life."

MARIE: Look sweetie...

handle this.

I got my ticket. People Magazine

I'm all set.

I'll see you at the gate.

(To Jaimie) You know sweet pea—

David and I have known each other for years.

We're steak and potatoes

and you're just a candy bar.

(Exits.)

JAIME: I like how you really step in and take over.

DAVID: I like women to fight over me.

JAIME: So?

DAVID: So what?

JAIME: So what should I do besides stand here feeling like a total idiot?

DAVID: Excuse me—but you did walk into the middle of my life unannounced and started making demands.

JAIME: Tsk, tsk, tsk. Do I believe my ears?

Are you talking double standard?

I thought that dialect was defunct.

DAVID: Marie's waiting.

JAIME: I thought you invited me?

DAVID: I thought you were otherwise engaged. If I'm not mistaken, your last words to me were— "We never met."

JAIME: Right. Well.

Great. We're even.

Nowhere together.

I thought you like women who give you a hard time.

DAVID: Sure. I like women who give me a hard time.

I couldn't love a woman like that.

JAIME: I should've seen this coming.

Lord have mercy—

You want a sweet young thing.

DAVID: Right.

JAIME: With a heart of gold.

DAVID: Helps.

JAIME: What other specifications?

DAVID: Gold...I like gold. Maybe some silver...You got fillin's ma'am?

(*Jaimie nods.*)

Maybe some copper in her hair...

JAIME: Oh, I get it.

DAVID: You do?

JAIME: To find true love...

DAVID: Yes?

JAIME: You need...

DAVID: Yes?

JAIME: A metal detector.

(*David kisses her. People walk up including the tourist group of foreigners with their leader...all of whom are walking very carefully single file staring at their shoes. Suddenly a large cutout of a mountaintop descends. It should hit with a thud. Sammy is sitting crosslegged meditating. Hughie approaches.*)

HUGHIE: So how're you doing?

(*Sammy looks up then ignores him.*)

Are you deaf?

SAMMY: Only to counsel.

HUGHIE: What?

SAMMY: I thought we were through.

HUGHIE: Why?

SAMMY: After what I said.

HUGHIE: We solved the case, didn't we?

SAMMY: Yes.

HUGHIE: Aren't you glad?

SAMMY: Delighted.

HUGHIE: So?

SAMMY: We're not meant for each other.

HUGHIE: It comes to that?

SAMMY: Yes.

We have irreconcilable differences.

HUGHIE: Sammy, would you explain what's really going on?

Don't you know you're hurting me?

SAMMY: Not enough.

HUGHIE: What?

SAMMY: I said not enough! I'm not hurting you enough.

Now get away. You're ruining my meditation.

HUGHIE: What do you want?

Why can't you tell me what you want?

Isn't it important to discuss things, openly, fully?

Haven't we always treated each other that way?

SAMMY: If you ask one more question, I'll punch you in the face.
(Rises.)

HUGHIE: *(Backs away.)* Ahhhhh.

So, you want me to change my whole philosophy?

SAMMY: Tell me you love me.

HUGHIE: *(Pulls out a flask.)* How about a drink?

SAMMY: Hughie!

HUGHIE: *(Drinks)* Do I insist that you alter your behavior for me?

Change your approach, your outlook on life?

Just for me?

Do I?

SAMMY: Coward.

Take a stand.

Express a belief.

Make a commitment.

HUGHIE: What's gotten into you?

SAMMY: I'm serious.

HUGHIE: Is it too much time in the West?

SAMMY: If you don't do it right now, this minute...

HUGHIE: *(Crosses his arms on his chest.)* Yes?

SAMMY: We're finished.

HUGHIE: Have you thought this through?

SAMMY: Life is change.

HUGHIE: But if I make a statement, don't I lose my posture as a seeker
of truth, a humble observer and prober?

Don't I, with a simple statement, wed myself to a specific reality?

SAMMY: Yes. Me.

HUGHIE: Ahhhhh.

SAMMY: Life is change. *(Sammy takes off her cap. Her hair flows to her shoulders. Her mannerisms become more womanly.)*
We're changing. *(She faces Hughie, challengingly.)* So?

HUGHIE: Yes ? *(He copies her stance, but takes a quick sip from the flask.)*

SAMMY: So tell me you love me.
(A long, long, very long pause.)
Hughie?

HUGHIE: *(Guiltily)* What? *(He can't meet her eyes.)*

SAMMY: Never mind. *(She wipes her eyes and turns away.)*

HUGHIE: *(Taps her on the shoulder.)* I do love you, you know.
(Black out. Lights up.)

END OF PLAY

MOE'S LUCKY SEVEN
by Marlane Gomard Meyer

*This play is dedicated
to my father Robert Punohu Gomard,
my mother, Corinne Gomard, to my uncle Joe Keawe
and to Barry Del Sherman.*

Biography

Ms. Meyer wrote plays for fourteen years before writing *Etta Jenks,* her first professional production. It received its world premier in 1988 as a co-production with the Women's Project at the Los Angeles Theatre Center. It's been awarded the Joseph Kesselring prize, a Dramalogue Award and was a finalist for the Susan Smith Blackburn Prize. It was first published by Methuen Drama to coincide with it's London premiere at the Royal Court Theatre. Her play *Kingfish* was first produced at the Padua Hills Playwright's Festival and had its first equity production at the Los Angeles Theatre Center. It has had subsequent productions which include the Public Theatre, the Edinburgh Fringe Festival, and the Magic Theatre. *Kingfish* was also a finalist for the Susan Smith Blackburn Prize, received a Dramalogue award and a Penn Center USA West award. Her play *Geography of Luck* won the California Playwriting Competition sponsored by South Coast Repertory where it premiered. Subsequent productions include the Los Angeles Theatre Center, San Jose Repertory and the Steppenwolf Theatre in Chicago. It was also a finalist for the Susan Smith Blackburn Prize. Ms. Meyer received an NEA Playwriting Fellowship and an NYSCA grant. Her play, *Why Things Burn* was a commission for the Mark Taper Forum. It was workshopped at the Bay Area Playwright's Festival. It received its premiere at the Magic Theatre in January of 1994. Her play, *Moe's Lucky Seven,* was a commission from South Coast Repertory. It had staged readings at the Mark Taper Forum's New Works Festival, Circle Repertory and Playwright's Horizons, where it received its premiere in May of 1994. *Moe's Lucky Seven* won the Susan Smith Blackburn prize finally in 1993. Ms. Meyer divides her time between New York and Los Angeles where she writes for television. She has also taught Playwriting at the Yale School of Drama. She is currently at work on a commission for Playwright's Horizons.

ORIGINAL PRODUCTION

MOE'S LUCKY SEVEN was directed by Robert Levitow, Produced by Don Scardino and Tim Sanford at Playwright's Horizons in May, 1994 and was originally commissioned by Jerry Patch at Southcoast Repertory Theatre.

MOE'S LUCKY SEVEN, in order of appearance:

Tiny/Divina	Jodie Markell
Knuckles	Steve Harris
Moe	Mark Margolis
Patsy	Deirdre O'Connell
Drake	Barry Del Sherman
Drew	Rick Dean
Mokie	Jefferson Mays
Kurt	Lanny Flaherty
Benito	Ismael 'East' Carlo
Eggs	Bruce McCarty
Janine	Phyllis Somerville
Lon	Sean San Jose Blackman

CAST

TINY, storyteller, female, also doubles as Divina
KNUCKLES, storyteller, male
MOW, a retired actor
PATSY, a descendant of Eve
DRAKE, a snake in the form of a man
DREW, a descendant of Adam
KURT, a married man
JANINE, a retired actress, Moe's wife
Benito, president of a union local
EGGS, an organizer for an international union
MOKIE, a working stiff
DIVINA, a ripe female
LON, a young snake

MOE'S LUCKY SEVEN

PROLOGUE

*Early morning. An old bar. Moe's Lucky Seven. Knuckles enters,
Tiny trails after him. Tiny sits at the bar, he sets her up. He sweeps
the floor throughout the prologue. As he sweeps, we see, beneath
the sawdust, a giant snake that's painted there. When he's finished
he throws down fresh sawdust.*

TINY: I like snakes.

KNUCKLES: What is it?

TINY: Snakes.

KNUCKLES: 'Cause you're a woman.

TINY: So?

KNUCKLES: They are an ancient ally.

TINY: You know, back in the old days snakes could talk?

KNUCKLES: You used to dance with a snake.

TINY: *(Irritated.)* It was a professional relationship.

KNUCKLES: That dancing snake business still embarrasses you, doesn't it?

TINY: Knuckles?

KNUCKLES: Woman and snakes, it's an ancient instinct.

TINY: I'm not ashamed...

KNUCKLES: It happened with that first woman, she got attracted by that
snake, remember her?

TINY: I'm trying to tell that story right now.

KNUCKLES: I mean, she had her purpose in nature, right? She was built
to be the companion of Adam.

TINY: To that shlub? A guy with no experience, with his trust and
innocence? What kind of talking can lead to love with a man like
that? Where was his evil? To love him in spite of what? Where
was the obstacle that gives love its power? His complication was
not yet in place.

KNUCKLES: So she went for the snake?

TINY: Oh, at first she was repulsed by his cool touch. But eventually it came to be what she loved best.

KNUCKLES: How could that happen?

TINY: He could TALK to her for one thing.

KNUCKLES: What could he have said?

TINY: He said, touch me.

KNUCKLES: That's what everybody says!

TINY: Yeah, but by the time he said it they had been talking for a long time, and she had been thinking of him for a long time, and because of that, it made it easy for him to ask and the way she looked at him let him know that she had thought through all the obstacles 'cause that was the kind of creature she was and the way her mind moved reminded him of his own corporeal nature...

KNUCKLES: They had inner affinity...

TINY: So when she stroked him, and he curled around her body, she came into an awareness of herself that was separate from her function as a mother.

KNUCKLES: Sex for pleasure and not for procreation.

TINY: It scared her to death.

KNUCKLES: So what did she do?

TINY: She ran away from the snake and went back to the man where she thought she could feel safe.

Knuckles: Anatomy is destiny, she wanted to have the baby.

TINY: But in order to do that she had to put that part of herself to sleep that contained the memory of snakes.

KNUCKLES: *(Out)* And the years rolled by.

TINY: *(Out)* And the times changed.

KNUCKLES: And the man changed.

TINY: And the woman changed.

KNUCKLES: And the snake?

TINY: He just kept crawling back. And everytime the woman saw him, she screamed *(Screams.)* and ran away...

KNUCKLES: I've had women do me like that, it burns.

TINY: So when he finally decided she had put him from her heart, he crawled along the earth to the sea, intending to do himself in. But as he was sliding through the waves he felt a cradle of seaweed lift him to the shore, and having failed even to die, he began to cry giant salty tears, and at that point he was possessed of a sorrow that had within it, transforming properties.

KNUCKLES: Transforming properties?

TINY: He was given the choice to remain a snake or become a man. Subject to the ills of men, to the temptations of the earth, and to the joys of the flesh.

KNUCKLES: I know what I'd choose.

TINY: Why do you always bring the question back to you?

KNUCKLES: 'Cause if I can't identify with the story what's the point of listening?

TINY: Okay, so what would you choose, Knuckles?

KNUCKLES: I would stay a snake, then at least, I'd know my place in nature.

TINY: Okay, but if he chooses to stay a snake, this play is finished.

KNUCKLES: *(Out.)* I knew that.

(Knuckles hits the juke box, Hawaiian music comes up, they move to a table Up Right of the bar. Knuckles turns on a light, we see the name "Moe's Lucky 7". The bar has a tropical jungle motif, lots of foliage, fishnets. Behind the bar is a scrim painted with a jungle motif. Behind the scrim is the garden of Eden, which is invisible for most of the play. Moe enters with a small portable typewriter, he sits at a table Downstage, types.)

SCENE ONE

We hear the sound of a woman's footsteps, a shadow on the door, Patsy enters, she moves to the bar. She watches Moe, waiting, till...

PATSY: Moe!

MOE: What.

PATSY: Look who's back.

MOE: *(He looks at her, unimpressed.)* When'd you get out?

PATSY: Outa what?

MOE: I thought you were in jail?

PATSY: I been up to 'Frisco, stayin' at my aunt's, Drew been in?

MOE: Haven't seen him.

PATSY: You haven't.

MOE: I think he met somebody.

PATSY: Get me a shot and a beer, will you?

> (*He begrudgingly leaves his stool, sets her up, she drinks.*)

PATSY: So. Drew's shackin' up.

MOE: Portuguese gal, name of Divina.

PATSY: I know Divina.

MOE: He's been stayin' up to her place.

PATSY: I know Divina, shit!

MOE: It looks serious.

PATSY: Drew can get that way.

MOE: Oh you mean like with you?

PATSY: Yes.

MOE: This is nothing like that. This is serious with a future, not serious like first degree murder with no possibility of parole.(*Drake opens the door, peers around the corner. He looks like a dog without its skin. Patsy and Moe turn, Patsy screams. Moe beckons to Drake.*)

MOE: (*Cheery.*) Come on in.

> (*Drake makes his way to a table Downstage. He wears a snakeskin vest and glasses with tinted lenses.*)

MOE: Yeah, I figure the longer Drew stays away the better things must be for him. He only comes in here when she's put him out.

> (*To Drake.*) There's no table service.

> (*Drake moves to the bar, tries not to stare at Patsy.*)

DRAKE: I'll have an egg in a glass of milk.

MOE: You got a protein deficiency?

DRAKE: Excuse me?

MOE: You want it blended?

DRAKE: Uh. No. (*She looks at him.*) Okay.

MOE: A blended drink costs more.

> (*Moe makes the drink.*)
> You from around here?

DRAKE: (*Hopefully.*) Do I look familiar?

MOE: You don't look like anybody I ever seen.

DRAKE: Then I must be from out of town.

MOE: You work on the docks?

DRAKE: Docks… (*He looks at his hands.*) No.

MOE: You some kind of union official?

DRAKE: Let me just say that I don't know where I've been or what I've been doing. I have a wallet with a driver's license. The license has a picture of me. An address. I have a key to an apartment at the address. Along with a key to a car called...Mustang. I seem to have information that comes out when people ask me questions. I sense at times that what I'm saying is false. That I'm repeating something I've heard or read. Some people look familiar. *(To Patsy.)* Like with you, you seem familiar...

PATSY: I look like everybody.

(Moe serves him a glass of egg milk. Drake downs it.)

MOE: You want a shot 'o whisky to cut that scum?

DRAKE: I don't drink.

MOE: You're a bartender.

DRAKE: *(Surprised.)* Yes. Yes I am.

(Moe takes a Hawaiian shirt, puts it on Drake.)

MOE: I was just typing an ad but if you could use a job, if you like the work, I don't like to wait on people myself, I'm a retired actor and a student of the occult sciences and this is my metaphysical workshop.

DRAKE: I believe there are better single malt scotches.

MOE: Oh. An epicurean. I see. Tell me something, Jellyfish, where are you from, San Francisco?

(Drew enters with Kurt and Mokie.)

DREW: And so I told her, like... if you don't like that, you don't like me and then she just starts crying 'cause she says, *(Imitating her.)* you don't even know yourself, you don't even know what you're like, and like she does, right? Why do women think they know everything...?

PATSY: Hey, Drew.

DREW: *(Looks.)* Oh, shit... *(Turns away.)* Gimme a beer.

MOKIE: Gimme a beer...

KURT: Gimme a beer, no fuck a beer, shit.

MOE: What are you doing off work?

KURT: *(Irritated.)* It's a walk out.

MOE: Two weeks before Christmas?

KURT: I bought my wife a fur stroller I don't know how I'm supposed to pay for that.

MOE: Whose idea was this?

KURT: Who else?

DREW: It was everybody's idea, not just mine.

MOKIE: We still gotta vote on it.

DREW: But we'll vote to strike.

PATSY: I just got my casual card, does everybody have to strike?

KURT: Benito said we'd be stupid to turn up our noses at the new contract with shippin' the way it is.

DREW: Benito's getting paid off by management to scare us.

KURT: It's part of the job.

MOKIE: Kurt, that is so cynical.

DREW: Benito is keeping us down.

(Benito enters.)

BENITO: You're keeping yourself down with that big mouth.

DREW: We shoulda merged our union with the M.I.U. two years ago but you talked us out of it.

BENITO: It was like a big fish eating a little fish.

DREW: If we'da done that we'd be getting the money we're striking for now and you'd be out of a job...

BENITO: You sound like Eggs talkin' now...

DREW: What's wrong with Eggs?

BENITO: He's a crook.

(Eggs enters.)

EGGS: Who's a crook?

BENITO: You are.

EGGS: I am not a crook, I'm an organizer for the M.I.U. and as such I might be able to offer a solution.

BENITO: Just leave us alone.

EGGS: Benito, you come in with us and we can leverage these guys, alone you can do nothing.

BENITO: That's not the way it works, and you know it.

DREW: Will the M.I.U. honor our picket line?

BENITO: There's not gonna be a picket line...

DREW: Oh yes there is.

BENITO: You go out on strike and they'll replace you, is that what you want? No job at all?

DREW: Company profits are up why can't we get a raise?

BENITO: It's a recession. Everybody's out of work.

EGGS: Did you tell them about the pay cut?

DREW: What pay cut?

BENITO: The company said if you take this cut everyone can keep their jobs... otherwise, we're gonna lose about half our places.

DREW: Oh man...

PATSY: What are they gonna shut down the division?

BENITO: I'm not sure.

EGGS: Quit tryin' to scare 'em.

BENITO: Will you get out of here?

EGGS: Look, why don't you guys come in with us, we get more jobs, better benefits...

KURT: Pay more dues.

DREW: Hey, you're two years from retirement. A merger means in future we can work anywhere, the Gulf, Seattle, 'Frisco...

MOE: You'll be Mafia owned and operated with Eggs.

EGGS: They'd be east coast affiliated.

MOKIE: Sounds good to me.

DREW: Yeah, what's wrong with that?

PATSY: There'll be no more rank and file vote.

DREW: You can't vote, you're casual.

KURT: We lose the vote if we merge?

EGGS: We used to let 'em vote but they never voted.

DREW: So who elects the officials?

EGGS: What difference does it make?

PATSY: The president, he appoints the officials and they elect him.

EGGS: Hey, take a look at our benefit package if you have any problems with the leadership...stock options, health care, longer paid vacations, our pension fund is a third of a billion dollars, that's a lot of vacation property.

MOKIE: I could buy a boat.

KURT: You can't even swim.

BENITO: Quit trying to bribe 'em.

DREW: I don't like losing the vote.

EGGS: If you're getting everything you want, what do you need with a vote?

DRAKE: It's democratic for one thing.

DREW: Who's that?

MOE: It's a bartender.

EGGS: The democratics have been selling you guys out for years.

BENITO: It's a concept, for chrissakes. Brotherhood? We care about each other, your guys don't even know each other.

(*The men are quiet, Eggs watches them a beat, smiles.*)

EGGS: You're an old fashioned idealist, Benito, and I admire that, I do. So. Best of luck, I wish you all success in your endeavor.

(*Eggs exits.*)

KURT: Can't we just go back to work?

DREW: No, we can't just go back to work.

BENITO: Let them vote on it!

DREW: We're having a meeting.

BENITO: Oh, really?

KURT: *(Beat.)* At two o'clock.

BENITO: You cuttin' me outa the loop, or what?

DREW and MOKIE: Yes.

KURT: No!

BENITO: Man. *(Beat.)* I'll see you guys at the hall.

KURT: Bye Benito. *(Beat.)* You guys! Poor Benito.

MOKIE: Poor Benito! Benito has coffee cans filled with ashes of cremated union members whose families have paid him to provide a burial at sea. Do you know what he does with those ashes…?

DREW: What?

MOKIE: He fertilizes his roses!

KURT: Who cares, let's eat. Drew?

DREW: Naw, you guys go on, I'm gonna hang out with my old man. I'll meet you over at the hall, save me a seat.

(Kurt and Mokie exit, beat.)

So what is it you keep comin' back here for?

PATSY: Maybe I missed you.

DREW: The only thing you missed was the heart nobody could find when they put that restless body together. "Hey, where's the heart? Anybody seen that little black heart?"

PATSY: Let's stop talking like this, okay?

DREW: Okay. Small talk. WELL. I been workin' pretty steady, doin' okay. I put some money by, thinkin' I was gonna maybe get MARRIED to this chick I met.

PATSY: Divina's a nice girl.

DREW: Nice? This woman loves me. You know? I never had that before. Somebody who really loves me.

PATSY: Screw yourself in every orifice.

DREW: Oh did I say the wrong thing? Shoot. Well, anyway, this woman has a good job, wonderful personality, very nicely put together, she's a little on the gabby side but she's congenial and her cooking more than makes up for any unusual clothing choices.

PATSY: I hate it when you talk to me about other women, it makes me feel that at some point in the future I'll be a conversation about the past and it makes me feel lonely right now.

DRAKE: Oooh, well said.

DREW: Hey?

DRAKE: What?

DREW: This is private.

DRAKE: Sorry.

DREW: *(Thinking.)* Okay. So anyway, everything's... *(Beat.)* What are you two together?

PATSY: No!

DREW: I don't like how you're looking at her.

DRAKE: I'm hungry is all it is.

DREW: Have an egg.

DRAKE: Oh well, don't mind if I do.

(Takes an egg off the rack of hard boiled eggs, puts it in his mouth, swallows it.)

PATSY: Well, I sure am glad you're happy.

DREW: Oh I'm overjoyed. And you?

PATSY: Well, I got my K card, and I was gonna be countin' bananas and drivin' a truck... but now I guess, I'm just... livin' with my mom, *(Pointedly.)* tryin' to find a job.

DREW: She still with Russell?

PATSY: No, and she's drinkin' pretty steady. So. I don't know. I mean I have to find my own place is what's happening... and... like, I been doin' a lotta thinking about, homes, and what it takes to have one and what you gotta be like.

DREW: You mean like normal?

PATSY: A thing I have resisted. And I came to this feeling in myself recently, of, like, maybe I could do that, that maybe I need to.

DREW: What?

PATSY: You know, whatever, walk upright, like the two leggeds?

DREW: *(Smiles, grins, laughs.)*

PATSY: What are you laughing at?

DREW: What are you talking about?

PATSY: I am talking about...transformation.

DRAKE: She wants to get married.

DREW: Patsy is not the marrying kind.

PATSY: Why not?

DREW: 'Cause you're not!

PATSY: People change...

DREW: Not you...you're too smart.

PATSY: Lots of the stupid ideas we make fun of when we're young seem like the logical choice as you get older...

DREW: Like marriage?

PATSY: Yes.

DREW: Why are you wasting your time trying to find value in a dead tradition? Why are you trying to seduce yourself with a fantasy? What are you thinking? A nice house, cute kids, happy husband, settle down, live in chains, get a mortgage, dirty diapers, nine to five, too tired to have sex, the dog dies! Why do you think I live in my car?

PATSY: 'Cause you're cheap.

DREW: 'Cause I'm smart. Sure, I was thinkin' about marriage and then bam, it hit me, why wreck my life? Let's smoke...

PATSY: I gotta quit...

DREW: What for, take it... take two...

PATSY: Just give me that pack if you want to kill me!

DREW: Naw, you don't want to get married, you want to be free! Like me! So we'll have another beer, and maybe an egg, 'cause you look tired, you been watchin' too much T.V.?

PATSY: I was watching kick boxing all the way from Thailand last night and it was just so weird to be able to see that, you know, feeling like this is so twenty-first century? Together yet isolated. Made me feel lonely.

DREW: Kick boxing made you feel lonely?

PATSY: Television has a distancing effect on how we perceive reality.

DREW: Damn, Patsy, I missed you!

MOE: Shit shit shit shit shit.

DREW: Little lamb chop...

MOE: Shit shit shit!

DREW: The reason a personal life is personal 'cause it's PERSONAL, so butt out.

DRAKE: Your father is voicing his concern.

(*Drew looks at him, shakes his head, stands, steps to the middle of the bar, clears a place, motions Drake over.*)

DREW: Come over here.

DRAKE: No.

DREW: Don't you want to die? Patsy says that everyone has a death wish.

PATSY: Leave me out of it.

DRAKE: Don't you think that good manners are the beginning of civilization and bringing that civility to our closest relationships is our first priority as custodians of the culture?

DREW: *(Beat.)* What's the point of making a civilized choice in a corrupt world?

DRAKE: It has a civilizing effect on the chooser and the world of the chooser because people follow you with their inner eye.

DREW: Okay, first I'll kill you then I'll kill myself 'cause I'm such a BARBARIAN now come over here.

DRAKE: This is human stupid.

DREW: As a gentleman, you should respect my wishes for I am the son of the man you work for.

MOE: We have only your mother's word on that.

DREW: Come here!

DRAKE: God *(Drake comes toward Drew, Drew hits him in the stomach, he goes down, stays there.)*
Ow. Okay?

DREW: What do you mean, okay? Get up.

DRAKE: If I get up you'll hit me again.

DREW: What are you going to do when you have to kick somebody outa here, wish him into the cornfield?

MOE: Drew's right, you gotta be able to take care of yourself.
(Drake stands, takes off his glasses, fixes him with a stare.)

DREW: *(Transfixed)* Father, these are not the eyes of a human being...
(Drake head butts him, he falls.)

MOE: Nice butt!
(Drake offers his hand to Drew, Drew knocks it away, Moe comes over and helps him up.)

MOE: That's enough, okay?

DREW: No, I hit him he hits me and on it goes till one of us is dead.

PATSY: This is what I hate about men.

DREW: I go down in front of my dad and my girl and that makes me look like a what?

MOE: A guy who can take as good as he gives.

DREW: It's not enough.

MOE: Yes, it is.

DREW: NO IT'S NOT.

MOE: YES IT IS!

DREW: This is a free country and I'm allowed to be as much of myself as I can be within the confines of the law.

DRAKE: Liberty offers us the freedom to self-discipline.

DREW: Quit lecturing me!

PATSY: Stop acting like a australopithecus.

(*Drake and Drew look at each other, Drake extends his hand, Drew starts to shake it...*)

DREW: Why are you so cold?

DRAKE: Metabolism.

PATSY: Drew?

DREW: Okay! New thing. Patsy! So... I gotta go vote... (*He slaps some money on the bar.*) Why don't you buy yourself somethin' to eat, boozebag.

(*He kisses her, and kisses her again, starts off, stops, looks at Drake.*)

DREW: If I catch you giving her one more hungry look I will grind you beneath my heel. (*Drew exits.*)

MOE: (*Irritated, to Patsy.*) You happy now?

PATSY: So what?

MOE: You happy?

PATSY: I don't think it'll be bad like you think why not just relax, okay Moe?

(*Patsy moves Downstage to a small table.*)

DRAKE: She seems like a nice girl.

MOE: They all seem nice before they get their claws so deep inside your guts you don't know where they begin and you end. I been married twenty-seven years, I know from whence I speak. You ever buy somebody a ring?

DRAKE: No, but I've rolled myself in a circle around a woman's body and squeezed her till I thought I'd disappeared.

MOE: Oh, that will be quite enough of that, old stick.

(*Janine enters, spies Drake.*)

DRAKE: What's that?

MOE: What's it look like?

JANINE: It looks like a secret that just won't keep. What's your name, jellyfish?

(*Janine extends her hand, he takes it. His hand is cold, she reacts.*)

DRAKE: Drake.

JANINE: Drake. Elegant with a whisper of contempt. (*She hisses.*)

MOE: What are you doing?

JANINE: Shut up.

DRAKE: I recognize you from the movies.

JANINE: You must like to stay up late, me too.

DRAKE: Let go of him!

(*She drops his hand, glares at Moe.*)

JANINE: Patsy, let's get drunk!

(*Janine takes a bottle and two glasses to Patsy's table.*)

MOE: We'll never make a living giving the booze away.

JANINE: Up yours. (*Beat, to Patsy.*) This Drake reminds me of a kid I knew who was so mysterious that when I finally got him into bed it made me feel smart 'cause I had knowledge of something complex.

PATSY: Like algebra?

JANINE: More like physics. (*Giggling.*) All that matter and energy?

PATSY: (*Giggling.*) Converging and colliding?

MOE: Knock it off.

JANINE: Drew been in?

PATSY and MOE: Yeah.

JANINE: (*To Patsy.*) Don't get us in trouble.

PATSY: You can't be where you're not.

JANINE: Sure you can. You can be in a dream, or a memory... Or television? Yeah. I saw myself the other night in this Adam and Eve movie, I was wearing this fig leaf bikini, you know, and walking through this fake garden. I mean, it was totally stupid, right? But I had that scene where I was talking to the snake and I swear to God, I played the shit out of that scene, I mean, I was like... God... in the act of creating himself female. Oh! Man, I wish somebody could have seen that. (*Beat, wistful.*) I was such a child.

(*She drinks, freeze, blackout.*)

SCENE TWO

Several hours later.

TINY: Later that evening, everyone returned to the bar. The mood was somber...
KNUCKLES: What is this play about again?
MOE: Wait and see.
KNUCKLES: It's about the decline of the unions, all the different kinds of unions, right?
MOE: Jesus!
KNUCKLES: And since we're at the edge of the sea...
TINY: Knuckles...?
KNUCKLES: That's symbolic of...what? Rebirth? Regeneration?
TINY: What are you doing now?
    (*Everyone looks at Knuckles.*)
KNUCKLES: I'm trying to figure out what's gonna happen. 'Cause it started out I thought it was gonna be about temptation.
TINY: Temptation, is what perfects our resolve.
KNUCKLES: Oh. *(Thinking.)* Resolve, resolution...evolution. Okay. Let's go.
    (*Everyone turns back.*)
TINY: *(She watches him a beat, turns.)* Later that night everyone returned to the bar. The mood was somber.
DREW: It's like a planet in the future where they have these women that have been like genetically engineered in test tubes, wait, no, scratch that, 'cause if we have sex scenes it's easier to get European distribution, so these women are bred, like monkeys, in cages. And they are like, idiots.
MOKIE: Like morons?
KURT: I hate that word.
DREW: Retarded then.
KURT: My sister's just adopted a developmentally disabled child...
MOE: *(Impatient.)* Last call.
DREW: Okay, okay, so it's a planet in the future where this mad scientist has created this race of women mating these stud monsters with these developmentally disabled women, then those kids he breeds with playboy bunnies and he gets these killer looking chicks that are dumb but really nice, I'm gonna call it "Planet o' the Babes." And then like, what happens is this science dweeb

takes a space ship full of these bimbettes to Washington and gets them jobs as pages on the Senate floor, and like, they all start dorking these politicians, and these guys get so obsessed that the country gets so much, much worse that the really smart guys who were too ethical to go into politics are suddenly forced to run for office and find solutions to the really big problems in this country, and like... civilization? Flourishes.

MOKIE: I like a movie with political content.

KNUCKLES: It's a comedy, right?

DREW: It's a dramady.

TINY: It's sexist.

DREW: Ma, is it sexist?

JANINE: Of course it's sexist and don't call me "ma" like I'm one of the Kettles for chrissakes...

DREW: So what if it's sexist.

MOE: And you're gonna have to come up with the solutions for all the urban blight stuff.

DREW: I have the solution.

MOE: What?

DREW: Kill everybody who doesn't vote.

MOE: That's half the country.

JANINE: You erode your tax base, Mr. Wizard.

DREW: These people aren't participating why should they have a spot on the freeway, get their garbage hauled, collect social security...?

JANINE: 'Cause they paid in.

DREW: It's not enough!

MOKIE: I think we should get the Mafia to run the country.

PATSY: Another victim of this culture's anti-hero obsession. Everybody's idealizing people who are either dead or in the underworld.

KURT: You can't kill people 'cause they're lazy.

DREW: It's my movie I could do anything I like.

MOE: It's too quirky for an M.O.W.

JANINE: Maybe for network but what about cable?

TINY: I think the women should get brain transplants.

DREW: 'Cause you're snobby, you think you have to be smart to be happy.

KNUCKLES: It helps.

DREW: You think stupid people can't figure out how to get rich.

MOE: No, you think that.

DREW: That's right. And you know why…?

MOE: Christ…

DREW: You know why?

MOE: Why?

DREW: 'Cause they're stupid.

(*Drew laughs.*)

KURT: I gotta go… *(He kills his drink.)*

MOKIE: It's early.

KURT: I told my wife I'd come home and tell her how it went. Man, is she gonna be pissed.

DREW: You act like you never been on a strike before. We'll be back at work by the end of the week.

KURT: We'd be back at work tomorrow if you'd kept your mouth shut.

MOE: What did you do?

MOKIE: He gave a speech.

DREW: It just came out, I opened my mouth and it was already there.

KURT: By the time we got around to votin', lotsa guys had changed their minds but Drew talked them back into it.

MOKIE: You shoulda seen Benito, man, was he steamed.

DREW: Benito is losing his juice.

KURT: Maybe you should run for office when he drips dry?

MOKIE: That's what Eggs was tellin' him out in the parking lot.

KURT: Oh man.

DREW: What?

KURT: The power brokers.

DREW: Get the fuck outa here.

KURT: Moe, am I crazy?

MOE: Don't make me think about this.

DREW: I told Eggs. My life is perfect. Why would I want to complicate it with business? I'm not that stupid. But if I were, this is the moment I would choose. This is a complicated time for the working man, a time when youth and energy might count for more than wisdom and experience. A time when we can no longer afford the luxury of high minded ideals like brotherhood and democracy…

PATSY: Shit.

DREW: We're too busy trying to feed our families.

PATSY: What family?

DREW: Now I'm not saying I have all the answers…

PATSY: Or any of them!

DREW: But neither does Benito.

KURT: Benito has experience.

DREW: Yes, but experience in a world that no longer exists. If the strike's a flop his career's over, and that scares him. But I'm not scared, because change doesn't scare me. But then that's the luxury of youth, is it not? That it will spend itself in the service of righteousness without counting the cost.

MOKIE: *(Applauding.)* God, I want to write some of this down...

KURT: Yeah, how do you spell ambition.

MOKIE: You got my vote, Drew.

DREW: Hey, nobody is gonna run me for office with a commie for a father, isn't that right, father?

MOE: I wasn't a commie, I was a socialist.

MOKIE: I heard you were blacklisted for ballin' Jose Ferrar's girlfriend.

MOE: Who told you that?

JANINE: I wasn't his girlfriend we just slept together for warmth workin' stock in the Catskills...

MOE: It had nothing to do with you.

JANINE: I think Jose had a little crush on me but who knew he'd take it out on your father...

MOE: It never hurt my career!

DREW: Your career as a saloon keeper.

(*Kurt exits.*)

KURT: 'Night all.

MOKIE: Man if this is what it's like after you get married...?

KURT: *(Off.)* You should have it so good.

(*Drew moves and sits with Patsy.*)

DREW: So what do you think of my movie idea?

PATSY: It's not a movie I would pay to see.

DREW: Don't tell Moe, but I got a call in to Burt Lancaster, him and Dad worked on Birdman and Burt owes him a favor, he's got his own production company and I thought...

PATSY: Just write it if you want to do it, just do it.

DREW: I can't really write, I mean, I can spell but it's not the same thing...

PATSY: Drew, can we talk?

DREW: Jesus, Patsy, like what, big talk or little talk?

PATSY: Never mind.

DREW: It's just I'm kinda talked out…

PATSY: Okay, fine, forget it…

DREW: Okay! But let's make it quick, 'cause I don't want to get hung up here wrangling all night…

PATSY: Then go home!

DREW: I thought we could take a drive.

PATSY: Don't you think I know what that means?

DREW: Oh alright. Let's talk.

PATSY: *(Beat.)* How do you figure out if you can live with a man for the rest of your life?

DREW: Okay, see, this is the kinda shit that screws us up…

PATSY: What, talking, talking screws us up?

DREW: I don't talk about things like this because it makes me feel stupid and then I get pissed off and we start fighting about things nobody even knows anything about, like how can you tell if you can live with a man for the rest of your life, how should I know?

DRAKE: You give him your power by revealing your feelings, you become vulnerable, and if he abuses that privilege you'll find yourself living in a constant state of defense, you'll be fighting a lot and bring children into the world who'll think that home and family looks like Armageddon, is that the point of the question, Patsy, children?

DREW: What did he say?

PATSY: Yes.

DREW: No, stop… *(To Drake.)* What did you just say?

MOE: What's goin' on?

DREW: I don't know.

JANINE: Patsy's pregnant.

DREW: She didn't say that…

PATSY: This isn't going well.

DREW: So you're gonna have a baby and that's why you came back.

PATSY: Yes.

DREW: God I'm so stupid I thought it was about me it wasn't about me…

PATSY: Who else would it be about?

DREW: IT'S NOT MINE, NOTHING IN THIS WORLD BELONGS TO ME EXCEPT MY CAR AND THAT'S THE WAY I WANT IT, UNDERSTAND?

(*He exits.*)

MOE: *(Referring to Patsy.)* See what happens with people like this, they don't have a plan so they screw up everybody.

(Moe starts after Drew.)

JANINE: Where are you going?

MOE: Stay here.

(He exits, Janine follows. Patsy and Drake look at each other, she pours herself a drink.)

PATSY: If something scares you, maybe it's best to run away. Like this. Bye bye... *(She starts to drink.)*

DRAKE: *(He holds her hand to stop her from drinking.)*

PATSY: I put the booze inside myself so the demon will get drunk and fall asleep, and dream of a beautiful garden where all the animals talk to her.

DRAKE: *(Irritated.)* Not all animals talk.

PATSY: You don't know what I'm saying so shut up.

DRAKE: And not all the animals would talk to you.

(She looks at him carefully.)

PATSY: When?

DRAKE: Before they got used to the upright walking, they would run away from you, remember?

PATSY: I remember that...

DRAKE: It made you cry.

(Patsy puts her drink down.)

DRAKE: So what happened to your fur?

PATSY: It fell off.

(She touches his face.)

Hey, ice cube!

DRAKE: I don't like to be handled scientifically.

PATSY: Don't you remember, science is my life.

KNUCKLES: See this is the shit that would drive me nuts.

TINY: They haven't seen each other for awhile.

(Janine comes in with Moe, Moe sees Patsy and Drake.)

MOE: *(To Janine.)* See what I mean?

JANINE: Patsy, knock it off.

MOE: *(Nicely.)* Why don't you two go home.

JANINE: Moe...?

MOE: *(To Janine.)* What difference does it make?

PATSY: I have to finish my drunk...

MOE: You want a baby with five eyes, go home!

(He tosses her drink, Patsy and Drake head for the exit.)

PATSY: Guess it's time to go home.

DRAKE: I'll go with you…

PATSY: Into the weird where the spooks live?

JANINE: ·Tell him to stay here.

MOE: I will not.

PATSY: Hurry, hurry…

JANINE: Patsy, you're really screwing up.

PATSY: *(She stops, looks at Drake.)* Stay here, Stupid, or you'll be out on your sumptuous rump.

    (Patsy exits, Drake stares after her.)

DRAKE: What is going on?

JANINE: She was just talking, taking a walk in the garden, when something appeared, just subtly appeared out of the midst of the garden.

MOE: Something WE are afraid of. *(Moe pours a shot.)*

JANINE: What are you doing?

    (He gives the shot to Drake.)

MOE: Welcome to the joys of the earth.

JANINE: He doesn't drink.

MOE: This isn't booze, it's medicine.

DRAKE: I like her.

    (Drake drinks, he has sharp intake of air, he lets it out in a hiss.)

    (Drew enters, he has a bouquet of horrible flowers. Drake pours himself another shot.)

DREW: She go home?

MOE: She knows you're gonna crawl back.

JANINE: Moe, I swear to God…

MOE: What?

JANINE: Stay out of it.

MOE: *(Innocent.)* I just… it's me, okay?

JANINE: Moe has issues with trust. Trusting people.

MOE: People? No, not people… well, maybe people but mostly women.

DREW: She's not the type to lie about something like that.

JANINE: You know her better than anyone.

MOE: She was gone for weeks, where was she?

DREW: San Francisco. She's got an aunt she stays with.

MOE: An aunt, you ever meet this person?

DREW: That's where she goes when she wants to think.

MOE: And drink.

JANINE: Drew likes that.

DREW: *(It's a toast.)* Let the good times roll.

MOE: You don't even know what she's talkin' about half the time.

DREW: So?

MOE: Does she?

DREW: I suppose.

MOE: How do you know that?

DREW: Motivation.

JANINE: Motivation...?

MOE: Messin' up your head. They like to do that. It makes them feel powerful.

JANINE: Drew, that doesn't sound right to me, does that sound right to you?

DREW: Well. Yes.

JANINE: She seems moody but that doesn't make her bad, that makes her complicated.

DREW: Like algebra? I flunked that.

JANINE: I wouldn't think about her like that if I were you.

DREW: Like how?

JANINE: Well. Like she's going to make a mistake so big that the love you have will not cover it.

(Moe looks at Janine, smiles.)

MOE: Yeah, put that right out of your head, that will hoist you by your own petard.

DREW: A man should be aware of his limitations.

Moe: True...so true.

JANINE: *(To Drake.)* Say something.

MOE: Stay out of it.

DRAKE: Nobody can tell you who to love, and you can't avoid it with strategy, that's God's work.

MOE: You dog!

DRAKE: Why not enlist an element of faith into the fantasy we've built around love. How could it hurt? The best you can do, any of us can do, is to try and have a little faith. Right?

MOE: No!

JANINE: Yes!

DREW: Yes. That's right, he's right. *(To Moe.)* He's right. And You, King Moe, are going to be a grandfather, whether you like it or not. And we're all going to live forever. *(To Drake.)* Right?

DRAKE: No.

DREW: Hooray! (*Drew exits.*)

MOE: *(To Drake.)* I had him and you let him go.

DRAKE: A holy war begins with each side being fully armed and equally defended otherwise it's not a fair fight.

MOE: Nobody ever won a war fighting fair.

DRAKE: I don't want the responsibility for another person's destiny unfolding or not by the influence I exert with talking, just talking them into or out of something.

MOE: Yes you do.

DRAKE: No I don't.

MOE: You just did it you big liar!

DRAKE: What time do you want me tomorrow, Moe?

MOE: I see the way you look at her, what do you think will happen? You think she's going to come around, to love you for yourself?

DRAKE: Well...yeah.

MOE: You are dreaming, Drake, of big fish now and chasing minnows, this is not the open sea, this is the tide pool.

DRAKE: I know what it's like to fall through the sea without hope or dreams, nobody up here lives like that.

MOE: But if these dreams turn to dust in the IMAGINING of them, day after day, losing the life that might bring them to pass, what then?

DRAKE: Then I'll still have my job.

(*He slams out the door. Blackout.*)

SCENE THREE

The bar is empty except for Knuckles and Tiny

KNUCKLES: Boy, Moe hates Patsy.

TINY: He doesn't think she can be made content.

KNUCKLES: I don't either.

TINY: So that's important to Drew.

KNUCKLES: But it's not his problem.

TINY: He thinks he should be able to make her happy.

KNUCKLES: Women let men think that to enslave them.

TINY: No they do not either.

KNUCKLES: A man has a box for you, in his head, it's about this big, this wide, this tall, and he looks around, and there you are, looking just about the right size. And you sort of squeeze into this place, in his head, and two things happen, either you fit or you don't. Mostly, you don't...

TINY: Sometimes you do...

KNUCKLES: You can make it happen by reshaping your expectations but mostly you don't fit and you don't say anything...

TINY: Sure I do.

KNUCKLES: No, because you have an agenda.

TINY: What?

KNUCKLES: The perpetuation of the species.

TINY: We're overpopulated.

KNUCKLES: I'm not faulting YOU, but that's what's happening with us now, we almost had a revolution, but now we're falling back into what is safe, what is traditional...

TINY: And what's your idea?

KNUCKLES: Get rid of the box altogether.

TINY: If you live with a box in your head you begin to see the world as one big box, and to lose that feels like death.

KNUCKLES: Of course you're sitting on the means of production in a world ruled by supply and demand, sure, you'll always have a job.

TINY: What are you, jealous?

KNUCKLES: Yes.

TINY: Can we get back to the story?

KNUCKLES: So the snake had a job.

(Drake enters.)

TINY: A pretty good job.

KNUCKLES: And he worked everyday. *(He sets up.)*

TINY: And he made a kind of life.

KNUCKLES: And he pined for the woman.

TINY: But he didn't let on.

KNUCKLES: Till one day he spoke to her of his feelings.

TINY: No he did not, Knuckles!

KNUCKLES: You said he was the temptor.

TINY: He is.

KNUCKLES: You said temptation is what perfects our resolve. It's the lynchpin of the story. But here he's gone and talked himself out of fulfilling his alleged destiny.

TINY: He has to restrain his instincts to evolve.

KNUCKLES: That's not much of a throughline.

TINY: A what?

KNUCKLES: An action throughline? It's what a good antagonist needs.

TINY: He's not an antagonist, he's one of several protagonists.

KNUCKLES: Who's the antagonist?

TINY: It's an amorphous desire for spiritual definition.

KNUCKLES: Wait, the antagonist is an amorphous desire?

TINY: An ineffable yearning for the divine.

KNUCKLES: How did the snake talk himself out of his slither?

TINY: Well, it was hard...

KNUCKLES: Because that is an animal thing.

TINY: The snake was becoming a man, he was domesticating his animal
nature.

KNUCKLES: Oh this is grim. Killing off your instincts... I feel sorry for
you, I do, I feel sorry for him...
(*Drake fixes Knuckles a drink.*)

TINY: And what with those dreams...

KNUCKLES: (*Out.*) Beautiful images of nature would spill out of his
unconscious as he slept reminding him of his purpose in creation...

TINY: He was the most miserable of all the creatures.

KNUCKLES: 'Cause if he wasn't sleeping and dreaming...

TINY: He was pining for this woman.

KNUCKLES: And occasionally when he did wake up, all by himself, tan-
gled up in the sheets of his bed...?

TINY: He would press his arms into the sides of his body and imagine
himself sliding through the moist, dark underbrush.
(*A light falls on Drake, he turns away from it, Knuckles shakes his
head.*)

KNUCKLES: I don't know if it's the real world that does us as much
harm as these dreams, Tiny.
(*Drinks. Light change. The garden appears briefly, blackout.*)

SCENE FOUR

Moe has a dreambook. Mokie plays solitaire Downstage.

MOE: Here we go. To dream of Snakes. "A snake is a symbol of transcendence and a creature of the underworld and can signify a passage from one way of life to another."

DRAKE: Will you leave me alone?

MOE: This dream often foretells a sudden reversal in one's expectations. If you dream of snakes coming from green herbs...

DRAKE: He didn't come from green herbs.

MOE: Where did he come from?

DRAKE: I can't remember.

MOE: Think.

DRAKE: He slithered down the side of a grass hut, the floor of which was sand. I was at the beach, and the snake was the color of the ocean, the skin itself had a rippling quality, reminiscent of water.

MOE: Water, water... *(He flips through the book.)*

DRAKE: The snake came to a bed on which I had been tied, and he traveled across my belly.

MOE: Repressed sexuality, subconscious understanding...

DRAKE: He was long and thin and cool and left a trail of salt on my skin.

MOE: Salt, skin, Lot's wife, don't look back...

DRAKE: At first I was afraid but he crawled up my arm to where the rope was chafing my wrist and the water from his body dissolved the tie and I was free. Then he crawled back to the ocean and I remember him telling me something important.

MOE: The snake was talking?

DRAKE: Water talk, a language only I could understand.

MOE: What did he say?

DRAKE: He said a viper cannot enter uninvited, or... or maybe it was a vampire cannot enter uninvited?

MOE: *(Beat, he laughs maniacally.)* You're weird, Drake! You're a freak! You know that, you scare me!

MOKIE: Moe, will you lay off him?

(Kurt enters, he moves to the bar, Drake gets him a beer.)

MOE: My bar, I could do anything I want, I'm the king!

KURT: Hey Moe, Eggs asked could he have a meeting here.

MOE: Eggs asked YOU to ask me?

(*Mokie and Moe look at each other, Kurt sits with Mokie, they play cards.*)

KURT: He said maybe a change of scene will break the deadlock.

MOE: I wouldn't trust that bastard, Kurt.

DRAKE: Drew hasn't worked in six weeks.

MOE: He's a doper, he could give a shit...

DRAKE: His car's been repossessed.

MOE: Adversity builds character...

DRAKE: Mokie can't pay his bar bill.

MOKIE: (*Irritated.*) I'm good for it.

DRAKE: Kurt's wife is living with her mother.

KURT: How does he know that?

MOE: (*To Drake.*) Big mouth.

KURT: So what'dya say, Moe? I already told him yes.

MOE: What's it gonna be like, a hit or what?

MOKIE: A hit? (*Giggles.*)

MOE: 'Cause I hate violence!

KURT: We're just gonna meet with Benito.

MOE: I hate melodrama.

KURT: Jesus...should I tell him find another place?

DRAKE: Moe, it's business.

MOE: Oh, listen to the young republican, go ahead,... make a big deal meeting...

DRAKE: They will eat, they will drink.

MOE: Oh sure, it's all about money these days, you young punks. It's all you can think of. I remember back in the old days, when MEN walked the earth and worked for the love of the labor, the love of the sea, you don't know what that's like.

DRAKE: I can imagine.

MOE: You know my father?

DRAKE: How could I, he's dead.

MOE: He named all of us, his sons, after Kings. The kings of France. I ever tell you that?

DRAKE: About fifty million times.

MOE: This was a very educated person. He was not like ANYBODY in this room.

DRAKE: You're lucky to have had a father like him.

MOE: He was a monster. If one of us did something wrong he would beat us all.

DRAKE: That's how you teach a group to police its own.

MOE: I never hit Drew enough, that's my problem, I'm soft.

KURT: Is he around? Eggs wants him at the meeting.

MOE: He's out in the car with that BITCH smoking SHIT.

DRAKE: I don't like him living in my car, Moe.

MOE: They're like animals I had to chase 'em outa the men's room.

DRAKE: That human smell gets in the upholstery you know and nothing will clean it.

MOE: I told him to get a motel. Find a place I said. Live like a homo sapien. But, he won't listen to me, why is that? What is wrong with people?

MOKIE: Gin.

KURT: We're not playing Gin.

MOE: What's HE doing with HER?

DRAKE: How should I know?

MOE: What were you waiting for, romance?

DRAKE: Yes.

MOE: Look at me, married twenty-seven years...

DRAKE: Big deal.

MOE: You don't care 'cause you're in love so what are you saying you're looking, you're not looking.

DRAKE: I didn't say anything!

MOE: Bullshit I could know it just from the goddamn phone bills, Drake, Christ, callin' her every five minutes... she's dorking him right now in your car.

DRAKE: At least somebody's getting laid.

MOE: White dog, white dog, always pissing, never fucking...

DRAKE: I like to call and make sure she's okay, okay...?

MOE: Oh she's okay. Yeah. Sure. Hah! She'll fall by her own weight. They always do.

DRAKE: She's not like you think.

MOE: She came on to me!

DRAKE: She wouldn't do that.

MOE: Mokie was there, he saw it all.

MOKIE: What did I see...?

MOE: Shit, thought she'd be doin' me a favor! I think my wife put her up to it, trying to screw me up, those bitches, sticking together, let them dork each other, right? Who needs it...?

KURT: Can we change the subject?

MOE: Sometimes when I see the two of you. It reminds me of a time I did this flick with the Duke, How The West Was Won? And I had this ingenue, and we were lookin' for a place to get fucked up, just the two of us, out in the sagebrush, and we come upon this she-wolf, pullin' apart a deer, just rippin' the guts out of it. I had to turn away, I had to turn my face, I felt sick to my stomach. But this chick I was with, she said...

KURT and MOKIE: She's pregnant, she needs to eat.

MOE: 'Cause it had a purpose, she could watch it. That's the way they are.

MOE, MOKIE, KURT: Predatory.

DRAKE: That's survival instinct, Moe. It's got nothing to do with gender.

MOE: She stepped on your head to get to the dead. Blue balls. What's she holding out for? Nothing, he takes it away, keeps it away...

MOKIE: What's he talking about?

KURT: I don't know.

MOKIE: I can't concentrate. *(He reshuffles.)*

MOE: She won't marry him.

DRAKE: You don't know that.

MOE: But you do.

DRAKE: No, I do not.

MOE: I'm thinking of a number between one and ten.

DRAKE: *(Involuntarily.)* Seven.

MOE: See how smart you can be if you let yourself you could play Lotto and win.

MOKIE: You always pick seven.

MOE: I'm only suggesting he use his gifts!

KURT: She will come around or she won't.

MOE: Sure! What difference does it make who she dorks if she loves him, right?

DRAKE: You think she loves me?

MOE: What does it matter?

DRAKE: Everyone likes to feel special.

MOE: It's an ego trip.

DRAKE: You think so?

MOE: No! I don't think so. I just said that to see just how really STUPID you are. You're a loser, Drake, you're a fuckin' loser...

KURT: Jesus Christ, Moe, will you shut up?

MOE: I'm helping him!

KURT: You're making me sick.

MOE: I am not.

KURT: Yes, you are.

MOE: No, I'm not.

DRAKE: Who wants a drink, I'm buying...

(*A door slams, Patsy enters, desheveled, barefoot, carrying her shoes. She sits at the bar, fixes her face. A door slams, Drew enters, he's half dressed, disheveled, he wears a pajama top and one dirty bedroom slipper.*)

DREW: What just happened?

PATSY: You enjoyed yourself.

DREW: We both enjoyed ourselves, we were having a good time...

PATSY: YOU were having a good time...

DREW: What's wrong with that?

PATSY: I came back here to work, I can't work and it's your fault!

DREW: My fault?

PATSY: Talking people into things just because you can, you don't give a shit, it's just an ego trip...

DREW: It is not, it's part of a larger plan.

PATSY: What plan?

DREW: A secret plan...

PATSY: You put everybody out of work.

DREW: It's not my fault I'm the voice of the group mind.

PATSY: Oh god...

DREW: Patsy, why can't we just have fun?

PATSY: 'Cause I have to pay for it is why!

MOE: You eat here, you drink here, it's on the house!

DREW: Stay out of it.

MOE: I'm gettin' back in show business I'm startin' my own band gonna be called Mealticket Moe and the Goodfornothing's...

DREW: I'll get some money if that's what's bugging you, Drake's got money... Drake?

DRAKE: I'm not loaning you any more money.

DREW: It's an emergency, okay, I gotta take Patsy to a motel.

(*Drake fishes through his pockets.*)

PATSY: Motel, Jesus! That's not what's wrong with me... You don't listen is your problem, you know that?

DREW: Listen to what?

PATSY: Me!

DREW: Oh wait a minute, are you mad 'cause you didn't get off?

MOE: Oh! This is one gruesome twosome.

KURT: She's upset 'cause she's gonna have a baby, IDIOT!

DREW: Is that what's wrong with you? Is it? 'Cause I told you...GET RID OF IT!

MOKIE: Ouch.

DREW: I'm a baby and I don't want a baby and I told her how I feel and now she's mad at me... right? Right? Patsy, look at me...

PATSY: NO. No. No more YOU and YOUR life taking up all the room in MY life, replacing ME and what I need to have happen...!

DREW: Don't raise your voice in my father's bar.

PATSY: I'M SICK OF YOU! I want to get away from you. You have too many problems, you're sad and it makes me feel weak. You mope around here waiting for what? You and your stinking father talking about your famous fucking famous friends they never even call you up!

MOE: What is she talking about?

DREW: Don't talk about my father if you don't have a father.

PATSY: I have a father!

DREW: He only married your mom 'cause he felt sorry for her. *(To Moe.)* Right...?

MOE: *(Lie.)* I never said that.

(Patsy throws her shoe at Drew, misses him.)

DREW: Come here, come here...

PATSY: No!

DREW: I shoulda killed you when I had the chance.

(He lunges at her, Drake grabs him, they struggle, Mokie and Kurt move their game, Patsy gathers her things, drops some of it, picks it up, hits him on the head with her remaining shoe.)

PATSY: Yeah kill me, go to prison, ruin your life...

DREW: My life is already ruined from knowing you!

PATSY: We just don't love each other enough, that's all, it's nobody's fault, it just happens.

DREW: It has not happened just 'cause you say it doesn't make it so if anybody decides to fall out of love it will not be by mutual consent it will be MY decision, I'm the boss!

(Janine enters with a case of vodka.)

JANINE: Hey boss, I can hear you all the way in the parking lot.

(The struggle ceases, Patsy takes one last hit at Drew.)

PATSY: I'm leaving Janine, I have to leave.

DRAKE: Why not sleep on it, Patsy.

PATSY: I sleep twenty hours a day as it is!

JANINE: That's right, get out while you can still walk out.

MOE: Oh please...

JANINE: Before you get carried out!

MOE: It's not about you, none of this is about you!

JANINE: I shoulda never got married.

MOE: Here we go...

JANINE: To be taken for granted day after day, nothing you do surprises or delights, a person could lose their life wasting it on bums like this.

(*Janine punches the register, takes out a twenty.*)

MOE: What, are you doing?

(*She slams the money on the bar.*)

JANINE: There's nothing worse than being broke, you know that so shut up!

(*Patsy takes the money, exits. Drake watches her, turns to Drew.*)

DRAKE: Hey...?

DREW: What?

DRAKE: DO something.

(*Drew reaches across the bar and grabs a bottle.*)

DREW: I'm not goin' after her if that's what you're asking me. That's not me, 'kay? You want to go, go after her if you want to 'cause I am not going after her, no way.

DRAKE: (*Wildly irritated, controlled.*) Jesus!

(*Drake exits. Janine takes the bottle from Drew.*)

JANINE: You been smokin', shit you look like a pig.

(*He sifts through the change on the bar, finds a quarter, moves to the jukebox.*)

DREW: 'Course you don't know what you're talking about so what difference does that make, right?! (*Drew punches in a song.*) Talk about giving advice. What do you two know about being in love. HUH? (*Drew leans wearily against the juke box.*) NOBODY KNOWS SHIT AROUND HERE.

(*Music comes up. We hear Dean Martin sing "Memories are Made of This". Moe looks at Janine.*)

JANINE: What are you lookin' at? (*He nods his head toward the dance floor.*) Forget it... I'm not that hard up.

(*Moe grabs her and they dance. We watch them have FUN, dancing for awhile. Drake enters and pours himself a drink.*)

DRAKE: Women walk out of here, and they're gone. You get to the
    door and they're gone. Where do they go?

DREW: Back to hell where they can relax.

DRAKE: How come you're such a dickhead?

DREW: 'Cause life sucks.

DRAKE: I bet we never get married. I bet we live our whole life here
    living here with nothing. Nobody to miss, nobody to miss us...

DREW: What are you tryin' to make me FEEL bad?

DRAKE: Yes! (*They drink. Eggs enters, he look at Kurt, Kurt looks away.*)

MOE: Ah, the stale odor of corruption.

    (*Eggs takes a table, sits.*)

EGGS: Drew, come, sit and be social. Mokie, scare us up some refresh-
    ments.

    (*He hands him a twenty.*)

MOKIE: Okay, gimme six beers, a couple of those chick o'sticks, half
    dozen pepperoni, a dozen eggs, and some pork rinds... what do
    you guys want?

EGGS: Get a bottle.

DREW: What's going on?

EGGS: This is America, everybody drinks.

    (*Benito enters.*)

BENITO: (*To Kurt.*) What's Eggs doing here?

KURT: It's okay, really. Sit down.

    (*Benito sits down. Drake serves them.*)

EGGS: Let us make a toast, to marriage.

BENITO: Marriage?

DREW: I don't want to drink to marriage.

EGGS: Marriage is the cornerstone of civilization.

DREW: I'd drink to civilization...

EGGS: It's more than a job and a paycheck that keeps us from falling
    through the cracks, Drew, a man should get married. At the end
    of the day, after a hard days work, a man needs a home, needs a
    base of support, needs a place to go at night, otherwise he drifts.
    Isn't that right?

DREW: I suppose.

EGGS: You have to think of marriage like you would a good suit. A
    good suit disguises a man's limitations.

BENITO: Nobody in this bar owns a suit.

KURT: I do.

EGGS: *(Congenial.)* You know, Benito, back in the old days I'da had your nuts in a coffee can by now.

BENITO: Screw yourself.

EGGS: If I could I would, that's the kind of guy I am, practical. But we're not here to talk about me, I'm not in the shit.

DREW: To marriage.

(They drink.)

KNUCKLES: What is all this about marriage?

EGGS: Marriage is a way of defining a relationship. We get married to show our commitment, sometimes we get married to discover our inability to make those commitments. But however you view it, marriage works best when the individuals involved are unified and working toward a common goal. Benito, what is the goal of the union?

BENITO: To create a brotherhood of workers that can collectively bargain for wages and safety.

EGGS: Drew, what is the goal?

DREW: Job security.

BENITO: Well that's part of it but that's not all of it...

MOKIE: It is, that's all of it.

BENITO: I don't like the feeling of what's going on here...

KNUCKLES: What is going on here?

EGGS: Benito, I want you to make Drew your deputy. I want you to bring him in during the transition.

BENITO: What transition?

DREW: I don't want to be a deputy...

EGGS: Yes, you do...

BENITO: What transition??

EGGS: You're stepping down.

BENITO: The hell I am.

DREW: Does a deputy get a car?

EGGS: Maybe if he could keep his big mouth shut.

BENITO: *(To Kurt.)* Is this what you got me up here for?

(Kurt moves away.)

EGGS: Benito, see this guy here, *(Referring to Drew.)* he talked your men into walking a picket line.

BENITO: He is a banana.

EGGS: People listen to him 'cause he speaks to the way they are feeling. He is a catalyst for transformation.

DREW: I am?

MOKIE: It's a gift.

MOE: It's a BIG responsibility.

JANINE: It's star quality and he got it from me.

EGGS: He's the new world, you're part of the old world. So, Benito, you can go quietly or you can die like bossie in the bullring, it's your choice.

BENITO: I'm not finished 'cause you say I'm finished...

EGGS: No, you're finished 'cause the strike is a flop.

KURT: See...I knew this would happen.

EGGS: If you'da come in with us two years ago, you'd be in good shape, as it is, you got no contract, you got scabs crawlin' up your spine, and men you started out with twenty years ago are selling you out.

(*Benito looks at Kurt, Kurt looks away.*)

DREW: So what's the deal?

EGGS: You guys come in with us and we get your contract back.

DREW: Same contract?

EGGS: Not exactly, no. You have to take a wage cut.

BENITO: Shit.

DREW: Then what was the point of the strike?

BENITO: Man you are so stupid.

DREW: (*To Eggs.*) You told me that engineering a chaotic moment was the first step in rehabilitating a stagnant situation.

EGGS: Change requires patience.

KNUCKLES: What's going on?

TINY: The big fish is eating the little fish.

DREW: It's not suppose to eat us it's suppose to assimilate us and then we become the big fish.

MOE: Theoretically.

EGGS: Everything starts with an idea or an impulse, depends on what kind of man you are.

DREW: I've lived my whole life by impulse.

EGGS: Then maybe it's time to grow up.

DREW: What about shutting down the docks till they give us a raise?

EGGS: What do want us all in the shit?

DREW: That's the point of the union.

BENITO: (*Smirking.*) No, it's not, it's job security.

KURT: So we're all getting our jobs back, right?

EGGS: Not exactly, no. We need a goat.

DREW: What's that?

BENITO: GOD DAMN IT!

EGGS: Look Benito, we put Drew in with you during the transition, that way you can exit gracefully.

BENITO: It wasn't even my idea to strike, you know that, don't you?

EGGS: C'mon, Benny, you don't want people feelin' sorry for you.

BENITO: You actually think in an honest election that my guys are gonna vote for him?

MOKIE: Yes!

BENITO: Kurt?

KURT: I just want my job back.

EGGS: These are not your guys anymore. These are men that have been raised on television. You can't hold them with sentimental notions about the way things should work, they want things, not democracy, or brotherhood, things.

KURT: I just want my job back.

BENITO: *(Beat.)* See? This is what happens when men don't have God, or a way of behaving themselves. They devolve. Back in the old days we'd never have known a man like this. A professional troublemaker. A man who rents his car, lives in a hotel, sleeps with strangers. Back in the old days, this guy would never have busted our ranks. We were tight. It was a community. We all knew each other, we had parties, we shared rides, we had houses in the brand new suburbs. I had a wife with enormous breasts and black lingerie who cooked every one of my meals. What happened?

JANINE: She got old and you dumped her.

TINY: What goes down comes around, eh, Benito?

(Benito takes out a handkerchief and…looks up.)

BENITO: What's that called?

KNUCKLES: Karma?

BENITO: Right. *(Benito blows his nose.)* You know, I was hauled down at the docks the other day, the fishermen had hauled in their catch, and I caught a whiff of that rotting fish smell from down in the holds, it reminded me of old Manila. You know? *(Laughs.)* I haven't been home in forty years.

EGGS: There's nothing about being homesick that going home won't cure.

DREW: Benito, there is no Manila like the one you remember, what do you think you're gonna do down there?

BENITO: Maybe I'll visit my ex-wife, see how she's holding up.

DREW: Come on, Benito…?

BENITO: Don't worry about me, Kid, you watch your back, they'll come for you some day, don't think they won't. (*Benito exits.*)

DREW: I don't like what we did to Benito.

(*Mokie looks down.*)

EGGS: We're all on the road to extinction. I wouldn't waste my time feeling sorry for people if I were you. (*He pulls out a wad of bills, drops them in front of Drew.*) Go get yourself a suit.

(*He exits. Patsy enters, she's missing a shoe, she speaks to Drake.*)

PATSY: I forgot my shoe.

(*Drake looks around, Drew finds the shoe and kneels in front of Patsy and puts it on her foot. Drake watches, motionless.*)

MOE: Oh shit!

DREW: Patsy, I want to be with you and I don't want anybody else to be with you. I want to be with you. You have to marry me.

KNUCKLES: Where have I heard that before?

TINY: It's from New York, New York. Robert DeNiro says it to Liza Minelli. Two people you'd never find dorking outside a movie.

DREW: Okay?

PATSY: Well… (*Clears her throat.*) Uh. Okay.

JANINE: Drinks on the house!

(*Drake remains in place as Moe sets everyone up with drinks. Music plays.*)

KNUCKLES: Jeez! What happened?

TINY: He thinks he needs to get married 'cause something in the future looks larger than he can face alone.

KNUCKLES: I don't think that's love.

MOE: Yeah but that's what happened to us. I met her at the Actor's Studio, we each put half in on a car to come to Hollywood. We fought the whole damn way. But after twenty-seven years, she still looks pretty good, don't you think…? She still looks pretty damn good to me.

Who's got gin and tonic?

(*Tiny raises her hand, blackout.*)

SCENE FIVE

The morning of the wedding. Patsy enters wearing her veil. She's sober. Drake is dressed in a tail coat. He's chilling a case of champagne. The bar has been decorated.

PATSY: Where do you think we go when we dream?
DRAKE: We go where we're afraid to go when we're awake.
PATSY: Which is where?
DRAKE: Into the weird where the spooks live.
PATSY: Do you ever dream about me?
DRAKE: No.
PATSY: Never?
DRAKE: No.
PATSY: Aren't you going to ask me if I dream about you?
DRAKE: No.
PATSY: What's the matter, don't you want to have a conversation about dreams?
DRAKE: I think you should go home.
PATSY: I think you should quit thinking about me.
DRAKE: Stop it.
PATSY: Stop what?
DRAKE: Stop trying to fuck me without touching me.
PATSY: Oh man...that was way off. *(She starts out, stops, turns...)* Just 'cause we have this kind of... (rapport.)
DRAKE: Go home...
PATSY: I mean we like to talk to each other...
DRAKE: You'll be married soon, you can talk to him.
PATSY: He's not a good listener.
DRAKE: Tough. *(She slams out. He waits, turns, watches the door a long beat, walks up to it.)* Did you know I was psychic?
PATSY: *(Off.)* Big deal.
DRAKE: It's a gift. This ability to know certain secret things, or to pick lucky numbers. If I let myself I could play Lotto and win.
(She comes back in.)
PATSY: Why don't you?
DRAKE: Would lots of money make you happy?
PATSY: No.
DRAKE: I don't use my gifts to acquire it 'cause I don't know what I'd

do with it if I had it. That's a more responsible attitude than you have, say, towards love.

PATSY: You don't know me like you think you do, but I like that you think you do. It's sexy.

DRAKE: Go home.

PATSY: 'Cause if you did, you'd know I'm just like everyone else, why do I feel like I have to defend myself to you?

DRAKE: 'Cause you're lying.

PATSY: When?

DRAKE: All the time.

PATSY: You mean about being knocked up.

DRAKE: About everything.

PATSY: I didn't lie about it, I lost it. I drink too much. (*Beat.*) Children are very serious! You need the right set up. A screwed up childhood changes people. For the better sometimes, obstacles, make people strong. Kid could come up a criminal... or an artist. No. I had to ask myself is Drew "the one"? 'Cause if you're going to be tied to someone for the rest of your life you should try and... (*Beat.*)

DRAKE: So is Drew the one?

PATSY: (*Resolved.*) I'm in love with Drew and we're getting married.

DRAKE: (*Silence.*)

PATSY: Just 'cause you're not saying anything doesn't mean I can't hear you.

DRAKE: When you have doubts about yourself you're hoping will disappear when you marry, I don't think that's love.

PATSY: I'm taking my place in nature!

DRAKE: Who's nature? Drew's?

PATSY: If I listen to you I'll end up all by myself, watching T.V. in the middle of the night, just like my mom, nobody to talk with and nothing to look forward to...

DRAKE: That could happen anyway, and you may find you like it, I do, I LOVE late night television...

PATSY: Quit trying to wreck my life...

DRAKE: Quit trying to scare yourself.

PATSY: That's the way I make decisions!

DRAKE: (*Beat.*) Okay. Ask me.

PATSY: What?

DRAKE: Patsy, you have to ask me.

PATSY: Why can't you just tell me?

DRAKE: Because a viper cannot enter uninvited.

PATSY: Vampire. A vampire cannot enter uninvited.

DRAKE: Is that it?

PATSY: Yes.

DRAKE: Oh. Well, then. There are three worlds to live in, Patsy, one is the one we let other people create, and we try to fit into, 'cause we're scared to be alone. One is the secret world we create to keep ourselves from getting too trapped in the first world. And the third world is the world we create when we get sick of lying. We let ourselves be who we are in the presence of strangers. Then these strangers will be able to see what we're like and may or may not choose to be our friends or guides and lovers in this world.

KNUCKLES: Get rid of the box...

TINY: Shhhh.

PATSY: I am not like you.

DRAKE: Our differentness is what gives love it's obstacle and makes it strong.

PATSY: I mortal love Drew!

DRAKE: Drew has a place for you in his mortal life.

PATSY: And if I can fit, why not?

DRAKE: 'Cause the genesis of the fit is...

PATSY: So what's wrong with sex?

DRAKE: Is he there, even when he's inside you, or is he in his head making love to an idea after all that familiarity.

PATSY: Hey, is this a conversation you want to be having?

DRAKE: No.

PATSY: It's more like a ritual these days. We go to his apartment. I cook dinner. He likes me to dress up and talk to him in this kind of baby voice.

DRAKE: Why?

PATSY: I don't know.

DRAKE: Think?

PATSY: To keep the part that scares him away.

DRAKE: The effort to find communion in what is unfamiliar is where God make's it's presence felt, that's the beginning of true love. But if otherness scares you, you settle for dominion.

PATSY: Are you trying to seduce me?

DRAKE: I am trying to make the truth so apparent... that you fall like ripe fruit into my hand.

PATSY: *(Smiles.)* I'm supposed to be getting married.

DRAKE: Marry yourself, for better or for worse, at least you won't be cruising on your wedding day.

PATSY: This is what my mom would call a Peter Pan moment. I'm standing on the ledge of a high window, in back of me is a house and a family, ahead of me, the night sky of London, and beyond that, Never Never Land. I have my shadow back, so I can go anywhere I want. What do I choose?

DRAKE: What scares you the most?

PATSY: Snakes. *(Beat.)* Remember a long time ago when we first met each other and you found out how much I loved fruit so you stole that fruit for me and we got in all that trouble?

DRAKE: Yes.

PATSY: Remember where we went?

DRAKE: *(Beat.)* I suppose.

PATSY: Into the weird where the spooks live.

(She steps back into the darkness and holds out her hand, she draws him to her...blackout.)

SCENE SIX

It's late at night. Everyone is dressed in wedding clothes, but nobody is happy.

JANINE: She's been moody. That's not right. A girl gets what she wants she's supposed to be happy, she wasn't. Of course neither was I...

MOE: Janine?

JANINE: They say a part of a woman dies when she gets married and that the first six months you spend in a state of mourning for that lost self.

MOE: REALLY?

JANINE: It's a big adjustment, Moe.

MOE: I'm still making it!

JANINE: Patsy couldn't face the music. Instead of the wedding march, she heard a dirge.

MOE: Oh, please!

KURT: Marriage scares a lot of people.

MOKIE: I almost got married.

KURT: You never did.

MOKIE: Yes, I had a girl I went with in the islands. Leilani? Big girl. Very big girl.

KURT: You have hidden depths.

MOKIE: Thank you.

(*Drake enters, he looks a little out of it. He stands center, beat.*)

DRAKE: Did you know that snakes have two penises and can copulate for up to twenty-four hours at a time?

MOE: Let's open the champagne.

DREW: Let's wait.

JANINE: Sweetheart, I don't think she's coming.

DREW: No, no, I can feel that.

DRAKE: Where did you get feelings?

DREW: What's the matter with you?

DRAKE: I'm a drunk.

DREW: Feelings are not something you can show everyone.

MOE: *(To Drake.)* You've had your chance, butt out.

(*Tiny moves into the scene as Divina.*)

MOE: Divina, you look like an angel.

KURT: Drew, look at how beautiful Divina looks.

DIVINA: Thank you, I made this dress myself.

MOE: As talented as she is good.

DREW: Divina?

DRAKE: *(Alarmed.)* Oh my god...

DIVINA: Yes, Drew?

DREW: Does marriage scare you?

DIVINA: Scare, I wouldn't say scare...

DRAKE: Scar, does Marriage scar you...?

DIVINA: It certainly can, if you let it. But I come from a big family where everybody's married. My parents, well you know those two, they've been married forty years, I have role models, marriage seems like not only the right alternative, but the only possibility for happiness. But, that's not everybody, like with Patsy...coming as she does from a broken home, a much married mother...

DREW: Divina…?

DIVINA: We learn to be adults from our parents and we learn to be parents when we are children.

KNUCKLES: What's that mean?

MOE: *(Firmly, to Knuckles.)* As wise as she is good.

DREW: Divina, I want to ask you something.

DIVINA: I'm ready.

DREW: Do you like kids?

DIVINA: I have kids.

DREW: I like kids too.

DRAKE: Since when?

DREW: Since about two minutes ago, okay?

DREW: Divina, I need a wife. Not a best friend or a drinking buddy or someone to fight with. I don't want someone who's different everyday. I can't get my bearings. I need a wife. Some children. A place to go home to at night. Someone to be with, to build something with. Now. Someday I may want to change. And that, well, that could be bad. But all I know is what I want right now. What do you say, Divina, will you marry me?

DIVINA: I'm not proud. Let's go for it.

(Knuckles moves downstage away from the group. The rest of the bar form themselves into a wedding tableau. Mokie takes a picture, flash. The group dissolves…)

KNUCKLES: I HATE this story.

TINY: Why?

KNUCKLES: It's poison, it's a poison story.

TINY: You're a baby.

KNUCKLES: I hate the way you trick me everynight into listening…

TINY: I don't…

KNUCKLES: And you never really tell me how it ends, I hate that.

TINY: I can't tell you.

KNUCKLES: Why?

TINY: 'Cause if you don't ask me everynight we can't do the play.

KNUCKLES: We never know what happens to Patsy and the snake, do we?

TINY: They disappear into the world.

KNUCKLES: What, they have a tumble and then boom, she takes off.

TINY: Yes.

KNUCKLES: What does that mean?

TINY: I don't know. Maybe you'll figure it out next time though.

(She smiles at him, smug.)

KNUCKLES: You gotta stop tryin' to control me through my ignorance, Tiny...

TINY: Oh nobody's doing that!

KNUCKLES: I'll never get any smarter if you don't trust me.

TINY: Knuckles?

KNUCKLES: I'll never get any smarter if you don't trust me.

TINY: I'm getting very sick of all these outbursts...

KNUCKLES: I am not manipulated by my fear of your anger. *(To himself.)* I am not manipulated by my fear of her anger. I am not manipulated by my fear PERIOD.

TINY: Alright!

KNUCKLES: Tell me what happens.

TINY: He went to look for her.

KNUCKLES: How did he know where to look?

TINY: He knew where to look.

KNUCKLES: How?

TINY: From himself, from inside himself.

KNUCKLES: And so one day he found her.

TINY: No.

KNUCKLES: I HATE this story!

TINY: He would find a room with lipstick stains on a glass and the smell of cigarette smoke. Those stinkin' clove cigarettes. He would find a T.V. dinner and some ripped up nylons. One shoe. But she would feel when he was about to show up, and they would slip away.

KNUCKLES: And the snake?

TINY: He went broke chasing her. He was down to his last dollar. So he played the Lotto.

KNUCKLES: 'Cause it had a purpose.

TINY: He bought a bar with all he won. This one here. Moe's Lucky Seven.

KNUCKLES: He went back home, so she would know here to find him, and he knew she would come back there eventually 'cause that is where she could feel...understood.

TINY: *(Impressed.)* Yes. Yes!

KNUCKLES: See?

TINY: You're a really good listener.

KNUCKLES: That's not so important, maybe, since I heard the story about a million times.

TINY: No, no. If you weren't such a good listener how could I keep telling this story? No, it is important to have someone who listens.

KNUCKLES: *(Shy.)* So. What happened next?

TINY: The snake plopped himself down and waited. And he waited such a long time that he forgot what he was waiting for. And the years rolled by. And then one day...

(Light change, Lon enters, he looks like a dog without his skin, he wears a snakeskin vest, he wears glasses with tinted lenses. He sits at a table downstage. Drake enters with Christmas lights, he's older.)

DRAKE: We're closed.

LON: You're open in five minutes.

DRAKE: Come back in five minutes.

LON: Can't I just sit here?

DRAKE: There's no table service.

LON: Okay. *(He moves to the bar.)* It's Christmas, I think I'll have an eggnog.

DRAKE: In five minutes.

LON: In five minutes then. Jeez, what a grouch. What's the matter, your cat die?

DRAKE: I would never domesticate an animal.

LON: I had a cat, I named it Puff Adder.

DRAKE: *(He looks at him.)*

LON: Some drunk sat on it and broke its leg.

DRAKE: You gonna tell me a sad story?

LON: We had the leg set, she limps but she is a wonderfully cheerful animal. Great thing about animals is how they adapt. You know about that, right? How a species will adapt?

DRAKE: You want some brandy in your eggnog.

LON: Liquors burn my throat.

DRAKE: You're too young to drink.

LON: Oh! Is that it?

(Drake fixes eggnog.)

LON: Do I look familiar?

DRAKE: You don't look like anybody I've ever seen.

LON: I've been everywhere.

DRAKE: I'm gonna be over here.

LON: Oh, I'm sorry, come back, no back story, I hate it when people carry around their story like it's some kind of key to the city. Why are bars so dark anyway...?

DRAKE: So people think it's night with the possibility that tomorrow things will be better.

LON: And sometimes they are.

DRAKE: You know what I hate about the two leggeds?

LON: That they are so goddamned hopeful.

DRAKE: *(He drinks.)* Yes.

LON: You should ease up on the juice, it has a cumulative effect.

DRAKE: That's what I like about it.

LON: Depression, ever hear of it?

DRAKE: Okay, that's it, you're too young to be here, I don't serve food so you'll have to get out...

LON: You serve eggs... can I have an egg?

DRAKE: *(Hands him an egg.)* If you eat it outside.

LON: I'm meeting someone.

DRAKE: If she shows up I'll tell her you left.

LON: I didn't say it was a woman. Swami.

DRAKE: But it is, and she's always late, sometimes she won't show up at all so, adios amigo.

LON: What happens then?

DRAKE: When?

LON: When she doesn't show up?

DRAKE: You wait. Like an old dog by the door.

LON: It's not like that. She's my keeper. She says she found me floating in the ocean. That's the way she talks about it. Like it's a kind of fable, or a fairy tale, she keeps the events surrounding my birth mysterious so that I could be, almost anybody.

DRAKE: *(He looks at him. Beat.)* I'm thinking of a number between one and ten.

LON: You're thinking of the number twelve 'cause I look so young.

DRAKE: *(Nods.)* That's a good gift you got there. That's a real good gift, you make use of a gift like that?

LON: Yes. Like now. Here. She's coming now. She stopped. *(Silence, they wait. Nothing, Lon looks at Drake.)* What are you doing?

DRAKE: Seeing what happens when she doesn't show up.

LON: She always shows up...

(Drake starts to drink, Lon holds his hand.)

DRAKE: Faith is for the two leggeds.

LON: I have faith in what is between us. This feeling I have in my heart has gravity, it's like an open hand, I hold it out and I trust that it will draw her back, I trust that it will keep us together, can you feel that?

DRAKE: No.

LON: Her heart with your open heart? (*Lon puts his hand over Drake's heart.*)

DRAKE: Owww, what are you doing?

LON: I'm opening your heart.

DRAKE: (*Sharp intake of breath.*) Owwww!

LON: C'mon Jellyfish.

DRAKE: You don't know everything, we can't know everything.

LON: Sure we can, we can know it all.

(*The sound of footsteps coming closer, the door opens, Patsy steps into the bar, it becomes the garden. Drake moves toward her as the lights come down.*)

END OF PLAY

THE FAMILY OF MANN
by Theresa Rebeck

BIOGRAPHY

Theresa Rebeck's plays have been seen in Boston, Philadelphia, Detroit, Chicago, London, and New York City. Her play *The Family of Mann* was seen at Second Stage in June of 1994; subsequently, *The Family of Mann* won the National Theatre Conference award for playwriting, and was named a finalist for the Susan Smith Blackburn Prize. Other works include *Spike Heels*, which was seen in readings and workshops at the Philadelphia Theatre Company, Ensemble Studio Theatre and New York Stage and Film before being produced off-Broadway at the Second Stage Theatre of New York in Spring of 1992, staring Kevin Bacon, Tony Goldwyn, Saundra Santiago and Julie White. *Sunday on the Rocks* was produced to critical acclaim in Boston, and was presented by the International Women in Theatre Conference there in 1987. *Loose Knit* was seen at New York Stage and Film, the Longwharf Theatre of New Haven, Second Stage in New York and The Source in Washington. Her one-acts have been produced by Alice's Fourth Floor, the Westbank, Manhattan Punchline, Double Image, New Georges, Naked Angels and Actors Theatre of Louisville, among others. She has collaborated with Bill Irwin on a piece produced by Seattle Rep in April of 1994, and she recently completed the book for a musical based on the 19th Century melodrama *The Two Orphans*. In television, Rebeck has written for the HBO series "Dream On," "Brooklyn Bridge," "L.A. Law" and "NYPD Blue." In film, she has written the screenplay for *Spike Heels* for Imagine Films; *Grounds for Dismissal* for Irwin Winkler, and *Kalamazoo*, an independent short starring Adrienne Shelley and Wallace Shawn. Rebeck earned her M.F.A. in Dramatic Writing and her Ph.D. in Victorian Literature at Brandeis University, where she met her husband, the stage manager, Jess Lynn.

Original Production

The Family of Mann was originally produced at Second Stage, directed by Pamela Berlin with the following cast:

Ed/Dave. . . . . David Garrison
Bill. . . . . Richard Cox
Belinda/Sissy . . . . Julie White
Clara . . . . Lisa Gay Hamilton/Chandra Wilson
Ren/Buddy. . . . . Robert Duncan McNeill
Sally/Ginny. . . . . Anne Lange
Steve/Uncle Willy . . . . Reed Birney

Cast

ED: The Executive Producer, mid 40's, large, friendly, a king.
REN: 31, boyish, good looking, likable.
BELINDA: 31, smart, opinionated, extremely emotional.
BILL: Mid 40's, the director; a hatchet man.
SALLY: Early 40's, feminine but determined.
STEVE: Mid 40's, a fierce has-been.
CLARA: Mid 20's, black, deferential but observant.

THE SIT COM
DAVE: Played by Ed
GINNY: Played by Sally
BUDDY: Played by Ren
SISSY: Played by Belinda
UNCLE WILLY: Played by Steve

The actress playing Clara grows wings in the second act. Although no one comments on them, she should wear them in every scene.

THE FAMILY OF MANN

ACT ONE • SCENE ONE
First Readthrough

*The lights come up, bright. Ed sits at the table, everyone else slightly
behind him. Everyone holds script binders in their hands.*

ED: Before we read through today's script, I just wanted to take a
moment to welcome our actors, our production personnel, our
talented staff of writers—all of you—to The Family of Mann. I
think we're all excited to be here today, embarking on a project
which will hopefully say something we can all be proud of, and
maybe give us all a couple of laughs in the bargain, since that's
what we're being paid for.
(*He laughs easily. Everyone else does too.*)
If you've seen any of the other shows we've worked on here,
hopefully you realize that what we're trying to do is quality
television that people can watch without being completely,
egregiously offended morally and intellectually. It's a crazy idea,
but we like to kid ourselves that stories about people living relatively decent, normal lives, the kind of lives I think most of us
had in our childhood, might be of interest to America. Anyway,
it's of interest to me, and I've had some success with this
approach, so we're going to try it again and see if we can prove

to the networks that Americans are not merely interested in amoral, sex-crazed psychopaths, or whatever it is they're putting on the air this week. Now, before we get started, I want to explain a few things about our organization. We really do consider ourselves a family here; mostly what we're interested in is creating a world where people can just enjoy coming in to work. If it's not fun, then I'm not interested in it, and I don't think you should be either. So I hope we can all just relax and enjoy each other and make some comedy here!

(*There is scattered applause.*)

I give you our director, Bill.

(*Everyone holds pencils and opens identical scripts. Bill, the director, starts to read.*)

BILL: Okay, here we are in the Mann family kitchen. It's a Saturday morning, the day is bright and lovely and Ginny, the lovely wife of Dave Mann, is talking to her husband. Scene one.

(*Lights change.*)

ACT ONE • SCENE TWO
BELINDA: The Writers' Room

All the writers sit around the table, scripts open before them. Everyone speaks very quickly.

ED: He's as big as a fucking cow. I mean, the last time I saw him was at the pilot, he looks great, and today, what, he's put on thirty pounds in two months.

SALLY: I put a call into his agent.

ED: Fuck his fucking agent. The man's old enough to know when he looks like a pig. Fucking actors. I can't believe this. He gets paid sixty thousand dollars a week to stay in shape and he shows up looking like Orson Welles.

REN: We have the same lawyer, I had lunch with him last week. First thing he says, so, how much weight has Jim put on? I'm like, what, I don't know what he's talking about; his last show, every hiatus he put on thirty pounds. Apparently he does this all the time.

ED: Oh, Jesus. *(To Sally)* Did you know about this?

SALLY: Of course not—

BELINDA: I don't think he looks bad—

ED: You put a camera on him, he's a mess. Six months ago, the guy is America's perfect father. This is making me sick. Get his agent on the phone.

(Sally picks up the phone.)

SALLY: *(Into phone)* Clara, can you get Andrew Stein for me, please? *(She hangs up.)*

STEVE: *(Overlap)* The script's in good shape.

ED: The script's phenomenal. As long as Jim doesn't sit on it.

(Bill enters as the phone rings. Sally picks it up and speaks while Bill and Ed speak.)

ED: How's it going?

BILL: Fine, except for the fact that Jim is as big as a fucking house.

SALLY: *(Overlap)* Andy? Oh, wonderful. Yes, it went very well; everyone's very excited. The network is very happy. Listen, Andy, we're a little concerned about Jim's weight.

ED: Could you believe it when he walked in? The guy's supposed to be our leading man, his gut is hanging over his—

BILL: And he's eating donuts, he doesn't pass the fucking table without picking up something. I think he's already had four or five.

ED: Jesus.

SALLY: *(Overlap)* So he is aware of it?

BILL: He's stuffing himself.

SALLY: Well, Ed's not sure—here, let me have you talk to Ed—

ED: Fuck him, I don't want to talk to some fucking agent. I want to talk to his trainer. If he's so fucking aware of it, how come he's still fat? The guy's being paid sixty thousand dollars a week to stay thin—

SALLY: *(Into phone, overlap)* Andy, we just wanted to make sure something was being done. Is he seeing a trainer, or—oh, good, good. So you'll tell him that we are concerned? Good. Okay. *(She hangs up.)*

BILL: I've seen this before. This is bad, this is fear of success. You can't start like this; if you don't come out of the gate like a fucking maniac it's all over.

BELINDA: I don't think he looks bad. He's incredibly appealing. My mother has the hugest crush on—

ED: Oh, Jesus, I feel sick. Can we get some lunch menus in here?
(*Sally picks up the phone again.*)

BILL: (*Overlap, to Belinda*) You don't understand; you can't start like this. If you start like this, it's all over. He's sabotaging the whole show.

ED: I didn't want to cast him in the first place. The guy looks like a weasel. Now he looks like a fat weasel. (*He and Bill laugh.*)

SALLY: Clara, can you bring the lunch menus in? Thanks. (*She hangs up.*)

ED: Fuck him. The script's phenomenal; it's going to be a great show. We'll just keep the camera on Monica all week, is she a beautiful girl or what?

REN: She has the most beautiful skin of any girl I have ever seen. She glows. She actually glows.

ED: What a punim. She good?

BILL: Unbelievable.

ED: Terrific.

(*Clara enters with a book of menus.*)

CLARA: You guys ready to order lunch?

ED: Skip the menus, do we need to see menus? Just pick up a bunch of pizzas. Six or seven, I don't care. Jesus, this is making me— and stop off at Victors for chocolate cake. We'll sit here and stuff our faces and make fun of how fat Jim is.

(*He and Bill laugh. Blackout.*)

ACT ONE • SCENE THREE
ED: The Family of Mann I

A suburban kitchen. Dad sits at a table, reading the newspaper while Mom chatters. They perform in a bright, skittish, sitcom style.

GINNY: Maybe I'll write a novel today.
(*Dad gives her a look. The laughtrack chuckles.*)

DAVE: You're going to write a novel, today? What are you going to write tomorrow, an encyclopedia?
(*More laughter.*)

GINNY: I mean it, Dave. I want to do something big today.

DAVE: How about we paint the living room?

(*More laughter. She glares at him.*)

What? We have a very large living room!

(*More laughter.*)

GINNY: Dave, we're finally free! We could do anything! We could travel, or go back to school, or learn how to ski!

DAVE: Go bungy jumping.

GINNY: Anything! Now that the kids have finally moved out, I feel so energized! Dave. We finally got rid of them.

(*More laughter.*)

DAVE: You sound like you hate your own children.

GINNY: No, hate would be too strong a word. Or maybe it wouldn't...

(*More laughter.*)

DAVE: Ginny!

GINNY: Dave, now that they're adults, it's time we faced facts. We have the most annoying children in America.

DAVE: I like them!

GINNY: I like them too, when they're not driving me crazy. Twenty-two years of Mom, it's your day for carpool. Mom, will you press my new blouse? Mom—

BUDDY: (*Off*) Mom, what's for breakfast?

GINNY: (*To Dad*) Yes, I especially hated that one. Mom, what's for breakfast. In that annoying nasal twang Buddy has. You sounded just like him for a second there.

BUDDY: (*Entering*) Moooooom! What's for Breaaaaakfast?

GINNY: (*Laughing*) Oh, stop! How do you do that?

(*Dad stares at her. She gets it, leaping to her feet.*)

GINNY: Buddy! What are you doing here?

BUDDY: I thought I'd come by for breakfast. (*He sits, expectant. Mom is confused.*)

GINNY: You live in Chicago, sweetheart. Why would you come all the way to Minneapolis to have breakfast?

BUDDY: Well, see, there's this little thing called a recession, Mom. Could I have some orange juice?

(*More laughter. She stares at him.*)

SISSY: (*Entering*) Moooooom!

(*Mom turns, desperate.*)

GINNY: Sissy!

(*Sissy throws herself on Mom's shoulder.*)

SISSY: It's so awful—oh, Mom—

GINNY: What is it, sweetheart, what's the matter?

SISSY: My husband is the most hateful man that ever lived.

GINNY: *(Sympathetic)* We've all known that for years, sweetheart. Why are you crying?

(More laughter.)

SISSY: Can I stay here, Mom?

BUDDY: Mom, I lost my job and my apartment, and I'm broke. It's okay if I stay here, isn't it?

GINNY: Oh, my poor sweet babies. I'd rather stick my fingers in a waffle iron than let you move back home.

(More laughter.)

(Beat.)

SISSY AND BUDDY: Daddy?

DAVE: Oh, she's kidding. Of course you can stay! Isn't this great. We're a family again! *(He puts his arms around Buddy and Sissy. After a moment, Ginny makes a running jump and leaps on Sissy, trying to strangle her. All try to pry them apart. Laughter and applause. Blackout.)*

ACT ONE • SCENE FOUR
BILL: It's Not Real Enough

The writer's room. Everyone is sitting around the table. There is food and coke cans everywhere.

ED: This doesn't, it just doesn't start right.

STEVE: Well, we talked about her, you know, her feeling of liberation when—

ED: Yeah, but a novel, it's too literary, everyone in America's going to be going who are these fucking people, writing novels, it's not real—

BELINDA: My mother tried to write a novel once.

ED: *(Not listening)* That's the mistake everybody makes, like all this sniping at each other, that's not real. Once you give into that sort of shit, you're dead.

STEVE: Well, we don't have to start with the novel, I just thought it would give a sense of her, you know—

ED: Yeah, but it's got to be real. This show is—we're bringing the family together in adulthood, now. We're showing Americans moving out of their adolescence into a deeper maturity.

BILL: I think we should start with Sissy and Buddy, that's where the heat is going to be. Either one of them could be a breakout. I say we just start with the heat.

REN: What, do you mean open with them already there?

BILL: Yeah, some sort of funny scene with the two of them plotting to get their old rooms back or something.

REN: Except he's after her room. Just getting back in the house isn't enough, he's—

ED: You mean, she's got the room with the view of Minneapolis?

REN: Something like that. A spectacular view of downtown Minneapolis, and he's after that room.

SALLY: Ren, that is a great idea.

BELINDA: So they get into some totally moronic juvenile fight about it? That could work. I mean, they start out as children and then—

ED: Yeah, but it's still—there's something not right about the tone. These people should not be mean to each other. They tease each other, but without meanness.

BELINDA: Well, if we started with the brother sister thing we would lose the section where Dave picks on Ginny, that's where I thought it was sounding kind of—

ED: No, that part's okay. It was the stuff about her not liking her kids that I thought really went too far.

BILL: The attitudes are reversed. Dave should be the one who doesn't want the kids back; that's where the comedy is. She's gotta be thrilled to see them.

ED: Yeah, this stuff about not liking her kids doesn't work.

BELINDA: *(Cheerful)* Well, I don't know. My mother hated me all the time. Didn't your mother hate you?

ED: No, I don't think—you're very nosey. Is this why your mother hated you?

BELINDA: It was just a periodic thing. You know, when you date drug addicts and come home trashed, parents tend to get upset. And isn't that like what we're going for with these two, that they're both—

ED: No, they're good kids, they aren't—

BELINDA: Well, I was a good kid too. I was just a good kid who got arrested a couple times. *(She laughs.)*

REN: You got arrested?

BELINDA: Oh, for buying cocaine. Big deal. I was a minor. It's not like I have a record or anything.

ED: Well, that's a big relief. You were buying drugs, but you were underage. I feel much better.

BELINDA: So, let's give Sissy a drug phase.

STEVE: Drugs aren't funny.

BELINDA: They're not?

ED: These are good kids. They're not drug addicts.

SALLY: Maybe if the opening is just more about Ginny's realizing the kids are gone—

ED: I need more coffee. Clara! Is there coffee? Clara!
   (*She enters.*)

CLARA: I'm in the next room, Ed. You don't have to roar.

ED: We need coffee.

SALLY: (*Overlap*) She doesn't know what to do with herself...

CLARA: I just made a pot fifteen minutes ago. (*She picks it up and looks at it, pours it into his cup.*)

ED: Oh, this is fresh? I didn't know this was fresh.

SALLY: (*Overlap*) There's a sense of confusion and loss—

ED: Oh yeah, those confusion and loss jokes are always such a scream.
   (*The guys laugh.*)

SALLY: No, I mean, if we tried to play it comedically—

ED: Comedically. Ohhhh. Now everything is clear. (*Off coffee*) This stuff is phenomenal. How do you make this?

CLARA: Well, you put the little white filter in the machine. Then you open the little silver bag and pour the coffee in.

ED: Phenomenal.

CLARA: I can't believe they pay you so much and me so little.

ED: I adore this girl.

BILL: Could I have some of that? (*Bill holds out his cup. As Clara pours, he puts his arm around her.*)

ED: She's phenomenal. isn't she?

BILL: Fantastic.

ED: So what do we have? Comedic confusion and loss.

BILL: I just think we gotta be careful not to lose Dave in all this. What I want to know is where Dave is.

ED: As played by Jim, Dave is standing in the corner with his fist up his ass.

(The guys all laugh.)

REN: Sitcom for the nineties. *(Doing Jackie Gleason)* "Norton! How would you like my fist up your ass?"

(The guys howl.)

BILL: "Alice! Why, I oughta just shove my fist up Norton's ass!"

REN: *(As Alice)* "You do whatever you want, Ralph. Trixie and I are going to go lick each other dry."

STEVE: *(As Norton)* "Hey, Ralph, Ralpheroonie, the girls are going to...lick each other dry! Don't you think we should, uh...watch?"

REN: *(As Alice)* "Why that's a great idea, Norton. You coming, Ralph?"

BILL: "Alice...you're the greatest."

(They are laughing uproariously. Belinda watches, puzzled, and Sally smiles politely. Clara does not respond.)

BILL: Oh, God. Oh, God...

REN: *(As Ralph)* "Norton!"

(They all laugh even harder.)

ED: So what do we have, Dave is standing around with Norton's fist up his ass? Well, at least it's funny.

(They continue to laugh. Lights change.)

ACT ONE • SCENE FIVE

BELINDA: Reality

Ed and Belinda are in his office.

ED: You like it here? I mean, everything's going okay? Need anything?

BELINDA: No, it's great. Everything's great.

ED: It's an amazing job, isn't it? I mean, the first show I got, I thought, they have to be kidding. I couldn't imagine how anybody would be willing to pay me for this. They put me in a room with three other guys and said all right, entertain yourselves all day, eat as much as you like, and while you're at it, if you write a few things down, we'll put them on television for you. Oh, and by the way, we'll pay you a zillion dollars for this. It's like stealing money.

BELINDA: It's pretty amazing. I mean, it seems—I'm still getting used to it, but, you know—I'm writing for a TV show! I'm sorry, I'm sounding like a moron—

ED: No, no—

BELINDA: Anyway, thank you for the opportunity. And, I hope I wasn't crossing lines in there, with the drug stuff—

ED: Not at all.

BELINDA: I just thought that might be an area for comedy, so I was—

ED: You'll figure it out.

BELINDA: I just, you know, I'm real excited about being here, so I want to do a good job, and I get—anyway. And on top of it all, to be making so much money, I—

ED: No, you can't do it for the money. That's the first mistake everybody makes. If you do it for the money, you're lost. If it's there, if it's not there, you have to be the same person.

BELINDA: *(Laughing a little)* Well, some day I hope to be the same person with a lot more money.

ED: You need money?

BELINDA: Oh. No, that's not— I'm fine. I'm doing fine. Thank you.

ED: I mean, the money's good. It's a good thing. To be able to support your family, and take care of the people you love. You don't have that worry right now, but you will. But for now, it's good that you can just learn the craft, and enjoy the opportunity. Television is so powerful; there's no other form of entertainment that reaches so many people. That's what's so great about what we do. We make a difference. We literally affect people's lives.

BELINDA: It's quite a responsibility.

ED: You're a talented girl. You're going to do fine out here. Los Angeles takes a little getting used to, but really, it's a wonderful place. It's possibly the last great cauldron of the American character, do you know what I mean? We're creating a landscape, creating an artform, creating ourselves. It's the essence of America. That's what I like most about Los Angeles. It allows you to create your own reality.

BELINDA: Oh. But—wow. I don't know. If you create it, is it real? I mean, I thought we were creating fantasies.

(She laughs, friendly. He stares at her. Lights change.)

ACT ONE • SCENE SIX
ED: Did You See My Name?

Belinda is at home. She is lit by the blue light of a television set. She is talking on the phone and drinking a beer.

BELINDA: *(On phone, excited)* Did you see it? Did you see my name? *(She laughs)* I know, it was wild, wasn't it? Did Grandma like it? *(Pause)* She thought it was too racy? Well, what do you want, she's near death, everything's racy to her. Mom. I'm kidding, Mom. Hi, Daddy! Yeah, it was great wasn't it? Well, not great, but for my first episode on television—yeah, it was exciting. It looked so real. And it's so weird, because it's what's not real, you know, but there it is on the television screen, and it's like, man, it's like you exist. It's so…Dad? Oh. Hi, Gigi! Yeah, it was great, wasn't it? Uh huh. Uh huh. No, I didn't write that, I didn't write that part. Well, you know, as a group, we rewrite things, and—*(Pause)* No, I—I didn't write that, either. Yeah, Ed wrote that. *(Pause)* Yeah, I wrote some of it—*(Lying)* yeah, I wrote that. That was my line. Good, yeah, I—Uh…who is this? Mrs. Markgraf! Yeah, it is fun being in Hollywood. No, uh, no I—I haven't met Tom Cruise. Could you put my dad back on? Thanks. *(Pause, laughing)* Dad, how many people are there? Well, yeah, but—. Of course I did. I had a, a bunch of friends came over and we watched it together. They're in the other room. Okay, you go back to your party and I'll go back to mine. Yeah. I love you too. Bye. *(She hangs up. Beat.)* Be right there. *(Beat)* I'm sooo pathetic.
(Lights change.)

ACT ONE • SCENE SEVEN
BELINDA: Phenomenal

Ed and Bill are in Ed's office.

ED: You see the reviews?
BILL: Phenomenal. We're gold.
ED: I can't believe it. You see the New York Times? The network guys, they're telling me they've never seen reviews like this. Not since *All in the Family.*
BILL: It just goes to show, people are hungry.
ED: Yeah, but now we gotta hit a home run every week. We gotta keep the heat on until we see what the numbers look like.

BILL: I'm not kidding, this is it, Ed. This is the way I felt the first week of *Family Business.* When it works, it works. We're going seven years.

ED: You think so?

BILL: If Jim goes on a diet.

ED: Fuck him. He can lose the weight or he's out of here. This isn't fucking *Designing Women,* or *Rosanne,* for that matter. Anybody can be replaced. Just make sure he knows that.

BILL: No, he's fine, he's going to the gym, he's going to be—

ED: Is he pulling anything? Come late to rehearsals or anything?

BILL: No, he's scared to death. He's desperate for this show to survive; he's got something like four mortgages to pay off. He's not going to fuck up.

ED: Is that why he's doing all those fried chicken commercials?

BILL: I guess.

ED: Jesus.

BILL: How's the table?

ED: Great. I mean, I'm still not sure this is Steve's kind of show, and Sally's not—you know, we're stuck with her, what are you going to do? They're friends; no one else will give them jobs. But Ren and Belinda are phenomenal. You read their scripts?

BILL: Phenomenal.

ED: First time out for both of them. Unbelievable.

BILL: Where'd you find her?

ED: In a stack. I mean, her spec came in over the fucking transom, I don't even know why I read it. I just pulled it out of a stack one day on a whim, and I thought, fuck, this is good, let's just hire her. She's got a fucking Ph.D., did you know that?

BILL: You're shitting me.

ED: Taught English at some university and got sick of it. I'm going to call fucking Cosby and say, fuck you and your Ph.D. I got a story editor with a Ph.D., take that and shove it up your ass.

BILL: *(Laughing)* That's perfect. You should, you should do it.

ED: Fucking Cosby and his fucking Ph.D. Anyway, I read her script, and I think, you know, she's good, and then that afternoon, I go to this psychic, who tells me, out of the blue, that a woman named Linda is going to come into my life and make a huge impact.

BILL: Linda?

ED: Is that amazing? I mean, it's not exactly the same, but—

BILL: No, but—you didn't—

ED: Nothing. I was there to ask about whether or not I should buy another house, Deb and I are thinking about buying a place in Santa Monica because the beach house is so far, and there are so many people at the house in Brentwood all the time we can't be alone, with the gardener and the housekeeper and Becky and the kids—

BILL: Yeah, yeah—

ED: So I hadn't said anything about hiring writers. I mean, we weren't even sure the show was going at that point.

BILL: That's wild.

ED: Yeah. A woman named "Linda." And what about Ren, he remind you of anybody?

(*Bill looks at him, actively thinking.*)

Me! Doesn't he remind you of me? About twenty years ago?

BILL: Oh—

ED: Yeah, I went back to that psychic today, to talk about the show, and you know what she told me? That I was going to have a son. Out of the blue, she says, I see a son coming into your life. A prince among men. And, you know, Deb's forty-six, she's not—

BILL: Well, you never—

ED: I know, but be realistic. I mean, with these psychics, you can't always be literal. She says a son, but that might mean a lot of things. So when I got back to the lot today, I bumped into Ren, and I thought: This is what she was talking about. A prince. Of course, I didn't know that when I hired him. That just happened today.

BILL: Ren's great. His script is phenomenal.

ED: And what a jump shot. Did you see him yesterday, making that shot from the corner?

BILL: See him? I was trying to stop him. I'm going, all of a sudden he's Michael Jordan—

ED: He played college ball.

BILL: You're shitting me.

ED: You didn't know? He made it to the Final Four. Twice.

BILL: Jesus.

ED: That's why I hired him.

(*They laugh. Lights change.*)

REN: The Numbers

Ren and Steve and Belinda are in the writers' room. Clara enters, carrying yellow sheets of paper.

CLARA: The numbers came in.
(*Steve and Ren jump, take the sheets eagerly.*)
STEVE: All of them?
CLARA: Just the overnights. We won our slot.
REN: All right! (*He gives Clara a high five.*)
STEVE: (*Studying sheet*) Not by much. Jesus. Not by much at all. A tenth of a point.
BELINDA: Now, how do you read these?
REN: (*Pointing*) This number is the percentage of available sets that were tuned into our show, and this one is—percentage of viewers. Of the sets that were tuned on, this is how many watched us.
BELINDA: What?
STEVE: This is not good at all.
CLARA: Bill says we'll bounce in the nationals.
STEVE: You didn't take these down to the set, did you?
CLARA: No, he came by before he went over—
STEVE: Never let an actor see a number. It makes them completely insane.
(*Ed and Sally enter. She is trying to show him polaroids.*)
SALLY: You can't tell from the polaroids, Ed. We have to go over there. It'll take ten minutes—
ED: I told you; I don't care what they wear.
SALLY: You say that, and then on show night all of a sudden nobody looks right—
CLARA: The numbers came in. (*She hands sheets to Sally and Ed.*)
SALLY: Oh, no. We fell four points off our lead.
STEVE: That fucking black show is a piece of shit, and then they blame us because everybody turns it off in the middle.
ED: It doesn't matter. Those assholes at the network will do whatever they want anyway. You have to ignore this shit. Is there coffee?
CLARA: What's the magic word?
ED: Clara, my love, is there coffee?
CLARA: Ed, sweetie, for you, there's always coffee. (*She goes to get it.*)
SALLY: I love your shirt, Ren. That's a terrific color on you.

REN: Thanks.

SALLY: All right, I'm going to wardrobe. I'll be back in ten minutes; don't start without me. *(She goes.)*

BELINDA: *(Still trying to figure it out)* This number is the percentage of what?…

ED: You can't pay any attention to them. Jesus, these numbers are for shit. Steve, look at what Empty Nest did, and that's a fucking hit.

STEVE: Back in the eighties, no one could stay on with the numbers.

ED: The networks are going down. Fuck 'em, they deserve to; they're as bad as the car companies. They put shit on year after year, it serves them right that people finally won't watch it. Shit, I don't want to talk about the numbers. Belinda, how's your script coming?

BELINDA: I'm proofing it over lunch. You'll have it this afternoon.

ED: Great. Did you put in that stuff we talked about? About Dave interfering with Sissy's boyfriends?

BELINDA: Yeah. It's a little creepy, but I think I figured out how to make it work.

ED: Creepy?

BELINDA: Ed, she's twenty-nine years old and her father won't let her date.

ED: So, what's your point? *(He laughs.)*

BELINDA: Right. So, I put that in and moved the dog food run to the top of the D scene; it's much hotter there—

ED: Great—

BELINDA: And I cut four pages out of the second act and reconceived Jimmy.

ED: Jimmy? I liked Jimmy.

BELINDA: He wasn't funny enough.

ED: Is he funny now?

BELINDA: This guy is so funny, he makes Robin Williams look like a big bore.

ED: You think Williams is funny?

BELINDA: Not as funny as you, Ed.

ED: I love this girl.

BELINDA: Yeah, yeah, yeah… *(She goes.)*

ED: *(To Ren)* She's great, isn't she? She's a machine. How's your new script coming?

REN: Great. You'll have it by the end of the week.

ED: She's gaining on you. *(Ed laughs. Ren laughs with him, sort of.)*

STEVE: Ed, I probably should get going on a second script, too. I mean, I haven't really done much since that first script, and I have a couple of ideas.

ED: Oh, well, yeah, sure Steve. Put them together and we'll talk.

STEVE: Well, is now a good time? I could pitch 'em now. It shouldn't take too long.

(*Ed is looking at the sheets again.*)

ED: No, why don't you hold onto them for a few days. Now is not really a great time.

STEVE: Oh. Okay.

ED: Fucking numbers. Ren, you want to go do some editing?

REN: Sure.

ED: Your episode is looking phenomenal. We just have to get another thirty seconds out of it.

REN: Great.

(*They go. Steve sits alone for a long moment. Sally enters. She looks around.*)

SALLY: Where is everybody? I thought we were working.

(*Steve looks at her. Lights change.*)

ACT ONE • SCENE NINE

SALLY: The Best Place to Work in Hollywood

Sally's office. Sally arranges flowers on her desk. There is also a teapot and cups. Belinda looks around.

BELINDA: What a lovely office.

SALLY: Thank you. I like to keep it pretty, so there's at least one place on the lot I can come to for a little—comfort, I suppose. Would you like some tea?

BELINDA: Oh, sure, that'd be great.

(*Sally pours and hands her a cup.*)

SALLY: So, how are you liking it here?

BELINDA: Well, you know, it's great, I just, a lot, it's real different.

SALLY: From the university?

BELINDA: Well, from anything, as far as I can tell. (*Pause*) I didn't know you knew about the whole...university thing.

SALLY: Oh, I'm sorry. Was it a secret?

BELINDA: No, of course not, I just—actually, I did ask Ed not to mention it. He found out about it through my agent, I didn't—

SALLY: Oh, Ed's telling everyone. You should be proud. It's quite an accomplishment.

BELINDA: Thank you. I just didn't want people to think I was an intellectual snob, or anything.

SALLY: Not at all. Well. A drug phase and a Ph.D. You're a very interesting person, aren't you?

BELINDA: It was a very small drug phase, I don't know why I even—

SALLY: You must miss teaching.

BELINDA: Well, yeah, I guess I do. There actually was something really comforting about discussing Victorian novels for twelve hours a day.

SALLY: I'm sure it was a much more intellectual environment.

BELINDA: Oh, no—I mean, yes, of course, but—

SALLY: We read too.

BELINDA: Oh, I know. I didn't—I really don't miss it that much. I was constantly broke and the politics—I didn't actually fit in.

SALLY: Oh, no. You're lovely! I'm sure you fit in everywhere you go.

BELINDA: Well, thank you. But I never actually felt comfortable as an academic. I mean, I loved teaching, but the faculty… I felt like a populist in elitist heaven. I prefer Dickens to Henry James.

SALLY: Really.

BELINDA: Yeah. And I just thought, writing for television, if Dickens were alive today, that's where he'd be, so—

SALLY: Well, you're very lucky to be with us on your first show. This is one of the best places to work in Hollywood. Ed is one of the few truly decent and supportive people in the industry, and he really does want you to consider this a home. You're lucky.

BELINDA: *(Cautious)* Everyone's been great. And I really am thrilled to be here.

SALLY: Well, good.

BELINDA: Of course, it's pretty different than I thought it would be. I guess I thought it was going to be sort of like the *Dick Van Dyke Show,* and, you know, it's really not.

SALLY: It does get a little rough sometimes. You must find that hard, coming from your ivory tower.

BELINDA: Oh, no. I love three hours of fist up the ass jokes. We used to kid about that all the time back at the old ivory tower. In between all the drugs we did.

(*Sally looks at her. Belinda smiles. After a moment, Sally smiles back.*)

SALLY: My first job, on *Happy Days,* the first day I was there, one of the other writers unzipped his pants, put his cock on the table and told me to suck it.

(*Pause*)

BELINDA: You're kidding.

SALLY: I was the only woman in a room of ten. They all thought it was hilarious, of course. I was twenty-four years old.

BELINDA: What did you do?

SALLY: Well, I certainly didn't oblige him. I laughed in a slightly uncomfortable way. (*She demonstrates.*)

After a month or so the joke wore thin and he went on to something else. The whole trick is going along with it, but not really. You know.

BELINDA: I don't think I do.

SALLY: You can't protest, because that would get in the way of the room's energy, but you also can't just pretend that you're one of them. Because, we're not. Are we?

BELINDA: Apparently not.

SALLY: Anyway, you don't have to worry about the really overt stuff here. Ed wouldn't tolerate it.

BELINDA: He wouldn't.

SALLY: Absolutely not. He's actually rather traditional.

BELINDA: Traditional?

SALLY: On the last season of *Family Business,* we had a staff writer, a woman, who told the filthiest jokes in the room. She also tried to play basketball with them in one of their pickup games. She didn't last the season.

BELINDA: (*Pause*) Are you warning me about something?

SALLY: I'm just trying to help. Ed is a complicated person. I hope you understand that.

BELINDA: You're kind of complicated yourself, aren't you?

SALLY: Not really. All I want out of life is to make a lot of money. More money than I can count. So much money that everyone will have to kiss up to me, and I can treat anyone I want like dirt. (*She laughs.*) More tea?

(*She pours. Lights change.*)

Sissy and Buddy are reading a newspaper. Sissy is circling items. Ginny bustles about the kitchen.

SISSY: *(Wistful)* I miss Benny.

BUDDY: Benny? The guy who chained you to the kitchen counter until you learned how to make a pie crust?

SISSY: That wasn't what it looked like.

BUDDY: It looked like about sixty pounds of wrought iron.
(More laughs.)

SISSY: You never liked him.

BUDDY: Well, no I didn't. And now that I find out he's been married to another woman the whole time he was married to you, I like him even less.
(More laughter.)

SISSY: Three other women.

GINNY: *Three* other women?

SISSY: Nobody's perfect!
(More laughter.)

BUDDY: I know nobody's perfect, but Benny isn't even in the ballpark! Why are you defending him?

SISSY: I just think that everyone has a good side, that's all.

BUDDY: Yeah, well, Benny's good side belongs in a federal penitentiary.
(More laughter.)

SISSY: What do you know about it?
(They start to argue. Ginny laughs.)

GINNY: Okay, you two! I don't want to have to separate you! *(Smiling)* Kids...
(More laughter. Uncle Willy and Dave enter.)

DAVE: Hey! Look who I found!

SISSY: Uncle Willy!

UNCLE WILLY: I was in the neighborhood, thought I'd stop by, visit my favorite brother and his gorgeous wife. You look fabulous, Ginny.

GINNY: Thanks, Willy. Have you had lunch?

UNCLE WILLY: Lunch! That would be terrific. Lunch, dinner, whatever. Breakfast. A chance to visit with my favorite niece and nephew for a few hours. A couple of days, weeks, months. Whatever! I'll just settle in a corner somewhere; you can throw me a bone once in a while. Sissy! You look fabulous.

(*Laughter.*)

DAVE: *(Threatening)* Willy...

UNCLE WILLY: *(Begging)* Just for a little while, Dave, till my trail cools off. I mean, till I get back on my feet!

DAVE: Alright. Everybody out! Not you, Willy!

UNCLE WILLY: Oh, that's not necessary, really, that's—

(*But they're gone. Willy turns, desperate, to Dave.*)

UNCLE WILLY: Dave. Dave, don't hit me, Dave. I'm not in a lot of trouble. A little, tiny misunderstanding with a loan shark.

DAVE: I'm sick, Willy. I just found out. I may be dying.

UNCLE WILLY: *(Pause)* What?

DAVE: I don't know how to tell Ginny, or the kids. I know we haven't always gotten along, but—you're my brother. Can you help me? (*They hug. Blackout.*)

ACT ONE • SCENE ELEVEN
REN: Real Money

The writer's room. Exhausted, Ren and Belinda are going through a mass of orange pages, copy editing with a pencil. Periodically, they pass pages back and forth. They keep reading as they talk.

BELINDA: What time is it?

REN: It's a little after two.

BELINDA: Oh, fuck. Jesus, fuck me. Where's the rest of this scene? (*She paws dully through the pages.*)

REN: What is it?

BELINDA: G. G. G, G, G. I only have half of it.

REN: That's the whole scene.

BELINDA: It's not the whole scene. What happened to the part where he tells them he's not dying?

REN: That's there.

BELINDA: No, it's not. (*She hands the pages to him. Ren reads.*)

REN: Oh, shit. Did we cut that? (*He starts pawing through the pages.*)

BELINDA: How could we cut it? The whole episode is about whether he's dying or not.

REN: Where is the old draft?

(*They both are pawing through white pages by now.*)

BELINDA: Fuck. Fuck me. We're going to be here all night. It's a good thing they pay us a fortune.

REN: My deal is fucked. I have a terrible deal. Ed is—I mean, he's a great guy, he's been great to me, but he's—you know, he's made a lot of promises that he doesn't keep. I was supposed to be a producer on this show.

BELINDA: Oh, yeah? And instead you're just a shitty little story editor like me.

REN: No, I mean, it's great being here, I'm just saying. I'm never going to make any real money here.

BELINDA: We're making four thousand dollars a week. That's not real money? What's real money?

REN: Four thousand dollars a week is not real money?

BELINDA: How did you end up here, anyway?

REN: My sister in law was a regular on *Family Business* the last season. She played the nun who tried to teach the twins to tap dance.

BELINDA: Oh, right. I missed that.

REN: So Ed and I got to know each other. We started playing basketball together.

BELINDA: Then you never did this before.

REN: Well, you know, I had a couple guest spots on *Who's the Boss?* and *Full House.* Here it is. Is this it? (*He reads off of some pages.*) Dave says "I just sat there and heard the doctor say, you don't have cancer. It's nothing. And then I thought, if it's nothing, how come you're charging me an arm and a leg?"

BELINDA: Oh, God, did we leave that terrible joke in there?

REN: Hey. I wrote that terrible joke.

BELINDA: Oh. I'm sorry—

REN: It's okay. It is a terrible job. But it's two-fifteen, and it's all we got. Where's the first half of the scene?

BELINDA: No, come on, we gotta fix it. I mean, there's got to be a way to fix this. (*She takes the page and stares at it.*)

REN: Belinda—

BELINDA: How about if we just take it out?

REN: Belinda.

BELINDA: (*Preoccupied, looking at the page*) That'll work. Actually, this is a moment that should not have a joke at all, rhythmically it doesn't—He's facing his mortality, I don't want to hear one liners... *(She starts to block out a cut on the page)*

REN: We can't just change the script on our own! Ed is going to throw a fit—

BELINDA: Ed is gonna love this. Look, it clears out a moment for the two of them, and, you know, if we don't build an emotional context—

REN: An emotional *what?*

BELINDA: Look, just because it's a sit com doesn't mean it has to be shit. This will make it better, so what's your problem?

REN: Well, excuse me. I mean, it's just my script. What would *I* know about it?

BELINDA: Ren, you said yourself it's a bad joke! Why are you fighting for it?

REN: Why are you fighting against it? It's two in the fucking morning! *(Clara staggers in.)*

CLARA: Are you guys okay?

BELINDA: Yeah.

CLARA: Are you almost done?

REN: Yes.

BELINDA: No.

CLARA: You know, we're not writing *the Brothers Karamatsov* in here.

BELINDA: We're just working on a few...

CLARA: Great. I'm gonna be here till three. *(She goes. Ren stares at the pages, grim and exhausted.)*

BELINDA: I'm sorry. I just, I taught writing for so long, you know, freshman comp, I spent so many years telling undergrads how important good writing is, and so many people watch television — I just keep having this vision in my head of all these people gathered around it like a campfire and we're the storytellers— *(Pause)* Nevermind. We'll just leave it.

REN: No, take it out. You're right. It's better without it. It is.

BELINDA: I'm sorry, I didn't—

REN: It's fine. *(He takes the pages from her and crosses the section out. She watches him.)* Okay, Clara, we're done— *(Clara enters, yawning.)*

CLARA: Who won?

REN: Belinda.

BELINDA: It wasn't—

REN: Yes it was.

CLARA: Just don't start up again. Man, I'm tired.

> (*She takes the pages as Ren and Belinda collect their things. Completely energetic, Ed enters.*)

ED: Hey! It's my two favorite writers! Clara, my love, is there coffee?

CLARA: It's two in the morning, Ed!

ED: So where is everybody? Are these the proofs? (*He takes the proofs from Clara and starts to page through them.*)

CLARA: Oh, my god. Maybe if I drove a stake through his heart…

ED: I love this girl.

CLARA: I'll go make coffee…

BELINDA: Ed—we didn't know you were still here.

ED: I've been over in editing. So, what, are you quitting? Deadbeats. Nobody's got any stamina anymore. My first season in television, I worked with three guys who never went home. I mean, literally. We'd work until four every night, then they'd go back and sleep in their offices. I didn't have an office, so I had to drive to Santa Monica, and back three hours later. My marriage was the only one that survived the season… (*Reading*) Whoa, you lost the arm and a leg joke?

BELINDA: Oh—

REN: I just thought, you know, he's facing his mortality, we don't need to hear one liners. And it gives the scene a little more room so that there's an emotional context. For the characters.

ED: An emotional context? He's sounding like a real writer, isn't he? It's a great script, Ren… (*He chuckles, looking at the pages before him.*) So, you guys didn't do anything to the A scene?

BELINDA: Oh—

ED: The lawnmower run doesn't work, does it? I mean, it's a good area, it's just not real enough…

REN: Yeah. I had some ideas but…

ED: Well, you want to do this now? I mean, we're still working, right?

REN: (*Enthusiastic*) Yeah! Great…

BELINDA: Great!

ED: Great.

> (*Lights change.*)

Clara and Belinda sit at a table with several empty glasses on it. They have been drinking Scotch, and are quite drunk. Periodically, they look over their shoulders. They are clearly afraid that someone might overhear them.

CLARA: ...So I go over to Bill's house, right, he's the fucking director what am I supposed to say? Besides, why the hell not, he makes the whole thing sound like an afternoon around the pool with his wife and kids, fun, I could stand to go swimming, this city is so hot and disgusting. So I get there and it turns out that Marguerite and the kids have gone to Jackson Hole for the week. Okay. I'm cool, I'm acting like no big deal, it's still a swimming pool, I'll stay for an hour or something and at least get wet. So he's sitting here and I'm swimming, and I get out of the pool and he's acting like my dad or something, smiling like—it's just creepy. And he keeps talking about what a great group we have on the show, it's such a family, do I want something to drink? Do I want to try out the Jacuzzi? And I'm like, no, Bill, I just want to get some sun. So he gets kind of jolly and paternal, and he says, come over here. Let me give you a hug. I'm like, excuse me? I'm in my bathing suit, I'm all wet, he's in his bathing suit, and he wants to give me a hug? And he's just sitting there smiling and holding his arms out like Buddha or something—

BELINDA: Oh, gross—

CLARA: And he just keeps sitting there, you know? He doesn't move. So to give him a hug, you have to sit on his lap.

BELINDA: No. Come on.

CLARA: It was completely creepy.

BELINDA: So, did you do it? Did you sit on his lap?

(Clara looks at her, then away.)

Oh, fuck. This town is amazing. It's like they've institutionalized sexual harassment.

CLARA: Welcome to Hollywood.

BELINDA: But they're so blunt about it out here. I mean, at least in academia the harassment was—subtle.

CLARA: And it doesn't get you anywhere, either. I mean, the whole point of putting up with harassment is that you get something out of it, right? Explain that to Bill. He had my spec for three weeks. That's why I went over there. Guess what? He still hasn't read it. Next time he asks me to sit on his lap, I'm going to tell him to fuck off and die.

BELINDA: You should've told him the first time.

CLARA: Look, don't give me that shit, I'm just doing the best I—

BELINDA: No, I'm sorry, I didn't—fuck, I know, it's—

CLARA: I shouldn't care, you know? I shouldn't even be out here. This town is bad. The first week I'm here, I'm walking around these gorgeous neighborhoods, Santa Monica, Beverly Hills, thinking, where the fuck are the black people? I drove through Compton just for the fuck of it, and that scared me so bad I went back to Beverly Hills. I called my dad in Dallas, he pulled some strings and got me a job on the lot, so then I'm walking around this major fucking studio, thinking, oh man, I work in the big house now. Fucking Bill says sit on my lap, I almost said, Yassir, Massa. You walk around the lot, maybe catch a glimpse of Whoopi or Denzel off in the distance, they're like fucking gods, you know, we aren't even on the same planet. And everybody keeps telling me how lucky I am. All my friends. I get paid three hundred bucks a week to run errands for white people, and I'm a lucky girl because I got a job on the fucking lot. I saw an angel on a street corner, and I didn't even think twice. Wings and shit. The whole nine yards. I didn't even blink. She said, get out now, girl, the day of judgment is at hand, get the fuck out of LA, and I said, what, are you kidding? I got a job on the lot!

(*Pause*)

BELINDA: You saw an angel?

CLARA: Oh fuck, they're everywhere now, you see them all over, what's the big deal? They're in catalogues, for God's sake. Notecards and shit. There was some Broadway play about angels, they're making a mini-series of it over on the other side of the lot. The place is crawling with angels. Six hundred extras with wings; the whole soundstage looks like this huge, stressed out birdbath. I don't know. The whole thing, it'll kill you if you think about it too hard. Oh, who cares, right? Some of them are real. They have to be. Don't they?

BELINDA: I guess. Yeah, sure. (*Clara drinks, depressed. Belinda looks at her.*) You wrote a spec?

CLARA: Every PA on the lot has written a spec.

BELINDA: Well, I'll read it for you.

CLARA: Oh, that'll do me a lot of good. No offense.

BELINDA: Hey, I know a lot about writing and contrary to what those guys may think, writing is not a competitive sport. You should let me look at it.

CLARA: Okay. Thanks. *(Pause)* You're not going to last out here, you know.

BELINDA: What?

CLARA: I mean, what the fuck are you doing, having drinks with one of the PA's? What is the matter with you? Don't you have a brain in your head?

BELINDA: What?

CLARA: You're not going to last.

(They stare at each other. Lights change.)

ACT ONE · SCENE THIRTEEN
STEVE: What is Comedy?

The writer's room. Everyone is screaming at each other. Once again, Ed is not there.

BELINDA: The scene dies; the whole thing just grinds to a halt—

STEVE: It's just the joke, if we come up with a better—

BELINDA: It's not the joke, it's the scene. We've been waiting for fifteen minutes to find out if she got the job, oh, suspense is building, did she get it, did she—

REN: Maybe there's something in the perfume area, there's got to be a joke in—

BILL: Perfume, that's funny.

SALLY: Perfume that smells like cheese, maybe?

REN: That's funny.

SALLY: 'Cause it's the cheese state, right—

BELINDA: Wisconsin is the cheese state.

STEVE: They're right next to each other. We can fudge it.

REN: Perfume that smells like fudge.

SALLY: For chocolate lovers. *(They laugh.)* Oh, this is a terrific area, Ren. You are so funny.

BELINDA: Look, all I'm saying is, we're waiting for this information, so if it comes out at the beginning of the scene, there's nothing driving the rest of it.

STEVE: Wait, wait, wait. Everyone who smells the stuff hates it, right? Perfume that smells like chocolate. Who would buy this shit? Then a huge fat man comes up to the counter—

REN: Oh, that's perfect—

(*Everyone except Belinda is laughing.*)

STEVE: He's like, in a trance—

BILL: And Sissy's put the perfume on, right? She's been trying it on, while she talks about dating again—

STEVE: And the fat guy waddles over—

BELINDA: Oh, come on, you guys, not fat jokes; aren't we above anything?

STEVE: Not if it's funny.

BELINDA: Yeah, but come on, this isn't that funny, and besides, Ed keeps talking about the show being real, and there's nothing real about a fat man and chocolate perfume. Come on, you guys. We could make this really good. I mean, they're going to put it on television, television is where people now, in our culture, go to hear stories about our lives, and stories are what keeps us human. There are so many stories to tell, some days I feel like I'm just choking on stories, and if we're not...I don't know— diligent—if it's just shit, then, what (*She notices that they are all staring at her.*) I'm sorry. I just think that, you know, twenty-five million people are going to watch this, and it really does bother me that we're always turning Sissy into such a moron. We don't have to. The problem here is just a little more structural, and if we figured out a way to—

STEVE: Oh yeah, structure always makes me laugh. Those hilarious structures they teach you in graduate school always lay me flat.

(*They all laugh.*)

BELINDA: That was mean.

STEVE: What?

BELINDA: That was a mean thing to say. The joke is mean, and you're being mean. Now. Here. You're being mean to me.

SALLY: Oh, dear. Did you get up on the wrong side of the bed, Belinda?

BELINDA: No. I did not get up on the wrong side of the bed. I can't remember what side of the bed I got up on; it was so long ago. Look, I'm sorry, I just—this isn't funny. It's just mean.

BILL: Oh, brother.

STEVE: Well, comedy is mean. If you can't take it, then—

BELINDA: No, I can take it. I guess I just never understood it. Comedy is mean. Wow. See, I always thought comedy was wit, and surprise, and insight. But I guess if you can't come up with that stuff, mean will do just as well. Oh. Was that a mean thing to say? Gosh, you should write it down; maybe we could use it in the scene.

(*Ren snickers. Sally looks at him; he lets the smile drop and doodles. Sally picks up the pencil.*)

SALLY: All right, where were we? Perfume counter...

BELINDA: Fine. Go ahead and write that damn joke. It will never make it in. Ed is going to hate it.

STEVE: Look—

BILL: No, she's right. Ed is going to hate it.

SALLY: I think it's funny.

BELINDA: Well, let's just ask him. Let's call over to editing and ask him. That way we don't waste any more time; it's after midnight already—

SALLY: I think it's funny.

REN: Yeah, me too.

BILL: Oh, yeah, it's hilarious. But I think she's right. It's really not Ed's kind of joke.

(*Pause. There is a moment of tense silence.*)

REN: So, what else can we use there, there's got to be something else we can put in there.

(*Pause. They think.*)

ED: Hey, how's it going, you hacks? Anybody crack this thing yet?

REN: Ed!

SALLY: Ed, hi—

BILL: You finish the cut?

ED: (*Shaking his head*) It's not coming together. Jim's a fucking mess. Maybe if you took a look at it. (*Off script*) Whoa. You're still in the D scene?

SALLY: Well. We've been kicking around a few—We were talking about maybe finding a joke in the perfume area.

ED: Perfume jokes? Yikes.

SALLY: No. We had some really funny ideas.

BELINDA: I just think the problem is—

ED: I don't want to know what the problem is, I want to know what the solution is! Jesus! Fucking perfume jokes! Do I have to do everything myself?

(*Lights change.*)

ACT ONE • SCENE FOURTEEN
CLARA: Is There Coffee?

> *Morning. The writers' room. Clara is cleaning up. Belinda enters, frazzled. She carries a rough draft manuscript.*

CLARA: Hey. How's it going?

BELINDA: I don't know. Ed called me on Friday and said he needed my episode first thing Monday, so I spent the whole weekend writing. How was the weather?

CLARA: Gorgeous.

BELINDA: What a surprise. Can you type this?

CLARA: Sure. I can't wait to meet Benny.

BELINDA: (*Not quite hearing her*) What?

CLARA: Benny. Sissy's ex-husband.

BELINDA: What about him?

CLARA: Your episode's about Benny, isn't it? (*Belinda stares at her.*) Ed had a meeting with the network last week. They were about to cancel us, so he told them all the great scripts coming up, and he said you were writing this hilarious episode about Benny. He's been telling everybody.

BELINDA: What?

CLARA: That's why he needed the script this morning. They're casting Benny this afternoon.

(*Bill enters.*)

BILL: Hey, how's it going? How's our little machine? I can't wait to meet Benny. Clara, is there coffee?

CLARA: Do you have eyes? Look at the coffee pot. Look at it.

BILL: I love this girl.

BELINDA: Bill, I didn't know anything about Benny.

BILL: Benny, Sissy's ex-husband. It's such a hilarious idea, bringing him on. I can't wait to see what you did with him.

BELINDA: I didn't do anything with him.

BILL: Ed said he called you on Friday—

BELINDA: He did call me on Friday, but he didn't tell me anything about Benny! I thought Benny was an off-stage character, we've been talking for months about how we were never going to see Benny—

BILL: The network wanted Benny. We're casting Benny this afternoon.

BELINDA: There's no Benny.

BILL: You didn't write anything for Benny? Oh, Jesus. What the fuck are we supposed to use for sides?

(*Steve enters.*)

STEVE: Hey, how's it going? So, today's the big day we meet Benny. Clara, is there coffee?

CLARA: Why are people always asking me that?

BILL: *(To Steve)* She forgot Benny.

STEVE: She what?

BELINDA: *(Overlap)* I didn't forget Benny, no one told me!

STEVE: Aren't we casting Benny this afternoon?

BILL: Except we have no sides.

CLARA: You want me to type this, the way it is?

BILL: No.

BELINDA: It's all I've got—

STEVE: You forgot Benny? Whoa.

BELINDA: I didn't forget him.

BILL: Ed's gonna have a fit.

(*Ed enters.*)

ED: Hey, how's it going? Can't wait to meet Benny. Clara, is there coffee?

CLARA: I can't believe how difficult this coffee thing is for everybody. No one can tell if it's here. No one can pour their own cup...

ED: I love this girl.

BELINDA: Ed, you didn't tell me about Benny. *(Ed turns and looks at her. She forges ahead.)* I just spent the whole weekend working on my script, because you said you needed it today, but you didn't say anything about Benny. And I can't do it, if you want me to invent this guy Benny, that's fine, I can do that, I can write a whole episode about Benny, I can do anything with Benny that you want, but you have to tell me. You told everybody else. Why didn't you tell me?

(*Ed stares at her.*)

ED: Look, you've got an hour. It's no big deal. Just introduce Benny. Write a little scene for him. Maybe something on a stoop in the rain on a college campus. It can be a flashback, we'll give everybody funny hair. I wrote a scene like that for my movie and it never got in. It was hilarious.

STEVE: I remember that scene. It was.

ED: So, you guys up for some hoops this afternoon?

BILL: Isn't it supposed to get pretty hot today?

STEVE: I heard it was gonna be in the nineties.

ED: Wimps.

(*They go. Clara watches Belinda, who sits at the table.*)

CLARA: You want me to type that?

BELINDA: This episode's not about Benny. Benny belongs in it about as much as the fucking tooth fairy. I'm going to have to rewrite it from scratch, I just spent the weekend working on an episode that's completely USELESS, I was up till four last night, I haven't had a day off in MONTHS and he's acting like I'm the one who's nuts. What the FUCK is the matter with these people?

CLARA: Belinda…Don't let them get in.

BELINDA: What?

CLARA: You want some coffee? Let me get you some coffee. Here. Have some coffee.

(*She pours Belinda coffee. Lights change.*)

ACT ONE • SCENE FIFTEEN
BELINDA: After Two

Belinda sits in the writers' room. She smokes. After a moment, Ren enters.

REN: Belinda?

BELINDA: Oh, Jesus. You scared me.

REN: What are you doing here? Everything's done, isn't it?

BELINDA: Yeah, I was just having a cigarette. I probably shouldn't be smoking in here. You know Sally's just going to throw a fit. Don't tell her I said that.

REN: Are you okay?

BELINDA: Yeah, sure. *(She smokes. He watches her.)*

REN: You going over to the garage?

BELINDA: No, you go ahead. I'll be out of here in a minute.

REN: I don't mind waiting.

BELINDA: Look, I'm fine, all right?

REN: It's after two.

BELINDA: Yeah, so maybe we'll get lucky; maybe some nice little psychopath will find me alone and come after me with a hatchet. It'd be a real break for you, Ren; once I'm out of here they're going to make you a producer like that. *(She snaps her fingers. He looks at her.)* Sorry. *(Clearly, she's not. After a moment, Ren crosses, takes a cigarette and lights it. He sits. She watches him.)*

REN: So, what's up with you?

BELINDA: Nothing's up. I'm just a little depressed.

REN: How come?

BELINDA: Gee, I don't know. I just moved three thousand miles to the ugliest city in America, I work eighty hours a week, I don't get any sleep, my writing is for shit and everybody hates me. I don't know why I'm depressed. If you can't be happy here, you can't be happy anywhere. Right?

REN: What are you talking about? Nobody hates you. They all love you here.

BELINDA: Secretly, they hate me. Maybe I'm not depressed. Maybe I'm paranoid.

REN: Maybe you are.

BELINDA: *(Snapping)* Yeah, what would you know about it, Golden Boy?

REN: Belinda—

BELINDA: I'm sorry. I'm a little tense. I started therapy this week; I think it's making me—

REN: Really? You're in therapy?

BELINDA: Yeah, so what, you've never been in therapy? Everyone does therapy—

REN: Feeling a little defensive about it?

BELINDA: *(Beat)* Maybe. Defensive, depressed and paranoid. Good thing I'm in therapy.

(*Pause*)

REN: What made you go?

BELINDA: (*Matter of fact, almost good humored*) I couldn't get off the floor. Saturday morning. I got up and took a shower, and then I went back to my bedroom, and I was looking for this shirt, in a pile of clothes on the floor, and I just...put my head down and started crying, and I couldn't get up. I couldn't get off the floor, for like...three hours. (*Pause*) Pretty weird, huh?

REN: Jesus, Belinda. Why didn't you call me?

BELINDA: What?

REN: You should've called me. I could've come over and made you lunch or something. We could've gone to a movie. Something.

BELINDA: It's okay. I improvised and went into therapy instead.

REN: What is it, are you lonely?

BELINDA: (*Pause*) Look, I'm fine—

REN: Do you want to go have a drink?

BELINDA: Oh, no, come on—

REN: What, you're just sitting here anyway—

BELINDA: I don't need you feeling sorry for me.

REN: Yes, you do. You need someone to feel sorry for you and then be really, really nice to you for a whole hour or something. Come on, we'll go to an all-night supermarket, buy a bottle of champagne and drink it in the parking lot. (*He takes her by the hand and pulls her up. She leans her head against his shoulder for a second.*)

REN: Come on, you're okay.

BELINDA: I know! It's just—nothing. Thanks.

(*They look at each other. After a moment, he leans in slowly and kisses her. After a moment of uncertainty, she kisses him back. She pushes him away. They look at each other. After a moment, they kiss again. The kiss quickly becomes passionate and they wind up on the table.*)

(*Blackout.*)

END OF ACT ONE

ACT TWO · SCENE ONE
CLARA: The Angel in Los Angeles

Clara wears wings and sunglasses and speaks to the audience.

CLARA: This is the way the universe works: Everything moves from imagination to reality. Such is the force of creation. As soon as anyone imagines anything, it is only instants away from becoming real. Magic is the power that makes this happen. Science also has power, but in a smaller way. You think of objects—a telephone, a refrigerator, an airplane, and then, they exist. From the imagination, to the real.

In America, somehow this process has been reversed. Americans look at something that is only imaginary, and then transform the real into that imagined thing. Little girls look at billboards of impossible women and say, that is what I want to be. People watch moving images of beings who could never exist, and say, that is what we are. The real yearns to be imaginary. And so, America is evaporating. This problem is particularly acute in Los Angeles, a city which is, frankly, about to lift off. Maybe that is why they call it the City of Angels. Although that too is something of a misnomer. Really, we don't like it here.
(*Lights change.*)

ACT TWO · SCENE TWO
REN: The Rookie Phenom

Ren and Belinda are in bed. He is reading a script. She is going through catalogues.

BELINDA: You hear the one about the megalomaniac baseball team?
REN: No.
BELINDA: Norman Lear has first base, Jim Brooks has second, Cosby third, and Ed has the whole outfield.
(*Ren smiles, scribbling.*)
REN: Come on, he's not that bad.

BELINDA: You know what he told me about that stupid movie he made, I saw that thing, it's the worst movie ever, right? Am I right?

REN: It's not *Citizen Kane. (She gives him a look.)* Okay. It's the worst movie ever.

BELINDA: Exactly. He told me, it was his autobiography. The thing is an adaptation of somebody else's book, this other guy wrote the book, and Ed is running around telling everybody it's his autobiography.

REN: He was being metaphoric.

BELINDA: Ed is incapable of being metaphoric. I mean, with all due respect, the guy's a fruitcake, and you're just defending him because he's decided you're his "son". The fact that you grew up in somebody else's house notwithstanding.

REN: Hey. If Ed's decided I'm his son, who am I to say I'm not?

BELINDA: Oh, it's all bullshit anyway. And if I hear one more word about how decent it all is, I may truly puke.

REN: What is the matter with you all of a sudden? What happened to television being like a campfire and you're the great storyteller?

BELINDA: Oh, come on—

REN: No, you come on. You watch a rerun of *The Odd Couple* some night. That show was a thing of beauty. Tony Randall's commitment and, and timing and pathos—

BELINDA: Pathos?

REN: Yeah, pathos, you don't see that—I mean, I've read Moliere—

BELINDA: Moliere? How did Moliere—

REN: Yeah, big surprise, the dumb jock reads Moliere.

BELINDA: I didn't say—

REN: And frankly, I don't see the difference.

BELINDA: The difference? Between Tony Randall and Moliere?

REN: Yeah, that's right. What's so fucking different, Miss Ph.D. in English? You tell me what's so different.

BELINDA: *(Overlap)* Could we not bring my Ph.D. into this, I'm not—

REN: Just answer the question.

BELINDA: You want me to tell you the difference between Tony Randall and Moliere.

REN: That's right. Why is fucking Moliere so much better than Tony Randall?

BELINDA: I don't know, he just is.

REN: He just is, that's a real compelling argument—

BELINDA: All right. The sophistication of his language, his profound understanding and compassion for human nature even while he's satirizing social—

REN: He's telling the same stories we are. Who gets the girl. Fathers and sons competing with each other—

BELINDA: Oh, come on, Ren, theatre and television are completely different experiences. The theatre is much more—vivid, it's more humane—

REN: Yeah, I have seen some class A shit in the theatre.

BELINDA: Of course, but—

REN: In fact, most of what passes for theatre is Class A shit. The only people who write for the theatre these days are people who can't get work in television.

BELINDA: Oh, is that so?

REN: And I've read your fucking New Yorker, too. Boy, that's good writing.

BELINDA: Ren!

REN: What?

BELINDA: What's the matter?

REN: Nothing. *(Pause)* I just, I think there's been some great television, and I'd like to write some. Someday. I mean, we're telling stories, right? You're the one who made me feel like this. When you talk about it, sometimes, you make it sound like something holy.

BELINDA: Well, I'm full of shit.

REN: No, you're not.

BELINDA: Yes, I am! Christ, we spend all this time, as a group, going over and over these damn scripts—who ever decided that writing was a group activity, that's what I want to know. And you know what else I want to know? Why, if we're going to do ten drafts of a script, it doesn't get better! Why not just shoot the first bad draft? Why shoot the tenth? Why do Steve and Sally get to fuck up my work? Why does Ed? I mean, all of this—it isn't about storytelling. It's not even about product. It's just about power.

REN: Then why are you doing it?

BELINDA: *(Pause)* For the money. *(Pause)* I mean, I've never had money. I know, you think it's chicken feed, but this is more money than I've ever dreamed of, this is—. That's the thing about selling your soul. No one tells you how much they'll actually pay you for it.

REN: You're not selling your soul. I can't believe you. I'd kill to be able to write like you, and all you do is run it down. Nevermind. *(He goes back to the script. She watches him, uncertain, a little embarrassed.)*

BELINDA: I'm sorry.

REN: You don't have to be sorry. I'm sorry. I'm sorry you don't enjoy this more.

BELINDA: *(Making up)* I'm starting to enjoy it. I'm starting to enjoy it a lot.

REN: Well, you should. Ed is crazy about you. And you love him. Whether you want to admit it or not.

BELINDA: I never said I didn't like Ed. I think he's a nut, and I'm also desperate for his approval. It's an ongoing topic of discussion between me and my therapist.

REN: Well, stop worrying about it. You know, he's bumping up your next episode. He called me yesterday, raving about it.

BELINDA: *(Pause. Positively glowing)* He did? He liked my script?

REN: He loved it. He loves you. He loves the way you fight—

BELINDA: Forget Ed. What do you like?

REN: I don't like anything at all.
(They kiss.)

REN: Okay. That's all you get.

BELINDA: Come on…

REN: I'm working!
(Giggling, she falls back, watches him for a moment, then looks through her catalogues.)

BELINDA: *(Musing)* Hey, Ren? What did you do when you first started making money? I mean, was there a moment when all of a sudden, you had money? You didn't have any, and then you just, had a lot?

REN: Yeah, sure.

BELINDA: What did you do?

REN: I don't know, I…I bought, uh, a box of chocolates. You know, like, a five pound box of See's chocolates, and I…Fed Exed it to my grandmother.

BELINDA: You sent your grandma chocolates? That is so—

REN: Yeah, okay—

BELINDA: It's adorable!

REN: So what did you do?

BELINDA: I bought sheets. I realized I've been sleeping on the same sheets since college; they're so expensive, I could never justify buying new ones. So I bought these pretty sheets, with colors, and...I'm sorry, I'm embarrassed now. After that spectacular grandma story, I sound so—

REN: No, you don't.

BELINDA: It's just so weird, actually having it. I don't quite know how to spend it.

REN: Tell you what. This weekend, we'll go to San Francisco, rent a suite at the Ritz, and never leave. Order up room service for two days.

BELINDA: Oh, yeah? What will we be doing for two days?

REN: We will be watching basketball on TV.

(*She laughs.*)

BELINDA: You are so mean.

REN: Basketball is a beautiful thing.

BELINDA: So how come you quit? I mean, you were a big college star, right? Why didn't you keep going?

REN: Because I was awful. I was the worst basketball player, ever.

BELINDA: But you were in all those big games, weren't you?

REN: Yeah, "big games." That's the NC double A to you, babe. I didn't really play in those games. The coach basically kept me on the team because he liked me.

BELINDA: I don't believe you. Ed says you're great.

REN: Compared to Ed, I am. He is old and weak, and I am young and hard.

BELINDA: (*Laughing*) Ed's no good?

REN: Terrible.

BELINDA: How's Bill?

REN: Sucks.

BELINDA: Wait a minute. If you guys all stink, maybe I could play with you.

REN: No.

BELINDA: (*Baiting him*) Why not?

REN: (*Beat*) You're not tall enough.

(*He kisses her as she laughs. Blackout.*)

The Mann family kitchen. Dave and Willy are arguing.

UNCLE WILLY: The situation is not grim, Dave. Not grim at all.

DAVE: The car is a lemon. I took you into my home, put a roof over your head, and you sold my daughter a lemon. Your own niece!

UNCLE WILLY: Now Dave, you're not looking at this right.

DAVE: I'm looking at a lemon!

UNCLE WILLY: You know, cars are like people, Dave. Each one has a different personality and no one is perfect.

DAVE: Don't start this, Willy. I don't want to have to hurt you.

UNCLE WILLY: But we all try to make ourselves better. Don't we? I know I do. I know I'm always searching for my best self. Well, cars search too.

DAVE: Willy, she's had this car for less than twenty-four hours and the fuel line is leaking, smoke is coming from somewhere…every-where…

UNCLE WILLY: Is there ever a good time for trouble, Dave? For some of us, it comes early, and for some it comes late. But trouble is an important part of life's journey! You would never call a person a lemon, Dave.

DAVE: Oh, I might.

UNCLE WILLY: No, not you. Not my big brother Dave. I loathe you, you big lug.

(*Sissy enters, followed by Buddy, who has soot on his face.*)

UNCLE WILLY: Sissy! Aren't you looking like a fresh spring morning.

SISSY: Thank you, Uncle Willy. Uncle Willy, is there something wrong with my new car? It's spouting dust everywhere. Buddy was trying to help—

BUDDY: Anything for you, Sis—

SISSY: But it just keeps blowing up!

UNCLE WILLY: Oh, no, that's perfectly natural for—

DAVE: Sweetheart?

SISSY: Yes, Daddy.

DAVE: You know I love you.

SISSY: Oh, thank you, Daddy.

DAVE: Could you go back outside for a minute? I'm going to have to hurt Uncle Willy, and I don't want you to have to see it.

SISSY: Oh.

UNCLE WILLY: Sissy—you know, Sissy, what would go beautifully with your hair today? A 1982 Volvo with new whitewalls and a moonroof.

SISSY: *(Sweet)* Oh, Uncle Willy. You always say the sweetest things. *(Abrupt)* I'm sorry, do I have—do I have to say this? This is so stupid.

UNCLE WILLY: I don't even have that. What is that?

SISSY: I can't make this work. It's not even funny.

(*Willy looks at her script. Bill enters, flustered.*)

BILL: What's the problem? Jesus. What's the problem now? Monica, you're supposed to cross—

BUDDY: What? They cut my—I had a whole speech there.

SISSY: It's bullshit, Bill. Come on, you know it is.

DAVE: *(Overlap)* I don't have these pages, either. What color is that, salmon? I don't have salmon pages.

BUDDY: Salmon? I didn't get salmon pages.

UNCLE WILLY: I haven't seen any salmon pages.

BILL: Oh, Jesus. Could someone call up to the writers and—*(Yelling out)* Who the fuck fucked up this time?

SISSY: I mean, I can write better than this. Bill!

BILL: Look, Monica, this is not a fight you want to pick. Ed's under a lot of pressure right now, and besides, the writing on this show is excellent; you should see the shit they make you say on other shows. *(Yelling out)* Could someone take care of this, please? Are we getting new pages?

SISSY: "You always say the sweetest things" is excellent? What am I, a complete moron?

DAVE: Sweetheart, you want Shakespeare, go to New York. You can do it in Central Park; they'll pay you three hundred bucks a week. Here, you make ten thousand a week doing shit. So shut up.

BILL: People. People!

DAVE: And could you get him to say the line right? It's I love you, not I loathe you. He's doing it on purpose.

BILL: It sounded fine to me, Jim.

UNCLE WILLY: I say the line that's written.

DAVE: He said I loathe you!

BUDDY: So where are these salmon pages? I don't have 'em.

(*Clara enters, frantic.*)

CLARA: Here they are! I'm sorry. *(She starts to pass out pages.)*

BILL: So what the fuck is going on, Clara? This is, we can't have this. We lost, like, fifteen minutes here trying to figure out if everybody's even in the same scene.

CLARA: I don't know what happened, Bill. I wasn't here this morning when the pages were distributed.

BILL: So who's in charge of this, can you tell me that?

CLARA: I don't know, Bill; I'll find out as soon as I get this—

BILL: *(Snapping)* Don't you fucking raise your voice to me!

(There is silence on the set.)

I don't need some little shit PA talking back to me. You fucked up. You cost this operation thousands of dollars because you were fucking careless. And now you're going to stand there and tell me this isn't your fault?

CLARA: I think I have a right to defend myself.

BILL: You have no fucking rights, you little shit! What makes you think your job affords you any dignity at all? You're a PA! You're nothing! And you fucked up. Do you understand? Do you understand anything at all? You're shit. You are nothing but shit here. No one wants to hear what you did wrong. Get out of here. *(Pause)* Get out! *(She goes. He turns back to the actors.)* Okay, the show's over. Could we do some work here?

(He exits. Lights change.)

ACT TWO • SCENE FOUR
BUDDY: We Could Help

Steve is sitting in the writers' room. Belinda enters.

BELINDA: Oh, hi, Where is everybody?

STEVE: I don't know. I thought we were meeting.

BELINDA: Well, yeah, I thought so, too. Clara? *(Clara enters.)* Do you know where everybody is?

CLARA: Bill's on the set, Ren and Ed are editing, and Sally's at wardrobe.

BELINDA: I thought we were meeting.

CLARA: Ed postponed till after lunch.

BELINDA: Oh, okay. Great.

(*Clara exits. Belinda starts to go.*)

STEVE: As long as we've got time, we could go over your script.

BELINDA: Oh. By ourselves?

STEVE: Well, I took a pass at it last night. I mean, it's good. I just had some ideas about the second act. To pop the comedy a little.

BELINDA: Oh. Well, shouldn't we wait until the whole group is together so that we don't…repeat?

STEVE: Are you doing something else right now? I just want to help. This is your first show, and I've done this a lot, and I consider it my responsibility to—help. Is that a problem?

BELINDA: No! No, of course not, I—

(*Bill enters.*)

BILL: Is Ed in here? Where is everybody?

BELINDA: Ed's in editing with Ren, Sally's in wardrobe.

BILL: Great. Jim just had a major meltdown.

STEVE: What happened?

BILL: Apparently, Monica was on the *Today* show this morning, so he's livid. Some asshole reporter said, on the air, that she's the real star of the show. So now nothing's right. Jim's costume's fucked, the scene's fucked, I'm fucked—

STEVE: Oh, Jesus.

BELINDA: You want me to go get Ed?

BILL: Please. He's not going down to the set for this kind of shit. What are we doing for lunch?

BELINDA: I don't know. I was gonna grab Ren. I'll tell Ed you're looking for him.

BILL: Oh, you're going over there?

BELINDA: Yeah, Ren and I are supposed to have lunch.

(*Ren enters.*)

REN: Hey, you ready?

BELINDA: Oh, you're here.

REN: Ed had to go do an interview.

BILL: Where are you going? Commissary?

BELINDA: Actually, I think we were going to go off the lot for a change. You want to come?

BILL: No. You go ahead.

(*They go. Bill shakes his head.*)

BILL: Can you fucking believe it?

STEVE: What?

BILL: Ren and Belinda. They're sleeping together. Man, it didn't take them long.

STEVE: You're kidding.

BILL: You couldn't tell? Shit. I just hope Ed doesn't find out. He hates that shit. And Sally's going to have heart failure.

STEVE: Sally? Why should she care?

BILL: Jesus, Steve. Where are you?

(*Sally enters.*)

SALLY: I'm sorry I'm late. Oh, aren't we meeting?

STEVE: Ed postponed till after lunch.

SALLY: Oh, God. I hate it when he does this. We're falling behind already and it's much too early in the season. We don't even have our pickup yet, and he's already—

BILL: We're fine. Belinda's new script just came in; it's terrific. Did you read it?

SALLY: Of course I read it. I think it needs work.

BILL: What, are you kidding? It's great. It reads like a fucking *Cheers* episode. If we've got any Emmy script, that's the one. Well, I'll go see if Jim's calmed down. He's going to be hell until we get the pickup.

(*He goes. Sally and Steve sit in silence for a moment.*)

SALLY: What is he talking about? That script needs a lot of help.

STEVE: I agree.

SALLY: I can't believe this. I mean, where is she? We could be working on it, even if Ed's not here. We could take an initial pass.

STEVE: She's having lunch with Ren.

SALLY: You're kidding. It's eleven thirty in the morning. What are they going to lunch now for?

STEVE: Apparently, they're sleeping together.

(*They look at each other. Lights change.*)

Ed is in his office. Sally enters.

ED: Hey, what's up?

SALLY: Nothing major. I just have some polaroids for you to look at. Jim keeps changing his mind about what he's wearing this week. He wants you to look at it. *(She hands him the polaroids.)*

ED: Oh, Jesus. Like I got nothing better to do.

SALLY: I told him, but he's gone completely insane. Ever since Monica did the *Today* show, he's been impossible.

ED: He's just uptight about the numbers. Everybody's got a lot riding on this. Here, this one.

SALLY: Great, that's the one everybody likes. So, are we going to take a pass at Belinda's script before it goes to table?

ED: Well, there's not a lot to do on it. I thought she and Ren and I would just take a look at it tonight, see if we can punch anything up.

SALLY: Oh. Sure. You don't want Steve and I to stick around, then?

ED: Yeah, you know, you guys, we should get you going on another couple of scripts, so if you could put some things together, ideas, that's probably the best use of your time.

SALLY: Sure. That sounds great. *(Pause)* Belinda's script really is terrific. Everyone's saying it could be our Emmy.

ED: Really?

SALLY: That's what Bill was saying. The crew is wild for it.

ED: Well, Jesus. I don't know about any Emmys. She's a kid. It's her third script.

SALLY: Oh, I know. That's just what people are saying. I mean, she and Ren are just great. You know, Ren's good, and she's really good.

ED: They're both good.

SALLY: But she's special, she really is. Everyone's noticed it.

ED: Yeah. I was the first to notice it, remember? I hired her.

SALLY: Oh, I know. She's really a find. Oh, one other thing. I was talking to some reporter this morning, from *Redbook* or something, who went off on this kick about not knowing how Dave fit into the show. Now—I tried to get her off this, because that idiot on the *Today* show said exactly the same thing to Monica.

ED: Oh, Jesus. Jim's going to throw a fit.

SALLY: That's what I thought. Anyway, I'm just not sure I convinced her, and the next thing you know, we're going to be in one of those situations where everyone's saying the star isn't the star—

ED: Yeah, yeah, yeah—

SALLY: Do you want to give her a call?

ED: Yeah, sure.

SALLY: I'll have Clara send the number over.

(*Belinda enters.*)

BELINDA: Hey, what's going on?

SALLY: What do you mean?

BELINDA: Well— Ren and I are over in the writers' building. Where is everybody? Aren't we starting the rewrite soon?

SALLY: Steve and I are taking the night off.

BELINDA: You are?

ED: Yeah, I thought the three of us could handle it. There's not a lot. Mostly we just need to take a pass and see if we can't make Dave more central to the episode.

BELINDA: *(Slight pause)* What?

ED: Yeah, I just think, you know, we gotta keep our focus on our guy. Keep him central. He's the person everyone's coming to see. I just don't think this script really answers the question Why is this important to Dave? just yet.

BELINDA: Well—

ED: *(A little dangerous)* You have a problem?

BELINDA: No! I just, you know, it's—this episode's not really about Dave. Off the top of my head, I just don't see how we're going to graft him in.

(*Ed stares at her. There is an uncomfortable pause.*)

SALLY: Have a fun rewrite!

(*She goes. Lights change.*)

The Family of Mann IV

The lights come low on Ed.

ED: *(Quiet)* I don't feel good. I don't feel good. You think I don't know what's going on? You think I'm stupid? I know what they want. Fighting amongst themselves. Trying to destroy each other. When I'm the one they're really after. You think I don't know that? You think I can't see it in their eyes? They're cannibals! They'd eat me alive if they could. That's what happened to the gods, you know. Their children ate them. For their strength. Why should I be any different? Well, fuck them. Fuck them all. Not one of them could handle this. Not ONE. The networks. The fucking numbers. Reporters. The assholes who advertise on this fucking show. FUCKING ACTORS. Every fucking day I deal with shit, with FUCKING SHIT, I keep everyone from destroying those fuckers, I spend my life providing for all of them, and they TURN on me. You think I don't KNOW?

GINNY: Dave? Are you all right, sweetheart? Why are you sitting in the dark?

DAVE: What, darling?

GINNY: Oh, you poor darling. You're upset about something!

DAVE: Oh, no.

GINNY: But you are, sweetheart. Your little forehead is getting all bunched up. Oh. Let me take care of you. Let me make you a cup of tea. Buddy! Sissy! Come down here and take care of your father! He's upset.

DAVE: That's okay, Ginny. Let the kids sleep.

GINNY: No, I want them down here, Dave, so you can see what a fortunate man you are. Your whole family is with you. Your kids, your brother. A lot of people might think, what a lot of good for nothing freeloaders. But you're glad they're here!

DAVE: I guess I am.

GINNY: I must admit, I sometimes worry. Maybe it would be better for Willy and the kids if they went out and lived their own lives. But it wouldn't be better for you.

DAVE: You think so, honey?

GINNY: I know it. You like it like this. Everyone here, under your control.

DAVE: Under my power.

GINNY: It makes you feel great.

DAVE: That's true.

GINNY: And that's why we stay. To make you happy. That's the only reason. Kids! Where are you? Your father needs you!

DAVE: Is that true, Ginny? You're all here, for me?

GINNY: Of course it is, sweetheart!

(*Buddy and Sissy enter.*)

BUDDY: Hey! What's everyone doing up?

GINNY: We were just talking about how glad we are to have you kids back home with us. You see, most people don't understand how perfect our world is.

DAVE: What could be better? I'm the king, and everyone else serves my needs. In return, I protect you and give you things. Money. Presents.

BUDDY: We earn some of that stuff, Dad. Yesterday, I did mow the lawn.

DAVE: Yes, you did, son. Not as well as I would have. But what the hey.

SISSY: Oh, Daddy. I love you so much. Would you like some more tea?

DAVE: That would be great, honey.

GINNY: I'm just going to go stand off in the corner here, Dave. I know how much you prefer the company of these young, healthy kids. If you need anything, just give a holler.

DAVE: Thanks, Ginny. You're so understanding.

UNCLE WILLY: Hey! What about me?

Buddy and SISSY: Uncle Willy!

DAVE: Come on over here, Willy, you old coot, and let me shove my fist up your ass!

(*Dave and Willy laugh heartily.*)

REN: Hey, are you two having good manly fun over there? I want to get in on this! How about I shove my fist up your ass!

(*They laugh.*)

UNCLE WILLY: And then I'll shove my fist up your ass!

REN: And then I'll shove my fist up your ass!

(*They laugh.*)

DAVE: And then we can all play basketball! And you girls can cheer us on!

SISSY: (*Dry*) Yeah, that sounds like fun. (*The men all stop laughing. They stare at her.*) (*With forced enthusiasm*) I mean, that sounds like fun! That sounds like fun! (*They continue to stare at her.*)

BELINDA: I'm trying, all right? And how much longer am I going to have to hold this fucking teapot?

GINNY: Sissy!

BELINDA: Oh, come on, he's not actually buying this shit, is he? I mean, do you really need me here? Can't I just go read a book?

DAVE: Sissy, are you feeling left out?

BELINDA: Left out? No. Pissed off is closer to what I'm running into. I mean, this is so boring. Do any of you know people who are like this? And would you want to? Why are we doing this?

DAVE: *(Beat)* You're not Sissy. You're not my daughter at all. What have you done with Sissy?

BELINDA: I ate her. *(She laughs maniacally.)*

DAVE: Sissy? Sissy! SISSSSYYYY!

(As Dave howls and Belinda laughs, the others turn and scatter. Blackout.)

ACT TWO • SCENE SEVEN
CLARA: Ed Wants To See You

Belinda stands at the door of Ed's office.

BELINDA: You wanted to see me?

ED: Yeah, come on in. Have a seat.
(She does. Ed looks up and speaks easily but abruptly.)

ED: I've been thinking about this, and I don't think you'll ever be happy here, and I think you should leave the show. It's up to you, but that's what I think.
(Pause)

BELINDA: *(In shock)* Okay.
(Ed looks at her, stunned and outraged.)

ED: All right. Fine. *(Pause)* That's all. *(He gestures to the door. She stands and looks at him, confused.)*

BELINDA: Wait a minute. Is this really what you want? You want me to leave the show. That's what you want?

ED: I think...you are never going to be happy here, and...it's up to you, but I think you should leave.

BELINDA: Yesterday you told me I was talented, and valuable and—now you want me to leave? I don't understand.

ED: It's your decision.

BELINDA: For heaven's sake, Ed, you're the executive producer. If you want me to leave, it's not my decision!

ED: It's interesting to hear you say that. You didn't seem to feel that way yesterday.

BELINDA: Yesterday, what? You mean last night? What did I say? I said, I thought that grafting Dave into the episode might not—

ED: I don't graft. I DON'T GRAFT. And if you're not willing to rewrite, then—

BELINDA: You wanted to rewrite an episode that worked!

ED: I decide what works!

BELINDA: Two days ago, you loved that episode. Everyone loves that episode.

ED: *(Overlap)* And if one day I say it works and the next day I say it's shit, then that's the way it is. You clearly don't understand the process. When I was working on my movie, I would go home every night and rewrite scenes for the next day!

BELINDA: But I was willing to stay! I didn't think it was necessary, but I would have done it!

ED: You didn't think it was necessary? You're making these decisions now?

BELINDA: You were the one who called off the rewrite. You said we'd do it today! Ed, listen. I am not trying to contradict you. I have nothing but admiration for your movie and your...brilliance. But yesterday, I listened to you with that reporter on the phone, and I thought, you seemed to be panicking. I just thought it was my job to reassure you that the episode was good, and you didn't have to panic.

ED: I don't need some little girl telling me what's good and what's not.

BELINDA: *(Flaring again)* Look, if you're going to stick fruit loops in one of my episodes because someone crossed their eyes at you over lunch, I think I have a right to at least—

ED: Your episode? Your episode? Let me tell you something. There isn't any episode that's yours. There is only my show. I write this show. Don't you ever talk about your episodes again.

BELINDA: Oh, Jesus, everybody talks about their episodes, we always—Ren practically blew a gasket last week because you bumped his episode in the release order and you didn't ask him to leave!

ED: That was a different situation. I was in a different mood then.

BELINDA: So I'm being fired because you're having a bad day?

ED: It's up to you.

(*Pause*)

BELINDA: I'll have my agent give you a call.

(*She goes. Ed's head twitches for a moment, then he sits. Clara enters, carrying a script.*)

CLARA: Hey Ed, you wanted to look at proofs for next week? (*Pause*) Ed?

ED: Belinda's out of here. She's out.

(*Clara stares at him, stunned. Lights change.*)

ACT TWO • SCENE EIGHT
REN: Belinda Blows a Gasket

Ren's office. Belinda paces, furious and frantic. Ren sits, confused.

BELINDA: Then, THEN he gives me the line about that fucking movie, when he was working on his MOVIE, he went home every night and rewrote scenes for the next day and I'm thinking, oh, what a blinding achievement that piece of shit was, Ed.

REN: Belinda, you have to keep it down; the secretaries—

BELINDA: I don't give a shit who hears. That fucking piece of shit fired me over nothing; he's screaming at me that no little girl is going to tell him anything; can you FUCKING believe that prick called me a little GIRL—

REN: Belinda. You have to be quiet now. You just, you have to be quiet.

BELINDA: I'm sorry. I'm sorry. (*She starts to cry. He crosses and holds her.*) I just don't—what happened? I mean, you hear about this shit going on, but who the fuck knew it actually did?

(*Bill enters.*)

BILL: What's going on? We can hear you guys yelling in here all over the building, what's—

BELINDA: Ed asked me to leave the show.

BILL: What? Oh, fuck. Oh, Jesus.

BELINDA: That fucking prick—

REN: Belinda.

BILL: He didn't mean it.

BELINDA: He was very specific, Bill—

BILL: What did he say?

BELINDA: He said he thought I should leave the show! But it's up to me. Is that the most passive aggressive bullshit you've ever—

REN: Belinda.

BILL: No, he means it. I mean, he means you don't have to go. You have to go back there and apologize.

BELINDA: What? What am I apologizing for?

BILL: Look, you're upset, you're crying, just go back and tell him you're sorry, it's all he wanted. He doesn't want you to leave.

BELINDA: I'm not going to cry for him.

REN: You're crying now. *(She stares at him.)* What? If you can cry for us, you can cry for him, what's the difference?

BILL: Look. Ed is under a lot of pressure, his wife is bugging him to get out of television, the show isn't getting the numbers he wanted, he wants to get rid of Steve and Sally, but he can't—

BELINDA: So he got rid of me instead?

BILL: No, he doesn't want to get rid of you. That's not what he wanted. He just wants your loyalty. He needs you to say, I'm here for you, Ed.

BELINDA: While he's telling me to leave?

BILL: He didn't say that. He said it was up to you. You cannot leave him.

BELINDA: He told me to leave!

BILL: That's not what he told you.

REN: Look, what did he say? What did you do to piss him off?

BELINDA: I didn't—I don't know, it was—

BILL: Look, you can't fall apart on us, Belinda. The show needs you. There can be no ego involved here!

BELINDA: What do you mean, no ego, I don't even know what that—

BILL: You do not exist. Do you understand me? The only person who exists here is Ed. He is the executive producer. It is his show, his vision, and you do whatever he wants.

BELINDA: He wants me to leave the show!

REN: He said it was up to you.

BELINDA: Oh, man. Don't you both fucking gang up on me—

BILL: You cannot leave him. No writer has ever left Ed and gone on to work on anything of any significance. Anywhere.

BELINDA: What?

BILL: All I'm saying is no writer has ever left Ed and gone on to work on anything of any significance.

BELINDA: What are you saying, I only exist in relation to Ed? If I leave, I cease to exist, I'm no longer a writer, is that what you're fucking telling me?

BILL: This is not about ego, Belinda!

BELINDA: I mean, I love this! He fires me on a whim, and now you're telling me that if I don't get down on my knees and beg for my job back, I'm being egotistical!

REN: Okay, okay, I'm taking you home—

BELINDA: Don't you touch me!

REN: Belinda, Jesus, would you stop, would you just—

BILL: She cannot leave the lot. I'm telling you, I've seen this happen before; she has to go back now, before he gets used to the idea and can't even—

REN: I'm just saying if we send her in there now, while she's still acting like a raving lunatic, it's not going to—

BELINDA: Well, thank you very much and could you all not talk about me as if I'm not even in the room? Jesus, you guys are starting to sound like Ed.

BILL: Belinda, Ed is a genius.

BELINDA: He's not a genius, he's a TV producer! *(Pause)* And, a mega-lomaniac. And a madman. And what's more, everybody knows it. *(She leaves.)*

REN: Oh, Christ.

BILL: That's it. It's over.

REN: Come on, let's go talk to him. She's, they're both so emotional.

BILL: You don't understand. It was a test, and she failed it. *(Pause)* It's over.

(He shrugs. Ren stares at him, confused. Lights change.)

ACT TWO • SCENE NINE
BILL: A Whole Different World

Ren and Ed are in Ed's office.

ED: Hey! How's it going?

REN: Great. It's really—

ED: I'm glad you're here; I was gonna call you. You want to go do some editing?

REN: Yeah, sure.

ED: Also, we're going to have to stay late and take a look at next week's script. It's not quite working and Belinda's gonna leave the show, so I thought you and I could take a pass at it.

REN: Yeah, I just saw her. She's real upset.

ED: She's a talented girl; she'll be fine. Sometimes these things just don't work out.

REN: She really doesn't want to leave, Ed.

ED: I gave her a choice.

REN: Yeah, but, I, I think she didn't understand—see, I just think she's kind of insecure. This is all really new to her. I mean, we've all done it before, one way or another, and she's from a whole different world. That's all I think it is. And Sally really is—I know you guys have been through a lot together, but she's not been great to Belinda. You know how competitive women can be. She's—it's mostly when you're not around, but she gives her a hard time, and you know, it's clear to everyone else that it's because she's threatened, but how's Belinda supposed to know that? And she's good, everyone knows that, but she's just, she's figuring out how it all works, so she's a little...I don't know. She makes some mistakes. But she loves the show, I know she loves being here, that's mostly what it is, I think.

ED: So, what are you saying? Are you two sleeping together? Is that what you're telling me?

(*Pause*)

REN: Would that be a problem?

ED: No! Jesus, no, I told you, I think she's great. I'm just—I mean, personally, I wouldn't be able to sleep with someone who's a better writer than I am. But hey, I think it's great. She'll land on her feet.

(*They look at each other. Lights change.*)

222 ✳ THERESA REBECK

BELINDA: Producer

> *Belinda lies on Ren's bed. She holds a bottle of Scotch, out of which she drinks. Beside the bed, there is a beautiful ten-speed bicycle, wrapped in red ribbon. Ren enters. Pause.*

REN: How are you?

BELINDA: Fine. How are you?

REN: Okay. Not so great. You know. *(She doesn't answer. He sees the bicycle.)* What's that?

BELINDA: It's a bicycle. Someone delivered it about fifteen minutes ago.

REN: For me? I mean, it's...for me?

BELINDA: Well, it's not for me.

> *(Curious, Ren crosses to look at it. He finds a card and starts to open it.)*
>
> It's from Ed. He's making you a producer.
>
> *(Pause)*

REN: Yes. I know.

BELINDA: Oh. You saw Ed.

REN: Of course I saw him, Christ, what do you think, I went over after you left and—

BELINDA: You went to see him? Oh. Did you talk about me?

REN: Yes, as a matter of fact, we did. I told him this was all a huge mistake.

BELINDA: You told Ed—The Ed—that he was making a huge mistake? *(Pause. Ren does not answer.)* No, that's not what you told him. You told him I was making a huge mistake. By not begging for his love while he tromped all over me, I made a huge mistake. Thank you for your support. It means so much to me that you went in and explained that to your good friend Ed!

REN: Belinda—

BELINDA: Yeah, too bad it didn't work. I mean, you went in to beg for my job, and came out a producer. Poor Ren. You can't do anything right.

> *(Pause)*

REN: All you had to do was cry.

BELINDA: Fuck you. You think it's so fucking easy to cry for that creep, then you do it, you fucking woman.

(*Pause*)

REN: I'm not going to talk to you right now. You're drunk.

BELINDA: Oh, that's rich. You can talk to a man who is completely insane well enough to get yourself that precious fucking producer button, but one drunken female has you tongue-tied.

REN: Jesus, you are—you know, you are just as bad as he is.

BELINDA: Not possible. No one's as bad as Ed. No one's as good as Ed. Only Ed exists, remember? You better remember, or he'll get you, too.

(*She drinks from the bottle. He reaches for it. She pulls away.*)

REN: Give me the bottle.

BELINDA: You know what I think is interesting? You told me to fight. You said, he loves you. He wants you to fight for what you believe in. He wants you to fight for your script.

REN: Belinda—

BELINDA: You sent me in there, to fight, and I got fired, and now you're a producer. I find that very interesting.

REN: That's not what happened.

BELINDA: Isn't it? Then you tell me what happened. You—you tell me—

REN: Give me that. Would you give me that?

(*She shoves him away.*)

BELINDA: No. No. Get your hands off me. Stay—just don't—

(*Pause. Ren sits on the bed.*)

Why don't you tell me to go? Just tell me to go.

REN: I'm not going to do that. I don't understand any of this. I think I'm falling in love with you, and—it's not right what he did. I don't know what I'm gonna do.

(*He rubs his eyes. She watches him. Blackout.*)

ACT TWO • SCENE ELEVEN
BILL: Loyalty

Sally, Bill and Steve are in the writers' room.

SALLY: Well, I think it's definitely what needed to happen. She just wasn't fitting in. Already, you can feel how relieved everyone is.

BILL: I just don't know what we're gonna do for scripts now. I mean, she was a machine.

STEVE: I've got a lot of ideas. We can pick up the slack.

BILL: No, I know, I just—

SALLY: I think Ed always overrated her, frankly. I mean, she wrote fast, but we had to do a lot of work on her material.

STEVE: She wasn't funny. I didn't think. She just wasn't funny.

BILL: Well, she certainly wasn't loyal.

STEVE: And she just made everyone tense. I don't know what Ren sees in her.

SALLY: Oh, please. That's not going to last.

(*Ren enters, frazzled. Sally is immediately sympathetic.*)

SALLY: Ren! How are you?

REN: Oh, I'm fine. I'm sorry I'm late, I just, you know. Is Ed around?

BILL: He's at the network.

REN: Something going on?

BILL: You know. The usual shit. They're talking about the pickup.

REN: Oh, Jesus.

SALLY: *(Sympathetic)* How's Belinda?

REN: She's fine. A little rattled.

SALLY: She'll be fine.

REN: Oh, yeah. She's already got, like, six job offers.

SALLY: *(Too polite)* Really?

REN: Yeah, it's amazing how fast people hear somebody's available. You know, there's always work for someone who can write. She doesn't know what she's gonna do. You know, I don't think she's ready to just dive into another show.

BILL: Fuck her.

SALLY: Bill.

BILL: No, I mean it. We give her her break, Ed hires her when she's nobody and now everybody wants her. Ed created her, and now she's off fielding offers from every shithead in town.

SALLY: Look. We're all upset by what happened—

BILL: No, look, I'm sorry Ren, I know there's something going on between you two, but I'm not going to lie about how I feel.

REN: No, I know. I understand that.

BILL: I think a person should show a little loyalty. That's just how I feel.

REN: I agree, Bill.

BILL: I mean, Ed doesn't—Ed is not in this because he needs the power, or the money or anything. This is all a huge headache for him, and he has so much money, he doesn't have to do it anymore. He doesn't have to do anything unless he thinks it's going to benefit mankind.

REN: I know that.

BILL: So when she goes in there and tries to take over the show, how is he supposed to take that?

REN: I don't think that's what—

BILL: That's how it looked, all right? I mean, how else is he supposed to take it? And the next thing you know, she's calling her agents in. I don't think it's right. I think Ed deserves a little better than that.

REN: I understand what you're saying.

BILL: Do you?

(*Beat. Ed enters.*)

ED: Hey, you hacks, how's it going?

BILL: Great!

ED: (*Sober*) You guys got a minute?

BILL: Sure. Sure! What's up?

ED: Well, you know, I know things have been a little tense around here lately, the numbers haven't been what we hoped and I know everyone's been pretty worried and wondering about what kind of life *The Family of Mann* has to look forward to. So I wanted everyone to know as soon as it happened. I just got back from the network, and...we've got our pickup. (*He laughs. Everyone cheers.*) I think this is a real vote of confidence for us from the network. They're under a lot of pressure to come up with shows that they really think are going to fly, and they're backing us a hundred percent. So I'd like everyone to just take a minute to feel good about all your hard work, and I think that we can now look forward to a lot of years together. (*Everyone cheers again.*) And don't worry about the numbers; everybody at the network assures me that it's not going to matter. They're going to stand behind us no matter what, and we all know that there is someone out there who's eventually going to find us and say, thank god. Something real, and decent for a change.

(*They all hug and applaud.*)

SALLY: Oh, isn't it wonderful?

BILL: Fantastic.

REN: That's great news, Ed.

ED: Yeah, it looks like we got a show for our new producer to produce! Now, get back to work. Hacks... *(He goes, laughing.)*

BILL: Well, how about this?

SALLY: What a relief!

STEVE: I wasn't worried.

(They all laugh.)

SALLY: Ren, we never congratulated you on your promotion. It's terrific.

REN: Thanks.

SALLY: Well, I guess if we're going for a whole season—

BILL: Hey, we're going longer than that. Seven years—

SALLY: Then we better get back to work!

BILL: All right! So what's Jim doing in this scene? Besides standing around with his fist up his ass.

(Steve snickers.)

STEVE: You think that's physically possible?

BILL: It's the only way Jim's gonna get it.

STEVE: "Hey hey, Ralph! What are you doing?"

BILL: "I'm fucking myself, Norton! It's the wave of the future! You wanta watch?"

REN: "Hey hey hey hey hey!"

BILL: "Norton—you're the greatest!"

(Bill and Steve laugh. Ren tries to smile. Clara enters. She wears her wings and passes out yellow sheets, menus and scripts.)

CLARA: Here are the lunch menus. Polaroids from wardrobe. Casting sheets. New second acts. Anything else?

BILL: Yeah, how would you like to give me a blow job?

(Clara looks at him. The others laugh. The laughter dies out.)

CLARA: Actually, Bill, you know what I'd really like, is to cut it off and shove it down your throat.

(Steve goes, "whoaaaa...." Bill stares at her, cold. She stares back. Lights change.)

Belinda sits on a bench, smoking a cigarette. A bedraggled Clara, still wearing her wings, approaches.

BELINDA: Hey. How's it going?

CLARA: Fine. Shitty, fine. *(She picks up the cigarettes from the bench and takes one.)* This city is, you know, man. This city is smoking. They're finally rioting over on Rodeo Drive.

BELINDA: They are?

CLARA: They should be. I mean, if I was gonna riot, that's what I'd do. I'd fucking burn Beverly Hills to the ground, that's what I'd do.

BELINDA: Bad day, huh?

CLARA: Please. Would you look at this place? Earthquakes. Fires. Riots. Floods. It's downright apocalyptic around here. The city of angels, my ass. This is Sodom and Gomorrah, and all this bad behavior is having an impact on the weather. The day of righteousness is at hand. Armageddon is starting at the corner of Wilshire and Fairfax, right down there in front of the May Company. I think it's already started. *(She smokes. Belinda watches her.)*

BELINDA: Clara?

CLARA: Yeah?

BELINDA: You've grown wings. You know that, don't you?

CLARA: You can see them?

(Belinda nods.)

CLARA: Oh, thank god. Oh, Jesus. I thought I was losing my fucking mind, I got these major wings growing out of my back and nobody's even mentioned it! I mean, I go in that fucking room, and fucking Bill—I got fucking wings growing out of my back and he's asking me for a blow job!

BELINDA: He what?

CLARA: He asked me for a blow job. In front of everybody! Can you believe it?

BELINDA: What did you say?

CLARA: I told him I'd rather cut it off and shove it down his throat. Some angel I'm gonna make. *(They laugh.)* You can see them? You actually see these things?

BELINDA: Yeah, they're pretty.

CLARA: You like them?

BELINDA: I think they're beautiful. Are they real?

CLARA: I guess. I mean, they kind of itch, you know? And they don't come off, which makes it real hard to get any sleep. And sometimes, at night, they just move. On their own. They beat. They're anxious about something.

BELINDA: Me too.

CLARA: Yeah, me too.

BELINDA: Where'd they come from?

CLARA: I don't know. I was just sitting at my desk, right, everyone's screaming at me, and I start thinking about flying off, imagining what that would be like, to just float away. Fly off, into the sunset. The next thing I know, fucking wings. Growing out of my back. (*Beat.*)

BELINDA: You imagined them. (*Pause*) I can't. I can't image anything except buying a gun and shooting Ed, in an alley. (*Beat. Trying to collect herself.*) Clearly, wings are a much better way to go.

CLARA: I think so. And I'm going to use them. I'm getting out of this town. I don't know why I stuck around this long. Unfinished business, I guess. You want to touch them? Go ahead. You can touch them.

BELINDA: No, I—no.

CLARA: It's okay. (*Clara reaches over and takes Belinda's hand. She places it on one of her wings. Belinda starts to cry. Clara takes her in her arms and rocks her.*) It's okay. Shhh. It's okay. (*Lights change.*)

ACT TWO • SCENE THIRTEEN
REN: A Great Opportunity

The writers' room. Ren is looking at scripts. Belinda pokes her head in.

BELINDA: Hi.

REN: Belinda! What are—what are you doing here?

BELINDA: I just cleaned out my office. And, I was looking for you, actually. Everyone's gone, aren't they? I looked around, and—

REN: Yeah. Ed's over in his office. But everybody else left an hour ago. You're safe. *(Awkward pause. She looks around.)* So. What'd you do today?

BELINDA: I went to the tar pits.

REN: Again?

BELINDA: Yeah, you know there's something about it I really find comforting. I think it's that dramatic recreation of the mastodon getting sucked into the tar. You know, the one you can see from the street. Her husband, and her little baby bellowing woefully at her from the bank. I find it kind of touching in a way that's unusual for Los Angeles.

REN: So how many times is that?

BELINDA: I don't know. Five or six.

REN: Just this week.

BELINDA: I've only been out of work this week. Give me a little more time, I may set a record. *(Pause)* I bumped into Clara.

REN: You did?

BELINDA: Yeah.

REN: She had a kind of a run in with Bill. Did she tell you?

BELINDA: Actually, what she said was he asked her for a blow job. In front of a whole roomful of writers.

REN: Well, she gave as good as she got.

BELINDA: You notice anything different about her? About the way she looks or anything? Like, wings or anything?

REN: Wings?

BELINDA: Yeah, you know. Wings. *(Pause)* Nevermind. She says she's not coming back.

REN: Yeah. She made that pretty clear.

BELINDA: This city is smoking, you know? Clara told me that, at the tar pits. I thought she meant that they were rioting again, but that's not it. I figured it out. She's talking about television.

REN: Really?

BELINDA: I think so. It's us that's burning. You know, we're like putting our lives into this cauldron, and turning up the heat so high—with the pressure, and the money, and the power, it's making us all white hot until our essence just burns away. You know, the best of us, the stuff that makes us human, it evaporates. And we're left with sitcoms. Maybe that's what all the smog is. It's not car exhaust. It's us, burning ourselves up.

REN: Belinda,—

BELINDA: And then hanging there, in the air, like a disease. Like television.

What is it? What are we becoming?

(*Pause. The door bursts open. Ed enters.*)

ED: Hey, how's my new producer? (*Beat. He takes her in.*)

BELINDA: Ed.

REN: I was on my way over, Ed, she just stopped by for—

BELINDA: It's okay (*Beat*) I was picking up my stuff, Ed.

(*Beat. They wait for Ed to respond.*)

ED: (*To Ren*) I'll be in my office, okay? Whenever you're ready. (*He turns to go.*)

BELINDA: God, aren't you even going to let me say goodbye?

(*He stops and waits for her to continue. She crosses and holds out her hand. He turns to Ren.*)

ED: Whenever you're ready. No rush.

(*He goes. Beat. Belinda looks at her hand.*)

BELINDA: Whoa. I've been dissed. (*She laughs.*)

REN: Oh, shit. I have to go.

BELINDA: Oh, come on, Ren, relax. What's he gonna do if you don't hop, fire you? Pretty soon he's not going to have any staff left. (*She laughs.*)

REN: I don't have time for this! This is bad, don't you get it? It's bad that he saw me with you! (*Beat*) I'm sorry.

BELINDA: (*Beat*) Oh, no. (*She looks at him. He looks away.*)

REN: Look. I'm as sorry as anyone about what happened to you, but you have to understand, this is a great opportunity for me, and I need to protect myself here.

BELINDA: Don't do this.

REN: Don't—Oh, that's great. Now I'm the villain.

BELINDA: No, you're not the villain, that's not—(*Regrouping*) Look. I'm sorry I haven't been paying attention to what's going on with you, the position that you're in now, I—I've been so upset, it's like this whole place has poisoned me, and I'm trying to get myself back—

REN: This place is fine.

BELINDA: No, it's not, Ren, it's destroying people! And I think the longer you stay here, the more it infects you, and pretty soon you can't imagine anything else—

REN: What did you think you were going to find here? I mean, why is this all such a big surprise to you? I'm just a dumb jock from Illinois, and I knew it was going to be like this. Why didn't you just go back and tell Ed you were sorry?

BELINDA: Because he would do it again.

REN: Of course he would! He's the boss! That's what bosses do! I don't get why—how can you stand there and act like what's happened to you is so terrible? You had a good job, with people who admired you, and you gave it all up for pride—

BELINDA: Yes, I still have—

REN: So the boss blows off steam in your direction, so what? He's under a lot of pressure. He's entitled. What's your problem?

BELINDA: Apparently my problem is I do want people to be decent.

REN: It's a sit com, Belinda! It's a fucking sit com!

BELINDA: Well, this sit com is a lie, and you're selling your soul to write it!

REN: Oh, no. That was never me. That's you, remember? I happen to like this show. I think it's funny, and smart, and decent. I'm proud to write for it, and I'm proud to work with Ed. I think I can learn a lot from him. I intend to try.

BELINDA: *(Pause)* Ren. What are you—are we on feed? Is this being piped into Ed's office? *(She looks for the hidden mic.)* Eddd...

REN: I have to go. *(He goes for his knapsack.)*

BELINDA: No. Please, listen to me. If you just go along with it all, you'll lose yourself.

REN: Look, I can't do this. Really, I can't fight with you anymore. I just can't. I have to go. *(He heads for the door.)*

BELINDA: Hey. What are you and Ed doing? Are you rewriting my script?

REN: *(Beat)* Yes. We are.

BELINDA: Well. Have a good time.

REN: Look. We all do what we have to do.

BELINDA: I know, I know that.

REN: I'll call you.

BELINDA: Sure. *(He goes. She sits, for a moment, looking at the room. From the darkness around her, the Mann family begins to take shape. They move in, whispering their lines. She turns.)* What? WHAT? *(They fall silent. She turns and looks at them as they surround her. She turns, finally, and looks at the script before her.)* Scene One: The Mann Family Kitchen. *(She looks at them, throws the script on the table, picks up her box, and goes. The Family of Mann leans in to read the script. Blackout.)*

END OF PLAY

GIRL GONE
by Jacquelyn Reingold

For Bernie, Bobby, and Will.
And for Charles, who didn't get to see it.

BIOGRAPHY

Jacquelyn Reingold's play *Girl Gone* was produced by Manhattan Class Company in 1994. It received the Kennedy Center's 1994 Fund for New American Plays Roger L. Stevens Award, the 1993 Greenwall Foundation's Oscar Ruebhausen Commission, and was a finalist for the 1995 Susan Smith Blackburn Prize. Other plays include *Dear Kenneth Blake* (Ensemble Studio Theatre Marathon '94), *Tunnel of Love* (Ensemble Studio Theatre Marathon '93 and Naked Angels), *A.M.L.* (Manhattan Class Company), *Lost and Found* (Circle Rep Lab), *Freeze Tag* (Working Theatre), and *Rollers on Rhode Island*, a comedy with singing and dancing for 25+ actors in wheelchairs (Manhattan Class Company and Shake-a-Leg, a rehab center in Rhode Island). Her work has been published by Dramatists Play Service, Samuel French, in Smith & Kraus' *Ensemble Studio Theatre Marathon '94*, and in *The Quarterly*. She has written plays for inner city kids for The 52nd Street Project. Jacquelyn is a member of New Dramatists, Ensemble Studio Theatre, Manhattan Class Company, and Circle Rep's Playwrights Project.

AUTHOR'S NOTE

Girl Gone started as a short play for The Mortality Project, Manhattan Class Company's annual giant collaborative experimental event that, sadly, no longer exists. That year, each writer was given a theme, a group of actors, a rehearsal room, and about two weeks. My piece was a short collection of scenes about a topless bar, a group of dancers, and a murder. With the constant support from MCC and director Brian Mertes, I kept writing. For a long time. On each of many MCC playreading retreats I would bring the next *Girl Gone* installment—sometimes only a page—sometimes dozens. Countless actors did countless readings, and I thank them all. *Girl Gone* could not have come to life without Manhattan Class Company, its Mortality Project, its actors, its spirit, the cast and crew, and certainly not without the generous support of the Greenwall Foundation.

ORIGINAL PRODUCTION

GIRL GONE was produced by Manhattan Class Company, Bernard Telsey and Robert LuPone, Executive Directors; W.D. Cantler, Associate Director. It was directed by Brian Mertes with the following cast (in order of appearance):

Tish . . . . Kelly Wolf
Jean . . . . Brenda Bakke
Dancer 1/Carla. . . . . Adina Porter
Dancer 2/Baby June. . . . . Dina Spybey
Dancer 3/ Roxanne . . . . Bernadette Penotti
Danny . . . . David Thornton
Sam . . . . Seth Gilliam
Bobby . . . . Jack Gwaltney

Original Music . . . . Delfeayo Marsalis
Choreography . . . . Mark Dendy
Set Designer. . . . . Christine Jones
Lighting Designer. . . . . Scott Zielinski
Sound Designer . . . . John Gromada
Costume Designer. . . . . Karen Perry
Production Managers . . . . Laura Kravets Gautier and Ira Mont
Production Stage Manager . . . . James Marr
Stage Managers . . . . Elaine Bayless and John Garrity
Props Master . . . . Christa Kelly
Assistant to the Director . . . . Yana Landowne
Casting. . . . . Bernard Telsey

CHARACTERS

TISH: Topless dancer. Lost her best friend. Trying to put a shattered world back together.

JEAN: Tish's best friend. Was a dancer. Lived her life to its absolute fullest. Sexy. Fearless. Appears in Tish's imagination and memory.

DANNY: Tish's boyfriend. Nice guy, but. Tries hard. A little goofy, but a big heart.

BOBBY: Jean's boyfriend before her death. Plays the sax. Sexy, dangerous. Seems like trouble.

DANCER 1 (Carla): Topless dancer. Has seen it all. Tough. A survivor.

DANCER 2 (Baby June): Topless dancer. The new girl. Wants to be on Broadway.

DANCER 3 (Roxanne): Topless dancer. Very hot. Into heavy metal. Loves to dance.

SAM: A hustler. Jean went to him for good sex.

PLACE

Multiple locations:

Topless bar. It has high bars, swings, platforms, where dancers can dance.

Danny's apartment.

Sam's apartment.

Bobby's jazz club.

The street.

Jean's apartment.

TIME

Now.

GIRL GONE

(The stage is dark except where Tish is standing. She talks to the audience.)

TISH: I'm walking down the street. I'm looking for cracks. You step on one and you're gone. The whole sidewalk goes. Major earthquake. A bird flies by, you look up. Someone says your name, you look up. There's a knock at the door, you forget to to ask who it is. You think who could it be, it's the door, they knock, they ring, you open it. One step and you're gone. They put it on the news—"Girl Gone". Nothing beneath you—no Con Ed, no cable TV, no New York Telephone. You gotta watch your step. A piece of gum, someone's chewed up sugarless gum, you're crazy glued you can't move. Cracks, gum, subway grates. You think someone checks them—you think they send out an inspector to check them? You fall through you fry like bacon they eat you with their eggs. Front page—"Girl Fried. Scrambled Eggs." You don't think it can happen? Man hole covers—what man? Does he have a gun—a knife—a saxophone? *(Jean appears, dancing slowly.)* I'm walking down the street and you're not with me. I'm walking past your house, no one's there. I cross the street. I stop. Manhole cover. Big crack. Crazy glue, I can't move. Oh God, I'm in the middle of the street. *(Tish puts her hands to her head.)* Jean?

❊

(Burst of loud dance music. Lights up on the rest of the stage. Three women dance topless. Tish is several feet away from them, trying to dance. They address the audience. No pauses.)

DANCER 1: I'm thinking about the money. Which guy has the most money.

DANCER 3: I'm thinking about the guy in the corner. He wants me.

DANCER 2: I'm thinking I hope I do it right.

TISH: I'm thinking—

DANCER 1: Him. I can smell his money.

TISH: —Oh God.

DANCER 3: He'd do anything to touch me.

DANCER 2: What if I hiccup?

TISH: How do I do this?

DANCER 1: Hey Honey, give me all your money.

TISH: I can't—

DANCER 3: He'd give me everything.

TISH: —remember—

DANCER 2: What if my nose runs?

TISH: —how to do this.

DANCER 1: Midtown tunnel filled with money.

DANCER 3: You want me, Babe? You can't have me.

TISH: Jean—

DANCER 1: GW bridge covered with money.

TISH: —I forgot.

DANCER 2: What if I fart?

DANCER 3: Can't touch me can't smell me can't know my name.

TISH: Can't remember.

DANCER 1: I'm thinking about who's watching me.

DANCER 3: I'm thinking about who's watching me.

TISH: Uh oh.

DANCER 2: I'm thinking about who's watching me.

TISH: Uh oh. Someone's watching me.

*

(*Lights dim on Dancers.*)

TISH: (*to the audience.*) Sometimes you open the door. You think who could it be, it's the door, they knock, they ring, you open it. Sometimes they lie and say they are who they aren't. Sometimes they have uniforms, they dress like deliverymen firemen policemen exterminators, someone you thought you knew, might have loved. Sometimes the elevator opens, and as you fall down the shaft you wonder what happened and why you didn't see.

Sometimes you reach for the shampoo, but someone left the Nair there and you can't figure out why your hair's all gone. Or for your birthday someone leaves a present at the door, it's a thousand piece jigsaw puzzle—with no picture on the cover of the box. And then for Christmas you get a box with a pretty picture—and inside—a thousand pieces each from a different puzzle. Sometimes you wake up and think you got it figured out, the next day you realize it's just your figure that's out—big is back, small is in, your clothes just don't fit; your best friend went away so you're left with pieces that don't match, walking down the street looking for cracks. She was my friend. It's different when it's your friend. It's not like channel 5, page 3, 88 on your AM dial. It's. She was. My friend. I. See. She used to do my make up. We used to talk. And now I forgot. I. Right arm out. Left foot. Left arm. I forgot how to dance. I lost my friend. Her name was Jean. She changed by life. She taught me how to dance. "It's like ducks," she said. *(To audience.)* I'm watching you and you're watching me, and I'm wondering if you killed by best friend.

DANCER 2: *(To Dancer 3, who walks away.)* What if I get my period?
DANCER 1: You cut the string.
DANCER 2: Oh.
TISH: *(To audience.)* Did you ever keep doing something even though you don't know how to do it?
DANCER 2: Yeah.
DANCER 1: No.
DANCER 3: Maybe.
TISH: Did you ever lose the person that made your life make sense?
DANCER 2: Yeah.
DANCER 3: Maybe.
DANCER 1: Dollars and cents.
TISH: Why would they want to hurt her?
DANCER 1: She must've done something stupid.

(Danny's apartment.)
DANNY: Sweetie? What happened?
TISH: Jean.

DANNY: Yeah?
TISH: Dead.
DANNY: Oh no.
TISH: Yeah.
DANNY: What happened?
TISH: Jean.
DANNY: Yeah?
TISH: Dead.
DANNY: Yeah but what—
TISH: That's it.
DANNY: Oh.
TISH: Jean.
DANNY: God.
TISH: Dead.
DANNY: God. I'm sorry. *(Pause.)* Tish? Say something.

TISH: Why would they kill you?
DANCER 1: You need a vacation.
TISH: Jean?
DANCER 1: Take a week. Take two.
TISH: Why?
DANCER 1: I know what you need.
TISH: Why did they do it?
DANCER 1: You need a new friend.
TISH: Why'd you open the door?
DANCER 1: We should talk.
TISH: I walk fast, I look for cracks, I put new locks on the door.
DANCER 2: My breasts look like hamsters.
TISH: I call the police. Case 3678BX. June 23rd.
DANCER 1: Maybe if you plucked the hairs.
TISH: They'll get back to me?
DANCER 1: I'll sell you a tweezers.
TISH: They can't find the file?
DANCER 2: I mean the shape.
TISH: They don't care.
DANCER 2: Maybe isometrics.

DANCER 1: I know what you need.

TISH: Yeah?

DANCER 1: Spirulina.

TISH: What?

DANCER 1: It's like a vitamin but from the ocean.

TISH: Oh yeah?

DANCER 1: Yeah, make you feel like a different person.

TISH: How do you feel?

DANCER 1: Peachy. I'll give you a discount, 'cause I like you.

TISH: I have some peach lipstick if you want to borrow it.

DANCER 1: It's not my color.

TISH: I have lots of colors.

DANCER 1: OK, kiddo, sure.

TISH: I'll take some of the spiru-whatever.

DANCER 1: Smart girl.

TISH: Yeah?

DANCER 1: Yeah.

TISH: Did you used to um sell to Jean—what did you sell to her?

DANCER 1: Nothing.

TISH: But you were friends, right, I mean before I got here. And now you're my friend, right?

DANCER 1: Right. I take cash and I take checks.

*

(*Dressing Room.*)

DANCER 2: (*To Dancer 3.*) Hi, I'm June, like from June Havoc you know, Baby June? (*She sings something.*) (*Dancer 3 exits.*) (*To Dancer 1.*) Hi. I'm a triple threat. Actress, singer, dancer. Where do you get your g-strings?

DANCER 1: I sell em. If you don't buy from me I'll be unhappy, and it's a good idea to make me happy. (*Dancer 1 exits.*)

DANCER 2: Oh. (*To Tish.*) Hi.

TISH: First week?

DANCER 2: Yeah.

TISH: The person you replaced was a friend.

DANCER 2: Great.

TISH: Your locker, it was hers. You can have the stuff in it. The outfits.

DANCER 2: Really? (*Tish nods.*) Cool, this stuff is so cool. Like Gypsy.

That was my favorite movie. I watched it every year. You know the part when she comes out in that big powder puff? I love that.

TISH: Listen, be careful who you um sing to.

DANCER 2: Sure. Wow, your makeup is great. How's mine?

TISH: It's nice.

DANCER 2: Hey, I have this audition for South Pacific. It's in Iowa, but it's the lead. Could you help me—maybe something like tropical?

TISH: For a job in Iowa?

DANCER 2: Des Moines

TISH: I'd be glad to help. *(To audience.)* God, she's green.

DANCER 1: No greener than you were.

∗

(Flashback. Dressing Room. Tish's first day. She is about to go on. She is frozen with fear.)

TISH: Oh God—I just can't—this is not—I don't think—I just—there's no way. I can't move.

JEAN: First day?

TISH: Yeah and oh I can't I just—I'm gonna

JEAN: Hey—you don't have to, you can go home—or go back to being a receptionist.

TISH: Waitress.

JEAN: Whatever. Unless of course maybe you really want to do it.

TISH: Oh God. Were you nervous?

JEAN: Pissed in my g string.

TISH: Really? Wow. You seem really great now.

JEAN: What's your name?

TISH: Patricia.

JEAN: Your real name? *(Tish nods.)* I'm Jean.

TISH: Great.

JEAN: You gonna stick around? 'Cause I'm not gonna give away secrets and have you run off to another club. OK?

TISH: OK.

JEAN: First thing, we change your name. So when you're out there it's you but it's not, you know what I mean? So, how 'bout um…Tish, how's that?

TISH: OK.

JEAN: You're a pretty girl. Very unique, nice face, sweet body, you're a lovely girl. And I know about these things. Tish, you want to be my friend?

TISH: Yeah.

JEAN: Then you gotta listen to me right now. I like you, do you like me?

TISH: Yeah.

JEAN: See how that made you smile? That's the secret. If you want them to like you, then you gotta look at them and say, "I like you, do you like me?" So say it.

TISH: Now?

JEAN: Now.

TISH: I like you do you like me?

JEAN: Again.

TISH: I like you do you like me?

JEAN: Again.

TISH: I like you do you like me?

JEAN: Listen. What do you hear?

TISH: Music.

JEAN: Smart girl. Now, mirror me. Do what I do. *(Jean dances, Tish follows.)* And say it.

TISH: I like you do you like me?...I like you do you like me?

JEAN: How do you feel?

TISH: Um. Silly.

JEAN: That's good. Let's be really silly. OK, Tishie? Let's do it like we're um ducks.

TISH: What?

JEAN: Yeah. Come on. We're Daffys, and they're Donalds. We make lots of money they get to look at duck breasts. Who's stupid here? Come on, quack quack quack quack....*(They move and quack.)* Now sing. *(They sing quacks. They laugh.)* Hey Tish.

TISH: Yeah?

JEAN: I like you. Do you like me?

✳

(Loud heavy metal plays.)

TISH: *(Looking at Dancer 3 dance.)* Roxanne?

DANCER 3: Huh?

TISH: You look great up there.

DANCER 3: Thanks.

TISH: Jean thought you were really hot. She really liked you.

DANCER 3: Yeah?

TISH: I do too. You're the best. How do you do it?

DANCER 3: I don't know, it's fun.

TISH: How do you do that with your hips?

DANCER 3: This?

TISH: Yeah. *(Dancer 3 shrugs.)* Is there something you think about?

DANCER 3: No.

TISH: Maybe you could show me.

DANCER 3: Maybe.

TISH: We could make an exchange. I could do your hair for you, or your make up. I'm good with make up.

DANCER 3: Maybe.

✳

(Danny's apartment.)

DANNY: Hey, Beautiful.

TISH: Danny, do you still like me?

DANNY: Yeah.

TISH: What do you like about me?

DANNY: You know.

TISH: Tell me.

DANNY: You have soft skin. You're sexy.

TISH: What else?

DANNY: The way you look.

TISH: Uh huh.

DANNY: The way you move.

TISH: Uh huh.

DANNY: Your body.

TISH: You like it?

DANNY: Yeah.

TISH: What else?

DANNY: The way you breathe. Your smell. Your breasts. You have great breasts. You still like me?

TISH: Yeah. You're sweet. Like ice cream.

DANNY: That's nice.

TISH: Could you hold me.

DANNY: *(He does.)* I'm sorry about.

TISH: Tighter.

DANNY: About—

TISH: Tighter...Tell me you like me.

DANNY: I like you.

TISH: Tell me you want me.

DANNY: I want you.

TISH: Tell me you want to fill me up. Do you want to fill me up?

DANNY: Yeah.

TISH: I want you to. Remember when we met?

DANNY: Yeah.

TISH: *(To audience:)* I met him at a bachelor party. I'd known Jean a week.

(Flashback.)

JEAN: Did it feel good?

TISH: Yeah.

JEAN: Just to dance?

TISH: Yeah. Thanks!

JEAN: Sure kiddo.

TISH: It was fun. I mean, I feel different since I met you. You're different.

JEAN: I would say so.

TISH: A guy asked me out.

JEAN: Good.

DANNY: Hi, I'm Danny. I've never seen someone take off their clothes.

TISH: Ever?

DANNY: I mean like that, not like that, I mean, you know. I'm just nervous 'cause you were really good and I think you're really beautiful and in a really good way and maybe I shouldn't say all that.

TISH: No, you can say it. Um, this is my friend, Jean. Everything I know she taught me.

DANNY: Wow, well you did a good job.

JEAN: Well, I had a good student. What are you good at?

DANNY: Um. Liking Tish. I'm good at that. I like her a lot.

JEAN: Come here. *(She kisses Tish on the lips.)* That's a better color for you. Have fun. *(Jean exits.)*

DANNY: Cool! Uh maybe we could—I could, maybe we. I could call you. Maybe. A movie. I mean. I just like you. I like to watch you dance.

*

(Music. Dancers dance.)

DANCER 2: I want Madonna.

DANCER 3: I want Nirvana.

DANCER 1: Jody Twatley.

TISH: Maybe it's the music.

DANCER 3: Foxy Lady.

DANCER 2: Mariah Carey.

TISH: Juke box music.

DANCER 1: Titney Houston.

DANCER 2: Bruce!

TISH: I can't hear it anymore.

DANCER 3: Alice in Chains.

DANCER 2: Something from *A Chorus Line.*

DANCER 3: Pearl Jam.

DANCER 1: Or—

TISH: I can't make it make sense.

DANCER 1: Helen. Reddy. *(Music out.)*

DANCER 3: I hate her music.

DANCER 2: I hate her music.

DANCER 1: I hate her music.

TISH: I can't dance to this music.

(Dressing room.)

TISH: In India if your husband doesn't like you he burns you.

DANCER 2: Really?

DANCER 1: You watch too much television.

TISH: I read about it.

DANCER 2: Can I borrow your lipstick?

DANCER 1: Then you read too much.

TISH: They do it and and nobody cares, nobody. What do you think about that?

DANCER 2: Wow.

DANCER 1: So why don't they leave the country?

TISH: Where are they gonna go?

DANCER 1: Iowa. They can go to Iowa.

DANCER 2: Yeah.

DANCER 1: *(To Dancer 2.)* And you can go with them.

TISH: Did you read about the guy who stabbed people on the street if they bumped into him and didn't say 'excuse me'?

DANCER 1: That guy used to come here. Sharp tipper. Get it?

DANCER 2: That's not funny.

DANCER 1: Hey, if I say it's funny, it's funny.

DANCER 3: Are we laughing?

DANCER 2: *(Giggles, then:)* Did you read about all the money those women who got breasts implants are getting?

DANCER 1: You mean, the money their lawyers are getting.

TISH: Silicone disease.

DANCER 2: I use silicone to waterproof my boots.

DANCER 1: I was gonna get some of those. Ex-tend my career a little.

DANCER 2: But all those women got sick.

DANCER 1: Hey, I'm talking about the salt water kind.

DANCER 2: Still.

DANCER 3: Do I look sick?

DANCER 2: No.

DANCER 3: I get sick I'll go to a doctor.

DANCER 2: Yeah, but, I did research. You lose feeling, don't you?

DANCER 1: Hey, I fed my son with these. If I have to put salt water baggies in 'em to send him to college then so be it.

DANCER 2: Yeah, right.

DANCER 1: Are you one of those feminists?

DANCER 2: Um—

DANCER 1: A bunch of them came in here one night, like a tour group, a hairy leg convention, staring at me like I'm a victim. So I stared right back and started to talking to 'em right while I was dancing. Fucking feminists. Who the fuck are you to tell me what to do? You want to help women? You want to help the women who need help? Don't put us down. Don't say we are adding to the problem by showing our God given breasts. Don't tell me I'm less than you, you elitist bitch. Don't tell me the way I talk is making me a fucking victim, bitch. Don't tell me I can't say bitch, bitch. You act like you're better than me, smarter than me, more enlightened than me, well come from where I come from and see where you would have ended up. You want to be my sister? Get me better working hours. Get me a dressing room I can take a nap in. But don't tell me I'm not worthy. Don't tell me I shouldn't do what I choose to do. I make money with my body. You make money with your narrow mind. You don't want to be me, I don't want to be you. I don't tell you what to think, you don't tell me what to dance. Objectify, my ass. It's my ass. *(She turns around, pulls up her skirt, sticks her butt out.)* I've always been a bad girl. I'll always be a bad girl. That's who I am. That's what I do. It's no better and it's no worse. You want to be a feminist, then don't blame me, and don't try to rescue me.

DANCER 2: Oh, no, I'm not one of those.

✳

(Flashback.)

JEAN: What happened?

TISH: Some man tried to grab me—under my dress he almost—God.

JEAN: What'd you do?

TISH: I I ran in here.

JEAN: So you're safe, right?

TISH: Well—no.

JEAN: If you'd been on the street you might be dead by now, as long as you're here, you're safe. Ok?

TISH: Well—

JEAN: Hey, did he have a big nose that looks like a penis?

TISH: How'd you know?

JEAN: Cause I know that guy. He's a jerk. If dicks were as big as noses he'd have it made.

TISH: Yeah.

JEAN: His looks like it has a foreskin.

TISH: Eew.

JEAN: He wears a condom on it when he has a cold—looks like an elephant. *(Tish smiles.)* If he tells a lie, what do you think happens?

TISH: It gets hard?

JEAN: Maybe he'd pay us for a nose job. *(Tish laughs a little)* What do you think his wife calls him?

TISH: Um, Penisocchio?

JEAN: Go tell him he has a big nose.

TISH: No.

JEAN: Yeah, go ahead.

TISH: I can't.

JEAN: Yes you can.

TISH: No.

JEAN: Why not? You afraid? Hey, you want to be my friend you can't be afraid. You gotta put your arms out and laugh like an airplane.

(Jean puts Tish's arms out like an airplane and sends Tish to the door.)

TISH: Excuse me sir, yeah you, your nose looks like a dick.

JEAN: What did he say?

TISH: He said, it's snot! *(They laugh.)*

JEAN: Hey, Daffy, you wearing any make up?

TISH: Yeah.

JEAN: It's not enough. I'm gonna give you a new face. Watch. I want you to do this every day. *(She dumps out make up bag.)* They're not allowed to touch you, those are the rules, they break the rules, they got thrown out. I can't do this *(Jean touches her.)* unless you let me. OK? *(She puts make up on Tish.)*

TISH: Why do men like breasts?

JEAN: Oh, 'cause they don't have them.

TISH: Why do they like them to stand up?

JEAN: 'Cause that's what they want their dicks to do.

TISH: Why do they watch us dance?

JEAN: 'Cause they're afraid to dance with us.

TISH: Men.

JEAN: Hey, kiddo, there's no problem with men. You just have to know what you want. If you want money, dry hustle: take what you can get, but don't get wet. If you want good sex, buy it.

TISH: What?

JEAN: You get what you pay for.

TISH: You're kidding.

JEAN: No. Sammy Chuck, New York's best fuck. You want his number?

❋

TISH: *(To the audience.)* Did you ever keep doing something even though you forgot how to do it?

DANCER 2: Sometimes I forget how to walk and I almost fall, but then I remember.

DANCER 3: Sometimes I forget how to how to fuck. Right in the middle of it.

DANCER 1: I keep forgetting how old I am.

TISH: There's something I keep trying to remember.

DANCER 2: I forget which train to take.

DANCER 1: I forgot how to read.

DANCER 3: My bike.

TISH: Something.

DANCER 2: I keep forgetting the lyrics.

JEAN: I forgot to ask who it is.

DANCER 3: I forgot my helmet.

DANCER 2: I forgot to ask.

TISH: I forgot what I forgot.

JEAN: To lock the door.

TISH: Did you do it?

DANCER 1: What she looked like.

DANCER 3: Her name.

DANCER 2: My tweezers.

TISH: *(Pointing to the audience.)* Did you do it? Did you?

JEAN: I forgot the number for 911.

TISH: I forgot how to dance.

JEAN: I guess I forgot how to breathe. You know, after, I guess that's how you die. You forget how to breathe. Your heart forgets how to pump, your brain to think.

*

(*Sam's apartment.*)

TISH: Hi. My name is Tish.

SAM: Pay first.

TISH: How much?

SAM: 100 to start. What do you want?

TISH: I know this sounds like a cliché, but I just want to talk.

SAM: Oh yeah? What kind of talk?

TISH: I'm a friend of Jean's.

SAM: And you want to talk? Don't you like me? She does. A lot. She knows I'm the best. I get her very hot.

TISH: Don't you know what happened?

SAM: No, what happened? She find Mr. Right?

*

(*Flashback.*)

JEAN: I met someone new.

TISH: Doctor, Lawyer, Indian Chief?

JEAN: Musician.

TISH: Yeah?

JEAN: So I ditched Darren. Limp Dick Darren.

TISH: Wow.

JEAN: Told him he needed a twelve step program. Limp Dicks Anonymous. Where you find your harder power...I'm in love.

TISH: What?

JEAN: He's sweet like hot fudge.

TISH: You really like him?

JEAN: Love.

TISH: Wow, really?

JEAN: I would give him my heart.

TISH: Who?

JEAN: Bobby... ...I would give him my heart.

TISH: Yeah?

JEAN: I just hope he knows what to do with it.

TISH: Yeah.

JEAN: I mean. My heart. Now that's a handful.

TISH: Where did you meet?

JEAN: Club. Downtown. He's different.

TISH: She said.

JEAN: I'm in love. He's sweet. Like hot fudge. It'll be different.

TISH: What's his name?

JEAN: Bobby.

*

(*Tish's apartment.*)

TISH: Someone followed me. Someone was following me.

DANNY: You want to call the police?

TISH: I don't know.

DANNY: Let's call the police.

TISH: No. OK, I don't know.

DANNY: Do you want to? Or do you think you don't want to?

TISH: I don't know.

DANNY: How long do you think he followed you?

TISH: I don't know.

DANNY: When did you notice it?

TISH: I don't know.

DANNY: Are you sure there was someone there?

TISH: Yes, I'm sure. I have eyes, don't I?

DANNY: Yes.

TISH: Is that all you can say? Is that all you can say?

DANNY: What do you want me to say? I said we can call the police, that's the thing to do if someone was following you, you call the police, they make out a report, that's their job.

TISH: What are they gonna do? Huh? Have a cop follow me around? You think they're gonna do that? They won't even take my phone calls and you think they're gonna give me private protection?

DANNY: OK. What would you like me to do?

TISH: You just don't get it, do you? Every time I get upset you offer some practical solution so you don't have to talk to me. You say call the police, you say don't worry, if you're tired go to sleep, if it's broken fix it. What good is that? I don't see what good that is. Have a nice day and sweet dreams. What does that mean? What can that possibly mean? Don't take any wooden nickels. Look both ways before crossing and watch out for murderers.

DANNY: I'm sorry she died. I didn't do it. I don't know who did. I don't know anyone who would want to do that. If you want to know what I think, I think you should quit your job. I think there are a lot of other things you can do.

TISH: I can't quit my job.

DANNY: Why not?

TISH: Um. Because.

DANNY: Why?

TISH: Because, that's where she was. I have to be where she was.

DANNY: Why?

TISH: 'Cause. If—if I quit, I'll never know, I'll never figure it out. Something happened. There's something that happened, and I have to know. Danny, I need to know. Someone took her away. It was a man. Someone she might have known, might have liked, might have loved.

DANNY: OK, I'm gonna go look. I'm gonna go outside and I'll look. *(He exits.)*

TISH: Someone took her away. Her smile, her hair, her laugh. I want it back.

✳

TISH: *(Hardboiled with a detective hat.)* Where were you on the night of June 23rd?

DANCER 1: You look ridiculous.

TISH: What were your feelings for Jean?

DANCER 1: What were yours?

TISH: Do you have an alibi?

DANCER 1: Do you have your marbles?

TISH: It was late. It was the kind of late that announces itself as late. I walked home. Something was in the air.

DANCER 1: Too much TV.

TISH: A thick crust of apprehension. A looming dooming something.

DANCER 1: You need a vacation.

TISH: You been here the longest, right? You're the biggest cactus in this desert.

DANCER 1: What?

TISH: Who do you think did it?

DANCER 1: Have you been taking that spirulina I gave you?

TISH: I'm gonna find him.

DANCER 1: If you do, you'll be dead, so what good will it be? You won't even know that you know. Might as well stay alive and not know, than be dead and know, you know?

TISH: *(To audience.)* A girl worked crosstown. Her boyfriend boiled her. Why? For the broth?

❋

(Music and movement transition.)

TISH: I go to her apartment. I have the keys,

JEAN: In case I go away.

TISH: She said.

JEAN: It's good to have someone have your keys.

> *(Jean's apartment. Bright lights. Silence. Tish finds an appointment book. She opens it, reads.)*

TISH: June 23rd. "Bobby." *(Tish finds a flyer. She reads it:)* "The Neptune Bar's own House Band. Every night at 10."

❋

> *(Jazz club. Saxophone music plays. Tish listens.)*

JEAN: Look at him.

TISH: Yeah.

JEAN: I'm in love.

TISH: She said.

JEAN: A guy named Bobby.

TISH: Look at him.

JEAN: Yeah.

DANNY: Where are you going?

TISH: *(To Danny.)* Out. *(Bobby walks by her table. He stops.)* Hi.

BOBBY: Hi.

TISH: Look at him.

SAM: Mr. Right.

TISH: Hi.

BOBBY: Hi.

TISH: How do you play like that?

BOBBY: It's what I do. They're closing. The place, it's closed.

TISH: Oh.

DANNY: I made you pancakes.

TISH: All I can hear now

DANNY: Fresh blueberries.

TISH: Is that

DANNY: Warm syrup.

TISH: Music.

DANNY: Hello?

TISH: It sounded like her.

DANNY: Tish.

TISH: It was her.

BOBBY: What's your name?

TISH: Uh. Patricia. You?

BOBBY: Bobby.

*

TISH: Remember you were this close, you said did I ever think about it, you said don't be afraid, you said, and I couldn't. You were right there and I couldn't—your hair so red, eyes blue, skin soft, I wanted to touch, I did, to touch something as soft as clouds. Oh God, if I had one wish I'd wish I'd fallen asleep right then. I wish I'd fallen asleep and the rest of this has been a dream and I could wake up, right now if only I could wake up and be close to you. Jean. I miss the lines around your eyes when you smile, and the mole on your back. A kiss from God, you said. And I knew it was true.

*

(*Sam's apartment.*)

SAM: Hello, Sunshine.

TISH: Do you like what you do?

SAM: I like everything about me and everything I do. I wake up in the morning with a smile on my face and hard-on in my shorts, ready for the new day. Did they ever call you Tushie when you were a kid, Tish?

TISH: When did you two meet?

SAM: Five years and thousands of dollars ago.

TISH: Don't you care?

SAM: What am I gonna do, kill myself?

TISH: Did she really pay you?

SAM: This is a business. I don't do it 'cause I can't find anyone to sleep with.

TISH: She didn't exactly have a hard time finding men.

SAM: Not the kind she wanted. You think she liked fucking rich men with fat bellies who paid her rent, her dinners, and her bill at Bloomies? Or her old boyfriend P-O-T head? Think sex was good with Mr. No More Braincells? Or the guy before that who drank til the veins in his cock were waterlogged.

TISH: Then she met someone new.

SAM: Wasn't gonna last.

TISH: Why not?

SAM: 'Cause he decided to kill her.

TISH: Why do you say that?

SAM: Hunch.

TISH: Why?

SAM: She meets this great new guy, all she can say is how great he is, she lets down her well built up guard, and she's dead. Who do you think did it? Domino pizza boy? I think it was Mr. Too Wonderful.

TISH: Well if it was him, I'll find out.

SAM: Oh? How are you going to do that?

TISH: Maybe I'll just ask.

SAM: Take it from me, you don't just ask, OK? You want to dance with a killer, you better learn some new steps.

TISH: Do you give lessons?

SAM: Come again?

TISH: Lessons. You know, how to uh dry hustle. I'll pay.

SAM: Uh-huh.

TISH: So?

SAM: So. Keep your eyes open in the back of your head, don't let anyone in your heart, and whoever tries to hustle you, you out hustle them. *(Holds his hands behind her head.)* How many fingers?

TISH: Three?

SAM: Keep 'em open. Here, your wallet. I'm honest for a hustler. Hey Tishie. I like you.

TISH: Yeah?

SAM: Yeah. I like a lot about you.

TISH: Like what?

SAM: Time's up. You want to know, come back.

*

(Dressing room.)

DANCER 1: We're illegal in the state of Indiana.

DANCER 3: What?

DANCER 2: I always get Indiana, Iowa and Idaho mixed up.

DANCER 1: Supreme Court says we're illegal there, if they want to, they can arrest us.

DANCER 3: What?

DANCER 2: Indiana has a good music theater department.

DANCER 1: It's not the way we dance—

DANCER 2: *(She sings something.)*

DANCER 1: —'cause that's protected under the constitution—but it's the actual nipple. A woman's nipple is immoral, obscene.

DANCER 2: What's that from?

DANCER 3: What?

DANCER 2: Who wrote that?

DANCER 1: Rehnquist.

DANCER 3: Oh.

DANCER 1: So I brought this for the dressing room. *(She holds up a giant poster.)*

DANCER 2: Oh God.

DANCER 3: What is it?

DANCER 2: It looks scary.

DANCER 1: It's a nipple. My nipple I took it myself. It's illegal in Indiana—and New Jersey. I got it blown up.

DANCER 2: Oh.

DANCER 1: I'm hanging it here. Anyone have a problem with that?

DANCER 3: Doesn't look like a nipple.

DANCER 1: What's a nipple supposed to look like?

*

(Jazz club.)

TISH: Hi again.

BOBBY: You a music fan?

TISH: Sort of.

BOBBY: What brings you?

TISH: I uh like the way you play.

BOBBY: Yeah?

TISH: I don't know how you can do that in this world, I mean, with what's happened.

BOBBY: What's happened?

TISH: Just everything, the world, you know.

BOBBY: That's why I do it.

TISH: Oh.

BOBBY: It's not that bad.

TISH: Huh?

BOBBY: You look sad.

TISH: It's just the shape of my face. I um. Do you give lessons?

BOBBY: You want to learn the sax?

TISH: I'd like to be able to do that.

BOBBY: I don't think so.

TISH: How 'bout a tape? Could I possibly make a tape?

BOBBY: What?

TISH: I'd like to dance to it. I mean in my apartment. Could you make me a tape?

*

(Dressing Room. Tish puts on a scarf.)

DANCER 1: Gingko. That's what you need.

TISH: What?

DANCER 1: Better than that other stuff. Gingko. It's an herb. For clarity of thought. New here, old in China. Very expensive, but I have a special just today. You want some?

TISH: Sure.

DANCER 1: Oh, and I have some new G strings—they have pockets on the sides, so by the end of the night you feel like a cowboy.

TISH: You know a guy named Bobby? Friend of Jean's?

DANCER 1: Why?

TISH: I though I might meet him.

DANCER 1: Don't meet the guys she hung with.

TISH: Why?

DANCER 1: Don't go hanging where she hung unless you want to end up like her. She may have been well known, but she wasn't well liked.

TISH: Why?

DANCER 1: Y is the letter after X and before Z.

TISH: This guy he's a sax player.

DANCER 1: I've met a lot of players. When they're with me they keep their saxes in their pantses. Jesus, Tish, is that her scarf you're wearing?

*

(*Flashback:*)

TISH: Don't tell.

JEAN: I won't.

TISH: Oh God, don't tell.

JEAN: Who am I gonna tell?

TISH: OK. You swear? (*Jean holds up her right hand, crosses her heart.*) My father. I think about my father.

JEAN: When you're dancing?

TISH: Don't tell.

JEAN: I won't…Well, what about him?

TISH: Oh, if he were around, say, and I never knew him so maybe he is, what would he think.

JEAN: About?

TISH: Me. Would he like me? Would he think I'm pretty? Would he like me better than anyone else? Would he think I look like my mother? Would he like me 'cause I look like him—or her? Would he know who I am?

JEAN: Huh.

TISH: Can I tell you something else?

JEAN: Sure.

TISH: When I was a kid I used to think he was watching. That there was a hidden TV camera and he saw everything I did. Even if he was dead. I thought that's what heaven might be: a room with TV screens and fathers watching.

JEAN: How old were you when he left, baby?

TISH: Little. You know, little.

JEAN: If it helps you to think he's watching, then you think it. Cause who knows. Sounds like he's the kind of guy would like this place.

TISH: Yeah.

JEAN: No marriages, no weddings, no child support, don't even have to touch or talk or tell anyone your name. Don't even have to tip. He'd probably be a nontipper, huh?

TISH: Probably.

JEAN: Except you, Honey. If he saw you, he'd give you a big tip.

TISH: Yeah.

JEAN: At least a twenty. Fucker.

TISH: Yeah.

JEAN: Here. *(Hugs her.)* A hug from your buddy, Jean. Better than Daddy any day.

TISH: How 'bout you? What do you think about?

JEAN: Flying.

TISH: In a plane?

JEAN: No, just me, up in the air, arms out.

TISH: Where are you going?

JEAN: Oh, some place else.

TISH: Miami?

JEAN: Better.

TISH: Vegas?

JEAN: Better.

TISH: Hawaii?

JEAN: Better.

TISH: Where?

JEAN: Some place else, kiddo. Hey, Tish.

TISH: Yeah?

JEAN: I never told that to anyone.

TISH: Yeah. I know. You must have been something as a kid.

JEAN: I guess.

TISH: Did you read comic books? I read a lot of comics. Did you?

JEAN: Uh, Thor, I was into Thor.

TISH: I loved Archie. And I knew I was a Betty and he'd never love me. I wanted to be Veronica so bad.

JEAN: Didn't you ever look at them, Betty and Veronica?

TISH: For hours.

JEAN: Well didn't you see? They were exactly the same. It was just the color of their hair that was different.

✱

DANCER 2: *(Sings something.)*

TISH: You met anyone suspicious?

DANCER 2: Like who?

TISH: Like someone who's sexy and different, who you could really like, who smells like chocolate.

DANCER 2: Gosh, not yet.

✱

TISH: *(Tish tries to imitate Dancer 3.)* Is it like this?

DANCER 3: No.

TISH: Like this?

DANCER 3: You're trying too hard. *(She tries again.)* I don't think this is gonna work.

TISH: No, no, it's great. It's great. You're a great teacher. Really. Great. I think I got it now. It's like we're ducks, right?

DANCER 3: What?

TISH: Ducks: quack quack.

DANCER 3: What are you talking about?

TISH: You know. *(She starts to move like a duck and quack.)*

DANCER 3: Maybe you should quit, you know, do something else. You look like an asshole.

TISH: Maybe we could do it like assholes! *(Makes farting noises.)*

DANCER 3: No more lessons.

✱

(Danny's apartment.)

TISH: Dance for me.

DANNY: What?

TISH: Come on, dance for me.

DANNY: I don't think so.

TISH: I dance for you. Show me—I forgot. Come on. Babe, I want to watch you. I want you to watch me watching you. Come on.

DANNY: I don't know how.

TISH: Yes you do. We all know how. Try it. It'll be fun. You're very sexy, Danny, and I know about these things. *(He tries to dance.)* You look a little self conscious, Sweetie.

DANNY: I am!

TISH: Keep doing it....Yeah, like you like me and you know I like you.

DANNY: My hips don't do that—that thing you do.

TISH: What?

DANNY: That thing girls do with their hips—I can't.

TISH: Try.

DANNY: I am.

TISH: Take something off. Take something off—yeah—like you know what they want, you feel it, you see it, they want you.

DANNY: I feel stupid.

TISH: It's OK to be stupid. Be really stupid. *(He dances very silly.)* Good. Sexy. I think you're very hot. I want you. Feel how I want you?

DANNY: Yeah.

TISH: The way you move makes me me want to take you, feel you. That's it—save the best for last—that's it. How does it feel?

DANNY: Good.

TISH: You like it?

DANNY: Yeah.

TISH: You feel the music?

DANNY: Yeah.

TISH: What if I gave you money?

DANNY: I'd take it.

TISH: What if I wanted to touch you?

DANNY: I'd let you.

TISH: And grab you.

DANNY: Great.

TISH: What if I turned out the lights?

DANNY: Go ahead.

TISH: And tied you to the bed?

DANNY: Wow.

TISH: What if I took out a—
DANNY: —You like it?
TISH: Yeah, I like it.
DANNY: What do you like?
TISH: The way you look, you have soft skin, you're sexy.
DANNY: Yeah?
TISH: Yeah.
DANNY: This is pretty good, Sweetie. This is good.

(*Flashback.*)
TISH: Without you I never would have met Danny.
JEAN: Are you thanking me for that?
TISH: Yeah, he's sweet.
JEAN: So's a Milky Way, but who'd want to put it between their legs?
TISH: I really like him.
JEAN: Yeah well, I liked Darren. He wasn't even a Milky Way, he was more like taffy. Couldn't get him out from between my teeth. Danny and Darren, even the names are similar, you know? Thank God I met Bobby. I look at him and you know what I see?
TISH: What?
JEAN: Me.

(*Jazz club.*)
TISH: So how long you been working here?
BOBBY: A while.
TISH: I'm a waitress. Place in Jersey. Mornings.
BOBBY: Uh huh.
TISH: Must be hard on your family. Staying out late.
BOBBY: Nice scarf.
TISH: Thanks. My father gave it to me. So, where are you from?
BOBBY: Why do you ask?
TISH: Curious.
BOBBY: Well, you know what they say.
TISH: What?…Oh.
BOBBY: Meow.

TISH: Right...That last song. What's it called?

BOBBY: Don't know.

TISH: You wrote it?

BOBBY: Yeah.

TISH: It's um. It's very.

BOBBY: What?

TISH: I don't know.

BOBBY: Me neither. Can't give it a name.

TISH: Is it new?

BOBBY: Yeah.

BOBBY: Why do you come here?

TISH: I like the music.

BOBBY: Rose cinder.

TISH: What?

BOBBY: Your lipstick. Rose cinder.

TISH: I think so.

BOBBY: Frosted, right?

TISH: Yeah. How do you know?

BOBBY: Popular shade.

TISH: Oh?

BOBBY: That's the title.

TISH: What?

BOBBY: Rose cinder.

TISH: Oh, I like that.

BOBBY: You're not really a waitress are you?

TISH: I'm not?

BOBBY: You're an heiress and you want me to play on your yacht for a year.

TISH: Right.

BOBBY: Right.

TISH: Bobby.

BOBBY: Yeah?

TISH: Sit down. *(He does.)* When you play that song—Rose Cinder—

BOBBY: Yeah?

TISH: —It looks like you're angry. I mean I'm just interested.

BOBBY: Give me your hand.

TISH: Huh?

BOBBY: Give me your hand. *(She puts out her hand. He looks at it.)* When I think about what I don't have I get angry.

TISH: What's it got to do with my hand?

BOBBY: The way it looks.

TISH: Yeah.

BOBBY: Reminds me—

TISH: —Of—

BOBBY: —What I don't have—

TISH: —And—

BOBBY: —It makes me angry.

TISH: You want to—

BOBBY: —Grab you, actually. I want to grab you. You shouldn't come around here.

TISH: Why not?

BOBBY: You just shouldn't.

TISH: Why?

BOBBY: I'm not someone to be hanging around with. You don't come back, I'd say you were being smart.

TISH: Give me your hand. *(He doesn't.)* I like you, do you like me?

BOBBY: Is there something you want to know? What do you want to know?

TISH: Your secrets, I want to know your secrets.

BOBBY: Hey I'm an open book.

TISH: Maybe we should just head for the library.

BOBBY: You look like such a sweet girl.

TISH: Do you want a taste?

BOBBY: Maybe.

TISH: Yeah, where?

BOBBY: In the library.

TISH: No, where on me? My neck? Would you like to leave a mark? So everyone would know you'd been there?

BOBBY: I don't leave marks. *(He puts a cassette on the table, exits.)*

(Dressing room.) (Dancer 1 brings in another large poster.)

DANCER 1: This is to commemorate that New York has declared the nipple is legal.

DANCER 2: Great.

DANCER 1: The left one is in New York, the right one, is in New Jersey where the nipple has to be covered, even if with saran wrap.

DANCER 3: I used Vaseline in Jersey.

DANCER 2: It's because of the Pilgrims.

DANCER 1: Puritans.

DANCER 2: That's an oil.

DANCER 3: Oil doesn't work, it drips.

TISH: You know the guy with the big nose?

DANCER 1: Which one?

TISH: His nose looks like a penis?

DANCER 2: Eew.

DANCER 1: I don't care if his nose is his dick, and his dick is his nose, so long as his money is as green as his snot.

DANCER 2: Did you see the lap dancing place?

DANCER 1: Not for me. You're sitting on their lap, and they come in their pants? You think they wear condoms under those pants?

TISH: You get wet, you get stupid.

DANCER 1: Stupid? You get dead. All the whores in Thailand are dead.

DANCER 2: Did you say Thailand?

DANCER 3: She said Thailand.

DANCER 2: I have a callback for The King and I in New Jersey.

DANCER 1: Well, make sure to cover your nipples.

✳

(Sam's apartment.)

TISH: What was it like?

SAM: What?

TISH: With Jean.

SAM: Words cannot describe.

TISH: Oh.

SAM: I could show you.

TISH: You mean—

SAM: You want to know, I'm the one to show.

TISH: Maybe you could just tell me or maybe you could sort of show me.

SAM: There was no sort of about it.

TISH: Maybe if you just answered my questions.

SAM: You afraid? It won't kill you. She wasn't afraid. Right?

TISH: Tell me—how—what—did she like?

SAM: She liked to leave marks like a map. And she liked to have them left on her. What do you like?

TISH: I have a boyfriend. We're—fine.

SAM: Then what are you doing here?

TISH: Learning.

SAM: You're a bad liar, Tish. I can see you through you like Vaseline on Saran Wrap.

TISH: You think you can.

SAM: Ooooh, a challenge. I'll play.

TISH: You're all bark Sam, even I can see that. You're just a face with attitude.

SAM: You think I don't know that? Nice try.

TISH: You're everything that didn't work about her life rolled into one. A dry hustle. You are a dry hustle.

SAM: I am?

TISH: Do you even sweat?

SAM: Come here and find out.

TISH: Is there anything real about you?

SAM: Yeah. One thing. Come here.

TISH: I'm not interested.

SAM: You're lying.

TISH: Oh?

SAM: Can't you feel how I want you?

TISH: No.

SAM: She wanted me.

TISH: She stopped coming here, didn't she?

SAM: Don't you want to feel what she wanted? *(He moves his hand down her body.)*

TISH: God.

SAM: Yes?

TISH: What would she say?

SAM: Do you like me?

TISH: And you'd say.

SAM: Yeah.

TISH: And she'd say.

SAM: You're the best, you're the fucking best.

TISH: Did it ever go too far?

SAM: Hey. China and back wasn't too far. *(He kisses her. She pushes him away.)* You're a bad liar. You want to learn how to hustle, you better learn how to lie. *(He pushes her towards Bobby.)*

*

(*Jazz club.*)

BOBBY: So where do you live?

TISH: Why do you ask?

BOBBY: Curious.

TISH: Well, you know what they say.

BOBBY: Where'd you get the perfume, Patty?

TISH: It was my mother's. Where'd you learn to play like that?

BOBBY: Can I call you?

TISH: Well. I live in this place where they're not big on calling.

BOBBY: What is it a convent?

TISH: Ha—no.

BOBBY: I don't like to be lied to.

TISH: Oh?

BOBBY: Is it that you have a boyfriend or what?

TISH: Boyfriend.

BOBBY: Live together?

TISH: Not exactly.

BOBBY: Well if you have a boyfriend that you kind of live with, what are you doing here?

TISH: Maybe it's not working.

BOBBY: Why don't you go make it work?

TISH: Maybe I can't.

BOBBY: Then maybe you should leave him.

TISH: You always give such good advice?

BOBBY: Hey, I'm glad you have a boyfriend.

TISH: Don't you like me?

BOBBY: Is this the cha cha? I go forward you go back, I go back you go forward? Is that what you get off on?

TISH: Is that what you get off on?

BOBBY: Be a good girl and work it out. (*He steps away.*)

TISH: I would give you my heart.

BOBBY: What?

TISH: Bobby. I would give you my heart.

BOBBY: Forget that, you hear?

TISH: What?

BOBBY: It's your heart. You keep it.

TISH: I would. If you wanted it.

BOBBY: What am I gonna do with your heart? What are you gonna do
without it?

*

(*Tish is reading.*)
DANNY: (*Enters singing.*)
TISH: Sweetie, I'm reading.
DANNY: (*Sings.*)
TISH: Danny.
DANNY: OK. What are you reading?
TISH: "Why men kill and rape."
DANNY: Ah.
TISH: "Women in pieces."
DANNY: Want to go to the movies?
TISH: No.
DANNY: How 'bout a film where a man kills a woman. How bout that?
TISH: What?
DANNY: Joke.
TISH: Oh.
DANNY: Would you do this for me? If it had been me would you be
doing this for me?
TISH: What?
DANNY: I know you were friends, but this is crazy. It's like you were
in love. Is that it? Were you in love?
TISH: No. That's not it.
DANNY: Well, don't you think you're overreacting?
TISH: How can I be overreacting if this is how I'm reacting?
DANNY: Look. I I think if we moved out of the city, we wouldn't be
having these problems. I mean we could have a garden, go bike
riding. I know we've talked about it before, and you didn't want
to, but now I really think that's what we should do.
TISH: You think what we need to do is go bike riding. And do things.
DANNY: Yeah. You know, nature is important.
TISH: That's like telling a quadriplegic to just keep moving.
DANNY: Well, they do a lot now.
TISH: What?
DANNY: People in wheelchairs, they do a lot. They have races and
basketball, they go on the busses all the time. And there's this
new law, I mean a lot has been done. They are doing a lot.

TISH: What?

DANNY: OK maybe that sounds dumb, maybe sometimes I sound dumb, but it doesn't have to be like this. I mean, I think it's important to live somewhere you can see the birds out the window eating the worms, instead of seeing people eat each other. What I'm trying to say is I want to spend my life with you. I want to find a way so we can spend our lives together. That's what I want. But I want all of you.

TISH: You never said—

DANNY: I know I never said. Why do you think I never said? Do you want to get married? Do you want to look at this house? Do you want to come to bed with me? Do you want to get married?

TISH: Is it me you want to marry? Me? Now? *This* me? Or the me when we met? *(He doesn't answer.)*

DANNY: Sweetie?

⁂

TISH: I'm reading here.

DANCER 1: I'm thinking about the money.

TISH: I need to read.

DANCER 2: I'm thinking about Ethel Merman.

DANCER 3: I'm thinking about the guy in the corner.

TISH: "Why Men Kill Women."

DANNY: I'm thinking about her.

DANCER 2: Angela Lansbury.

TISH: I'm thinking about Bobby.

DANCER 2: Tyne Daly.

TISH: She loved him.

DANCER 3: Sometimes I forget how to fuck.

TISH: I can't.

DANCER 1: If you do you'll be dead.

TISH: Stop thinking.

DANCER 2: I want Madonna.

DANCER 3: I want Nirvana.

DANCER 1: Jody Twatley.

TISH: About him.

(Bobby's music plays.)

DANCER 1: Oh God.

DANCER 3: What is it?

DANNY: I'm thinking about him.

DANCER 2: I can't dance to this.

TISH: It was him.

SAM: Domino pizza boy?

DANCER 1: God!

DANCER 3: Tish!

DANCER 2: God!

TISH: She forgot how to breathe, I guess.

DANCER 1: I'm thinking about the money.

DANCER 2: I'm thinking about Tyne Daly.

DANCER 3: Sometimes I forget how to fuck.

SAM: He decided to kill her.

TISH: *(To Jean, facing audience.)* It was different with you.

DANNY: *(To Tish.)* It was different with you.

TISH: *(What Jean said:)* It was different with him.

✳

SAM: You need to relax.

TISH: What?

SAM: You gotta relax.

TISH: Yeah.

SAM: Yeah.

TISH: Like ducks.

SAM: I don't do pet tricks. I know someone who does. I don't think he's ever done a duck though.

✳

(Jazz club.)

DANNY: Hi.

TISH: Hi. What are you doing here?

DANNY: I followed you.

TISH: What?

DANNY: I want to know what's going on. What's going on?

TISH: What do you mean?

DANNY: What's going on?

TISH: Nothing.

DANNY: You a jazz fan all of a sudden?

TISH: Look, let's go, OK? Let's just go. *(She stands. He grabs her arm.)*

DANNY: No, I like this place. Let's stay.

BOBBY: You all right?

TISH: Yes. Fine.

BOBBY: Who's this, your boyfriend?

TISH: This is Danny.

DANNY: Who are you?

TISH: This is Bobby.

DANNY: Nice to meet you, but if you would excuse us. We're having a conversation. *(Bobby doesn't move.)* Do you have a problem?

BOBBY: If you're giving her a hard time in any way then you're my problem. You understand?

DANNY: What are you, her bodyguard?

BOBBY: Psycho saxophonist, so as long as you're here, you better watch the fuck how you touch her and how you talk to her. I'm walking away now, but I'm watching. *(He walks away.)*

DANNY: Who the hell is that?

TISH: Bobby.

DANNY: You already told me his name. Is that what's been going on?

TISH: No.

DANNY: Well?

TISH: He's a friend. Can't I have a friend?

DANNY: You call that thing a friend?

TISH: I like the way he plays.

DANNY: And what else?

TISH: I come to hear the music.

DANNY: And what else?

TISH: That's it.

DANNY: Why didn't you invite me?

TISH: I didn't think you'd want to come.

DANNY: So you didn't invite me? Next time, invite me.

✳

DANCER 2: Which eye shadow is better?

TISH: What?

DANCER 2: I did one mocha and one jade.

TISH: It doesn't matter.

DANCER 2: OK. Geez. I thought you were nice.

TISH: No, I can't be nice. I cannot in any way be nice. It's not that I don't want to it's just I can't. What I think you should do is just—go home. Wherever you came from, go back.

DANCER 2: Now just wait a minute. I have an audition for Beauty and the Beast next week. I mean that is a big deal. I am not going back home. It's none of your business to tell me to go anywhere. You are not my mother. You're barely old enough to be my older sister. I mean you work here, don't you?—you're still here. I mean, why don't you get a life?

TISH: You're right. Maybe I can have yours.

DANCER 2: What?

TISH: Maybe I'll just take yours. It could happen, you know. I might seem like a friend, but what does that mean? One minute you're close, the next you're dead.

DANCER 2: I take it back about your being nice. I thought you liked me. But I guess you're just jealous. And that stuff you gave me, you should have told me about her. I never would have taken it. I heard she was a hooker. I would never do that. *(She shoves Jean's clothes at Tish.)* Here, I don't want it, it gives me the creeps. Like you.

*

TISH: I like you. Do you like me?

SAM: Christ, you sound like her.

TISH: Oh yeah?

SAM: It's like hearing a fucking ghost.

TISH: I bet I even feel like her.

SAM: Oh?

TISH: Teacher, want to see how much I learned?

SAM: What does that mean?

TISH: Means I'm sweet like she is and if you want a taste I'll give you one.

SAM: You'll give me one?

TISH: Yeah.

SAM: Since when?

TISH: Since now. I've got your wallet in my pocket. I bet it has a lot of cash in it.

SAM: Bullshit.

TISH: Check your pockets.

SAM: Fuck. Well you better give it back to me.

TISH: Why?

SAM: Because I said so.

TISH: If I don't?

SAM: You will be sure to regret it.

TISH: Is that what happened to her?

SAM: Fuck you.

TISH: Those eyes in the back of your head, you should keep them open. It's on the desk, your wallet, you put it on the desk.

*

(*Jazz club.*)

BOBBY: Patty Cake. Here. (*He gives her a box. Inside is a pair of stockings.*)

TISH: They're very. They feel.

BOBBY: Silk.

TISH: Yes.

BOBBY: There's something about them, I don't know. 40s. Black and white movie, or something. I thought of you. I actually thought of you in them.

TISH: Oh. Do you like legs?

BOBBY: What?

TISH: Legs—women's legs.

BOBBY: Sure. and yours are—

TISH: What?

BOBBY: They would look nice in those.

TISH: What do you like about me?

BOBBY: Oh, your smell.

TISH: And what does that make you want to do?

BOBBY: You ask a lot of questions.

TISH: Something wrong with that?

BOBBY: You really want to know?

TISH: I'm dying to know.

BOBBY: What?

TISH: I said I'm dying to know.

BOBBY: What—what do you want to know?

TISH: Oh, how you look in the dark, what you say in your sleep, how it would feel to be with you. How you play like that. Where did you get the tune? (*She puts the stockings on.*)

BOBBY: What are you doing?

TISH: Putting on my present. What does that make you want to do? Tell me. Are you into anything, you know, any—

BOBBY: What?

TISH: —thing unusual?

BOBBY: Like what?

TISH: You tell me. I want to hear what you're thinking.

BOBBY: Now?

TISH: Now.

BOBBY: I want to paint this room with your smell. Lock the door. Tie you down.

TISH: What else?

BOBBY: Tickle you from your ankle to the inside of your thigh where the skin is soft and white.

TISH: If you could would you take off that white part—would you want to carry it around with you? Take it home with you? Would you?

BOBBY: What are you saying?

TISH: I'm saying I like you, do you like me?

BOBBY: And I'm saying, for the last time, to keep away. Do you understand? This is getting very—

TISH: —Real.

BOBBY: Yeah. So I hope you're not playing with me. I can't have you be playing.

(Jean appears.)

TISH: *(To Jean.)* If you were here, if it had happened to someone somewhere else you would have—

JEAN: —laughed.

TISH: You would have found a way to make it—

JEAN: —funny.

BOBBY: I hope you're not playing with me.

TISH: What? Step on a crack—?

BOBBY: Break your mother's back…

JEAN: *(Laughs)*

TISH: *(To Jean.)* I never had a friend like you.

BOBBY: Pattycake.

TISH: …Pattycake.

BOBBY: …Bakers man.

TISH: Bake me a cake.

BOBBY: As fast as you can.

(He touches her hair.)

*

(Flashback.)

JEAN: Rub my head, kiddo. *(Tish does.)* Mmmm.

TISH: Um, Danny has this new idea, about leaving the city.

JEAN: Uh huh.

TISH: Getting a house, you know, not far. I think he wants me to go with him.

JEAN: That's not a good color for you.

TISH: Oh... What do you think?

JEAN: I think it clashes with your hair.

TISH: No, about moving, about Danny—

JEAN: How'd you meet him?

TISH: You know how we met.

JEAN: Remind me.

TISH: Bachelor party.

JEAN: So that's what I think, as long as he's a customer, great, but don't forget why he liked you.

TISH: It's not like that.

JEAN: Uh huh.

TISH: It's not.

JEAN: Fine, so quit your job, move to Peekskill Hicksville Blankville, just don't expect me to come visit. What are you gonna do there, paint the white on the fence? Clean the toilet bowl? Dance naked on his birthday?

TISH: You can't have everything. You can't do everything.

JEAN: Here. *(Jean takes off her shirt.)* This is a good color for you.

TISH: What?

JEAN: My shirt, it's yours.

TISH: What—why?

JEAN: Take yours off.

TISH: Why?

JEAN: Oh come on, I want to trade shirts. Take it off. *(Tish takes off her shirt, Jean now has both.)* Smells like you. You're a lovely girl.

TISH: Thanks.

JEAN: I remember when we met.

TISH: Yeah.

JEAN: Didn't know how to dance, how to look out for yourself, how to laugh. You were afraid to be looked at. But now I think you like it, right?

TISH: I guess.

JEAN: Do you ever think about it?

TISH: What?

JEAN: What it means to be really close to someone?

TISH: What?

JEAN: How soft it would be. Listen, what do you hear?...Remember? Mirror me. Come on. I like you, do you like me? Come on. Friends. *(They start to move together.)* I like you do you like me?

TISH: Yes. *(They dance, Tish hesitates.)*

JEAN: Don't be afraid. What do you think's gonna happen? *(They dance. Jean gets very close to Tish, touches her, Tish pulls away.)*

TISH: I I can't. I just—

JEAN: Suit yourself.

TISH: I can't. I'm sorry.

JEAN: What are you sorry about? It was just a dance.

TISH: I know, but.

JEAN: I still like you kiddo, always. You hear me? *(Jean exits.)*

✸

TISH: She was my friend. It's different when it's your friend. It's not like channel 5, page 3, 88 on your AM dial. It's. She was. My friend. I. See. She used to do my make up. We used to talk. And now I forgot.

✸

TISH: Roxanne?

DANCER 3: Yeah?

TISH: Is that your real name?

DANCER 3: No. Marjorie.

TISH: Can I just.

DANCER 3: What?

TISH: Can I just—

DANCER 3: What?

TISH: —touch you.

DANCER 3: Oh.

TISH: Just. There. Where it's soft. I just want to feel something soft.

DANCER 3: I don't think so.

TISH: Please.

DANCER 3: How much?

TISH: What?

DANCER 3: For how much? *(Dancer 3 exits.)*

*

(*Dancer 1 is in a special performing spot.*)

DANCER 1: What are you doing? It's my set.

TISH: How do you do it?

DANCER 1: You're not supposed to be here.

TISH: How do you keep dancing in this topless tundra?

DANCER 1: Uh uh. Not now.

TISH: You're the oldest duck in this pond, right?

DANCER 1: Right and quack quack, I'm telling you to move. You are stealing my money.

TISH: Is that all you care about?

DANCER 1: If you don't get out of here—

TISH: What was it like to be really close to her?

DANCER 1: No such thing, ok?

TISH: But you two were friends, until I came along. What happened?

DANCER 1: Hey, I was not her friend, she didn't have any. She was too busy thinking she was better than everyone.

TISH: She was.

DANCER 1: No, Tish, she wasn't. No one liked her except you. And she only put up with you 'cause your nose was browner than my butt.

TISH: That's not true.

DANCER 1: Sure kiddo. "Why don't you run to the store, buy me some makeup with your money, then come back and rub my head for me."

TISH: Did you do it?

DANCER 1: What?

TISH: Kill Jean.

DANCER 1: Stupid. Really stupid.

TISH: Did you?

DANCER 1: You just broke the camel's back. And I promise you—you just lost your fucking job. You have two minutes to get out of here. And then I'll have you thrown out. (*Dancer 1 exits.*)

*

SAM: You running around asking people if they killed her. What are they gonna do, tell you? And what if they do, you gonna believe them? And what if you do, that's an answer, to what? What does that answer? You keep running around asking questions, you'll get your head cut off. Maybe if you stopped, opened your mouth and looked inside you'd see something. I didn't kill her, but maybe I'm lying. You gotta trust me, but you can't, but you gotta, 'cause what else is there? And what if I am lying? What if I did it, what if I killer her, what are you gonna do, kill me? What good is that? Huh? That's not what you're looking for, Tushie, it's written all over your made up face. It's not gonna bring her back, it's not gonna make you into her, it's not gonna make me into her. She's gone. Whatever she gave you, it's already yours. You're looking in the wrong place. Get yourself a three-way mirror, and take a look, you'll see the back of your head, the front of your head, the side of your head. You can dye your hair every day if you want, it's still your hair. But hey what do I know, I'm just a hustler, I'll lie to you til the day I die. But what I'm saying now is the truth. You don't have to believe it, but what else you got to go on? Time's up.

TISH: No, it's not.

SAM: Yeah, it is.

TISH: No it's—

SAM: Up.

TISH: When can I come back?

SAM: You can't.

TISH: What?

SAM: I'm doing you a favor, OK, in her honor. Cause I liked her. She was my friend, too. So, you can't come back. I just gave you all my best stuff. I got nothing else to give. You want good sex, then yeah call me. You want something else, you're looking in the wrong place. Here. *(Gives her a mirror.)* What you want I don't have. You can believe me or you can not believe me. All you got is my word, but what's that worth, huh? *(Sam exits.)*

*

DANNY: Are you seeing that guy?

TISH: What?

DANNY: Are you seeing that psycho guy? Tell me.

TISH: His name is Bobby.

DANNY: I know his name. You told me his name. More than twice. Is that what's going on? I'll go there—I'll go there right now and ask him.

TISH: I.

DANNY: Yeah?

TISH: He knew Jean he.

DANNY: What?

BOBBY: Hey Pattycake.

TISH: Hi.

BOBBY: Dance with me.

DANNY: What?

TISH: He might have done it, it seems like—I think he's the one.

DANNY: I can believe that. I really can...So tell the police.

TISH: They don't care.

DANNY: So what does that mean. Huh? That you're what—what—flirt-ing with him? Is that what you've been doing? Is it? Talk to me.

BOBBY: Dance with me.

TISH: I can't do that.

BOBBY: Sure you can.

TISH: No.

DANNY: No, what?

TISH: No, I.

DANNY: What?

BOBBY: Come on, this is a dance tune.

TISH: I I have to—

DANNY: What?

TISH: I don't know, I. Please.

DANNY: Are you gonna see him again?

TISH: I have to—

BOBBY: Let's go arms out, like an airplane.

DANNY: What?

TISH: I don't know. I have to—.

DANNY: This is not working. I mean this is obviously not working.

TISH: Wait.

BOBBY: Hey—I'm not gonna hurt you.

DANNY: I don't understand it.

TISH: Please.

DANNY: I can't find the way to talk to you anymore.

TISH: Sweetie.

DANNY: It breaks my heart.

TISH: I'll be the way I was. I swear.

DANNY: I don't know what else to do.

TISH: I'll do anything.

DANNY: I can't do it anymore.

TISH: You can't do this. Not now.

DANNY: It breaks my heart. *(He exits.)*

TISH: Danny? Sweetheart? Oh God. Please. I can't. Danny? Please.

BOBBY: Come on. You afraid? You wanna be my friend, you can't be afraid. Let me show you. One arm here, one here. *(He puts her arms out.)* See? It's just a dance.

TISH: *(Partly to audience.)* I've got my arms out and there's nothing to hold onto.

BOBBY: Patricia.

TISH: I look down, nothing below my feet.

BOBBY: Tricia.

TISH: I look up, can't get back.

BOBBY: Look.

TISH: What?

BOBBY: Beneath you. Look. It's me.

TISH: One step and you're gone.

BOBBY: *(They touch.)* Have you thought about it?

TISH: What?

BOBBY: What it would be like to be close?

TISH: What?

BOBBY: Come home with me. I want you to come home with me.

TISH: I um.

BOBBY: Tonight.

TISH: Um.

BOBBY: After my next set.

TISH: Um, why?

BOBBY: I want to be alone with you.

TISH: And?

BOBBY: Touch you.

TISH: And?

BOBBY: That's enough isn't it? Is that what you want?

TISH: Sure.

BOBBY: So?

TISH: Um. I. See this is getting very—

BOBBY: Real.

TISH: And I.

BOBBY: Come on, don't be afraid. What do you think's gonna happen?

TISH: I I. I just.

BOBBY: Look, I'm telling you the truth here. If you don't want to be with me, for real, then don't be here when I get back. *(He exits. Tish exits.)*

*

(Lights change to the street. The look is identical to the top of the play.)

TISH: I'm walking down the street I'm looking for cracks. One step and you're gone. The whole sidewalk goes. They put it on the news, "Girl Gone". You don't think it can happen? Manhole covers, what man, does he have a gun, a knife, a saxophone? I'm walking, I'm looking for cracks. I cross the street. I stop: manhole cover, big crack, crazy glue, I can't move. Jean? *(She puts her hands to her head.)* Oh God, I'm in the middle of the street. Oh my God, cars honking, people yelling, I can see them but I can't hear them. Jean? How does it go, right foot, left foot, and you fall, isn't that what happened? Jean?

JEAN: You better move.

TISH: Hi.

JEAN: You're in the middle of the street.

TISH: Yeah.

JEAN: These people aren't gonna wait all day.

TISH: I'm trying to remember, how did that go, right foot, left foot?

JEAN: Look where you are. You can't just stand here.

TISH: I know. Could you show me?

JEAN: Tish. You gotta move, time is short, right? If anyone knows that, it's me, so get out of the street and go somewhere.

TISH: I can't, OK? Jesus, you're one to talk. What did you do? Fall in love with a psycho? Couldn't you have, you know, checked if he had a record. Or or asked if he carried a weapon. I mean, did you look in his eyes? Did you think? Did you know what was going on? Huh? Damn it. Show me. You just show me. Now.

JEAN: If you hold on this tight, you're gonna fall hard when you let go.

TISH: Jean.

JEAN: Yea., Me Jean, you Tish.

TISH: I miss you.

JEAN: No you don't.

TISH: Yeah I do—

JEAN: No, it's you who you miss. My red hair is buried in the ground. It's like you thinking your father's watching you from heaven. It ain't him. It's you watching you trying to put it together. Put it together kiddo. Or you might as well be me, right? So, move, kiddo, move. You listening? Patricia, what do you hear?

TISH: You not talking, you not beside me.

JEAN: Listen harder.

TISH: You not laughing.

> (*Bobby's music plays Tish turns away from Jean to hear it. Jean gives her one last look and is gone.*)

TISH: I can almost feel you. If I just keep going, I can almost feel you.

✳

> (*Saxophone music. Jazz club.*)

BOBBY: Hi.

TISH: Hi.

BOBBY: You're still here.

TISH: Yeah. I'm still here. And.

BOBBY: Yeah?

TISH: I want to be with you.

BOBBY: And?

TISH: I want to touch you.

BOBBY: And?

TISH: That's enough, isn't it?

BOBBY: Yeah.

TISH: But my place, OK? That's what I want. 'Cause I have a surprise.

BOBBY: Oh?

TISH: For when we get there. I think you'll like it.

BOBBY: Well, what is it?

TISH: If I tell you it won't be a surprise. And I don't want you to see, so here. (*She pulls her scarf out of her dress.*) You have to put this on.

BOBBY: Um, I—

TISH: Come on Bobby. I want you to come home with me. Is that what you want? (*She touches him.*) I'll give you what you want, whatever you want.

> (*As she ties the scarf around his eyes, the setting changes to Jean's apartment. A bed. A door. A dresser.*)

> (*Lights up. Tish and Bobby in Jean's apartment. He opens his eyes. They stand on opposite sides of the bed.*)

BOBBY: Oh God.

TISH: Surprise.

BOBBY: Oh my God.

TISH: Welcome back.

BOBBY: I don't—.

TISH: Can I get you anything?

BOBBY: What is this, a joke? Is this some kind of a joke?

TISH: No joke.

BOBBY: What are you, a cop?

TISH: No.

BOBBY: Jesus fuck. Who are you? You better tell me who you are.

TISH: My name is Tish.

BOBBY: Tish who?

TISH: Her friend, Tish.

BOBBY: You're her friend, Tish, her puppy dog friend Tish? What are you—working for the cops?

TISH: No.

BOBBY: So, what the hell are you doing?

TISH: I wanted to know you.

BOBBY: What? What did you want to know?

TISH: You.

BOBBY: You're a fucking liar. Playing with me, you playing with me? You bring me here with that 'fuck me look' that 'I want to be with you look'—

TISH: I couldn't tell you who I was.

BOBBY: —And what're you thinking, I'm the Boston Strangler—Son of Sam Zodiac killer?

TISH: If I'd told you what would you have done?

BOBBY: Exactly what I'm gonna do right now. Leave.

TISH: Oh, I don't think you should do that. I don't think it would be in your interest to do that. Maybe you should stay awhile. Maybe you should tell me about the last time you were here. When was that, by the way? Was she on the bed? That's what they say. That she was—

BOBBY: I read the paper.

TISH: I like you.

BOBBY: Oh yeah and I like you.

TISH: Yeah?

BOBBY: Oh yeah.

TISH: I think about you. How you said those things about my legs.

BOBBY: Well I thought I was talking to someone else, you know.

TISH: I said I'd give you what you want. What do you want? I'm wearing your stockings...You don't like them anymore? Come take them off me. What's the matter? Think I might not let you? You might hurt me?

BOBBY: Someone is gonna hurt you.

TISH: Oh?

BOBBY: Someone is definitely gonna hurt you.

TISH: The same person that hurt Jean?

BOBBY: You're a cunt, you know that?

TISH: No, actually, I'm not. I have one, but I'm not one.

BOBBY: You're a fucking cunt.

TISH: You like to say those words together? Fuck and cunt?

BOBBY: Yeah, I'm just a murdering rapist and if you say the right combination of fuck me words I'll do it to you.

TISH: What kind of words do you like?

BOBBY: Nothing fancy. Your basic Penthouse variety. Mix in some s&m lingo and I'm sure to go off. Ted Bundy with a sax, that's me. You think I killed her?

TISH: Did I say that?

BOBBY: I didn't fucking kill her.

TISH: Who did?

BOBBY: Someone else.

TISH: Why? Why would they do that?

BOBBY: There is no why these days. There's only how.

TISH: Then how?

BOBBY: Shit happens.

TISH: And it doesn't matter? *(He shrugs.)* You cared about her didn't you? She cared about you. So I assume you cared about her.

BOBBY: She tell you that?

TISH: Sure.

BOBBY: And I should believe you? I should believe anything you say? Patty?

TISH: Bobby. I think about you. I think about you touching me the way you touched her. I think about you watching me, about going too far, about taking you and you taking me and it all being on her bed. What do you think about?

BOBBY: You get that out of a book? Is that your usual line?

TISH: I don't have a usual line.

BOBBY: Is it usually your way to pretend to be someone else?

TISH: I want you to touch me.

BOBBY: I can think of a lot of things I'd rather touch than you.

TISH: Maybe you'd rather just look.

BOBBY: I'd rather stick my hand into a bonfire.

TISH: I like you, Bobby. I want you to like me.

BOBBY: You think I don't know what you're doing? You trying to dry hustle me? *(What Jean used to say:)* "Take what you can get but don't get wet."

TISH: I already am.

BOBBY: You forget who I hung around with. You took lessons from her but I fucked her and you're a pale imitation, Patty. You're not even the pan the cake was baked in. If you were Jean I'd be begging for it by now. I'd be on my knees begging. But I'm not even hard. I'm soft as jello. I'm just jiggling in my jockeys. So you better work a little harder. Let's see who's hustling who.

TISH: You want me?

BOBBY: Find out. If I fuck you then I must've wanted you, right? Or maybe I just wanted to get in you to see if there was anything inside. Come on, you think I came here for a conversation? Have a nice day? I'd call a 900 number if I wanted that. Take off your clothes. I want to see you wet as a washcloth. Or maybe I'll just leave. Who cares. So what is it?

TISH: So leave. Bobby. I want you like hot fudge. I want you to drip all over me sweet and hot.

BOBBY: You girls talked about everything, huh?

TISH: I be the ice cream. You be the fudge. I'm wearing your favorite underwear, Bobby. But you can leave if you're not interested. You can leave. *(She touches his crotch.)* I thought you weren't interested.

BOBBY: Maybe you killed her.

TISH: Why would I do that?

BOBBY: Jealous.

TISH: Where'd I get the sperm?

BOBBY: From a man, I assume. From some man.

TISH: You mean I took out a deposit? Like from a bank?

BOBBY: No, like you jerked some guy off at the bar and carried it over in a cup.

TISH: Logic would say it was you.

BOBBY: Logic? Is that why you're here? Is that why I'm here? Is that why you won't move your hand? If logic had anything to do with it, I'd be getting drunk and you'd be home with your goofy boyfriend.

TISH: He's not my boyfriend.

BOBBY: Uh huh.

TISH: He was, but he isn't anymore.

BOBBY: Oh I'm so sorry, I can't imagine why. What did you tell him your name was—Pia Zadora?

TISH: You have protection?

BOBBY: Oh yeah, I got special poison tipped condoms.

TISH: No. Protection: a gun, a knife. You have one?

BOBBY: You?

TISH: You want your stockings back, cut them off me.

BOBBY: Wouldn't you be afraid?

TISH: Why?

BOBBY: I might kill you.

TISH: So?

BOBBY: Then you'd be dead.

TISH: So?

BOBBY: You don't care?

TISH: I'm the ice cream, you're the fudge.

BOBBY: Jesus.

TISH: Dry hustle—

BOBBY: Yeah?

TISH: Two way.

BOBBY: Don't you care? Is that it? There's nothing to you?

TISH: I think we talk too much. *(She puts on the tape player, it plays the tape he gave her of him playing the sax. It's loud. She takes off her clothes as the music plays. She leaves on stockings, her bra and panties. He looks at her. She wears the red underwear Jean wore when she was killed. She poses in a Jean-like position.)* You like me?

BOBBY: Turn around.

TISH: *(She does.)* What do you like about me?

BOBBY: Oh. Skin. *(She touches her skin.)* Hair. *(She touches her hair.)* Legs. *(She touches her legs.)* The way you look.

TISH: Yeah?

BOBBY: Reminds me.

TISH: Of.

BOBBY: What I don't have.

TISH: And—

BOBBY: —It makes me—

TISH: —Angry. You want to—

BOBBY: —Grab you—

TISH: Actually.

BOBBY: Where'd you get the underwear?

TISH: Don't you like it?

BOBBY: No.

TISH: So take it off me. Use a knife.

BOBBY: You still wet, Patty? Or was that a lie? *(She puts her hand in her panties, then touches his nose with her finger.)* I suppose she told you how I liked it best.

TISH: Remind me.

BOBBY: From behind.

TISH: Sure.

BOBBY: So I don't see your face. She tell you that?

TISH: Sure. From behind. So you can grab my ass.

BOBBY: Yeah, and I want it to hurt.

TISH: Sure.

BOBBY: And on the floor, not on the bed, on the floor, so your knees get rough.

TISH: Where?

BOBBY: *(Points by his feet.)* Right here. You do that, and I'll do what you want, I'll cut off the underwear, I'll cut off whatever you have on you. *(She walks towards him. She gets on all fours.)* You think I killed her? Tish? Do you think I killed her.

TISH: Did you?

BOBBY: Do you think I would kill her?

TISH: Shit happens.

BOBBY: Do you want to die?

TISH: I want you.

BOBBY: To—

TISH: Make me feel.

BOBBY: Yeah?

TISH: The way you made her feel. She—

BOBBY: Yeah?

TISH: She was different after she met you.

BOBBY: Uh huh.

TISH: Softer.

BOBBY: Uh huh.

TISH: Just waiting for you I feel soft. You touch me, I melt. Except my knees. My knees are rough.

BOBBY: Uh huh. What's your name?

TISH: You like me like this? *(She changes position.)* Or like this? *(She changes position.)*

BOBBY: What's your name?

TISH: I want us to go to China and back.

BOBBY: Your name.

TISH: I want to leave marks like a map on your back.

BOBBY: What is it?

TISH: Tish.

BOBBY: Tish what?

TISH: Tish Rivers.

BOBBY: Tish Rivers, I wouldn't fuck you if you were the last thing on this earth. It would be like sticking my dick into a dry wind. You understand? I don't want you at all. Not even for a second. I was lying. How's it feel to be lied to? Show you a taste of your own medicine. At least it was quick. What's the matter? Cat got your tongue?

TISH: My knees are rough.

BOBBY: I don't give a shit about your knees. You think I care about rough knees?

TISH: I still have your stockings.

BOBBY: You can keep em.

TISH: I would give you my heart.

BOBBY: What heart?

TISH: I would open my arms and legs and let you in in a way I never have.

BOBBY: Too late, Patty. Should have thought of that before.

TISH: Ok, you're mad. Show me how you're mad.

BOBBY: I'm not mad. I'd have to care about you to get mad. And I don't. I just don't care.

TISH: You're lying.

BOBBY: I'm lying? No. That's the truth. Can't you tell?

TISH: Did it feel good to put the knife in?

BOBBY: No, it felt like nothing at all.

TISH: Did it give you pleasure?

BOBBY: Not enough.

TISH: Was it better than sex?

BOBBY: About the same.

TISH: Did you come before, after, or during?

BOBBY: Who's counting.

TISH: I know you did it.

BOBBY: Oh, did she tell you that?

TISH: You did.

BOBBY: 'Cause you're willing to stick your ass in the air for anyone who asks means I'm a killer? Sorry, it just means you're a nobody. I bet guys like you a lot. I bet you do whatever they want. Well I'm not one of them. Patty, Susie, Betty, whoever you are. I don't like you at all. And I've seen all of you now, haven't I? Thanks for the fun evening. It'll make a good story at the club.

TISH: You can't leave.

BOBBY: Oh really?

TISH: If you leave I'll tell everyone what you did, how you killed me, you killed me. You took me apart. I am humpty dumpty, you are looking at humpty fucking dumpty, and I need to know, do you understand that? I need to know what happened.

BOBBY: Fucking lunatic, I'm here with a fucking lunatic.

TISH: You will tell me, you understand? I speak for the two of us, you get it? I am speaking for the two of us. She was my friend. It's like she gave me my life, like she gave me my life and you took it away, and I know you were here, she said, she said she was seeing you, and I have it, I have it in her book, her appointment book, I have it and your name is in it, you were here. It has your name in it. This. See? Your name. *(She gets the book.)*

BOBBY: And what does that mean? Huh? Nothing. That means nothing. We canceled. Did you ever think of that? We canceled. *(He goes to the door.)*

TISH: You cannot leave. You have to show me. We have to be shown. Because this is all that's left: me and this. *(She pulls down the covers on the bed revealing a large patch of dried blood.)* Hot fudge, dried up, room temperature.

BOBBY: Jesus.

TISH: This is her and this is me and I sleep there, that's where I sleep, we sleep together and at night my dreams are hers, we dream together.

BOBBY: You sleep here?

TISH: Who do you think makes the bed? Who do you think waters the plants? Not all the king's horses and all the king's men.

BOBBY: Jesus.

TISH: There was a crack and I fell, I reach out my arms and it's too late, it's just too late 'cause I forgot how to hold on, and when I look up and see her, pieces of her that I can't reach. And when I look down I see you, and I know there's only one way I can go. And there you are, you're already there. All you have to do is stay put. So if you try to leave someone is gonna get hurt. You were right. This is a dangerous world. You can't be too careful these days. You have to have protection. *(She opens a drawer revealing a knife.)* You can never tell who is who *(She opens a drawer revealing another knife.)* or what is what. *(She opens another drawer with another knife.)* Someone's gonna get hurt— if you try to leave I'll try to stop you and someone will get hurt. And if it's me, I don't care. You understand? I don't care. I have nothing to lose.

BOBBY: I didn't do it.

TISH: That's fine, maybe you didn't, maybe you just didn't, but you can't leave. You leave I call the police, I show them the book. Or you leave I try to stop you. *(She picks up a knife.)* Or you leave I cut myself, then call the police, tell them you did it and show them the book. *(She puts the knife to her wrist.)* Or I just kill myself. I kill myself, right in front of you, I go and join her on that bed, and you have someone else to write songs about. You show me what happened, and if you say you didn't do it then you just make it up, you understand. You just make it up. We do this. I'm her. You be him. You just come a little closer to the bed and we make it up. *(He crosses closer.)* It's Friday night. We have sex. Right? Right?

BOBBY: Right.

TISH: Did I like it?

BOBBY: I don't know.

TISH: Do I usually like it? Do I usually like sex?

BOBBY: Yeah.

TISH: So I liked it.

BOBBY: Tish—

TISH: Yeah, Babe.

BOBBY: I didn't do it.

TISH: I didn't ask you that. Did I ask you that?

BOBBY: I will go along with this. I will do this, but I'm making it up, all right?

TISH: Whatever you say, Babe. So we made love and I liked it. What would you say? I love you or what? What would you say?

BOBBY: Um.

TISH: What?

BOBBY: I would just look at her.

TISH: How? Not like that. Closer. *(He moves closer.)* I say…Babe…Yes. Just those. Babe. Yes…Babe. Yes.

BOBBY: *(Looks at her.)* Sweetheart.

TISH: Yeah. *(He pulls away.)* That's right. First we get close, and then you pull away, something happens—what? What? I will do it to myself if you don't answer. I will just do it to myself. I will show you. I will refresh your memory.

BOBBY: He cut her.

TISH: Where?

BOBBY: I don't know.

TISH: Where?

BOBBY: The paper said.

TISH: Where?

BOBBY: Hair, right? It said he cut off her hair.

TISH: What am I thinking?

BOBBY: Kinky, probably just thought it was kinky.

TISH: Then?

BOBBY: I don't know.

TISH: Come on, you read the paper. Tell me. Why would it be so hard just to tell me what you read in the paper?

BOBBY: Hands.

TISH: He.

BOBBY: Cut them.

TISH: Am I dead yet?

BOBBY: Uh. Probably not.

TISH: What am I thinking? Huh? What am I thinking?

BOBBY: Hurts. He's hurting me.

TISH: And?

BOBBY: Why is this happening?

TISH: And?

BOBBY: I have to make this stop happening.

TISH: But?

BOBBY: I can't. Jesus.

TISH: Then?

BOBBY: Nothing, then nothing.

TISH: No. Then?

BOBBY: Her.

TISH: What?

BOBBY: You know, her.

TISH: What?

BOBBY: Breasts.

TISH: They're —

BOBBY: Cut.

TISH: How is it to cut them?

BOBBY: Um.

TISH: How does it feel?

BOBBY: Soft.

TISH: Do I fight back?

BOBBY: Try.

TISH: But?

BOBBY: Can't.

TISH: Am I dead yet?

BOBBY: I don't know.

TISH: Maybe not. How do you make sure I'm dead.

BOBBY: Stab.

TISH: Where? Where would you stab me?

BOBBY: I—I don't know. Please I.

TISH: Guess. You have to make sure I'm dead.

BOBBY: Heart.

TISH: Yes.

BOBBY: I.

TISH: Yes.

BOBBY: Your heart.

TISH: Killed her.

BOBBY: Yeah.

TISH: Show me.

BOBBY: What?

TISH: Put the knife there. Show me.

BOBBY: I can't.

TISH: Do it. I'll help you. *(She takes his hand and with hers, places the knife. She lets go, he holds it over her heart.)*

BOBBY: I...Oh God.

TISH: What?

BOBBY: Baby.

TISH: Yeah, Babe, what is it?

BOBBY: Oh God, I'm sorry.

TISH: For what?

BOBBY: I'm sorry. It's—it's my fault. I'm sorry.

TISH: You did it?

BOBBY: I.

TISH: You killed me?

BOBBY: Please forgive me.

TISH: *(She gets up, steps away.)* Shit.

BOBBY: I'm sorry Baby, I —

TISH: Shit.

BOBBY: I should have.

TISH: Oh, shit.

BOBBY: Sweetest.

TISH: Why?

BOBBY: I—I—

TISH: Why?

BOBBY: I was mad.

TISH: Mad? Like the bus was late mad? What mad?

BOBBY: I came here.

TISH: Yeah?

BOBBY: I came here, I came here to—and she was with someone.

TISH: So you killed her? You cut her like a piece of meat?

BOBBY: No, I.

TISH: What? Show me, I want to see your face. You show me.

BOBBY: It was a surprise. I wanted to surprise her. I wanted to catch her getting dressed, I wanted to walk in with flowers. I. I knocked.

TISH: And?

BOBBY: No answer.

TISH: And?

BOBBY: I heard something, I knocked again.

TISH: Uh huh.

BOBBY: I said, it's me, Baby.

TISH: Yeah.

BOBBY: I heard noises, a man, I said, Jeanie, you all right, let me in, you all right? I thought what is it, what is it. I yelled, I'm gonna knock the door down. And she opened it. She had on a robe, she had on perfume, she said, hey Babe, what's up, I said you tell me, she said I was sleeping, I said you always sweat when you sleep? She said if I'm thinking of you. I said where is he? She said why don't you come back later. I said just tell me. She said come back later. I said if you think I'm ever gonna come back you tell me the truth. She said, later. I went home. The phone rang. She left a message. I thought there was something in her voice, but I was mad, I didn't pick up. She said come on over, I think you should come over now. I thought we'd have it out. The door was open.

TISH: And?

BOBBY: Pieces. All over. Her pieces. There, there, there, I mean someone had, I mean, they cut her up and tossed her around like she was a doll, like a fucking doll and I don't know what happened, I mean, it was my fault, if I'd answered the phone, and then I thought, I really thought I'd fix it, I mean I thought—something happened—and I was drunk or, and I tried to put her back. Shit, I tried to put her back. I took all all the parts of her, one by one, and put them together on the bed. And Jesus, Jeanie I'm sorry. I should have. I tried to make it better, see? And then, I wanted to—I wanted to make love, I still wanted her, even the way she looked, I wanted her. I knew how she liked it and how it made her smile and how she'd look at me and say yes. And I thought, I really thought that's what would happen, if we could be that close, she'd smile and say yes. If we could make love, if we could just make love, it would bring her back. And I I touched her, God, between her legs, and it was still there, the knife, he had left it in her, and I knew, I knew I couldn't, I couldn't bring her back. I knew it would only hurt her, my touching her would only hurt her.

TISH: God.

BOBBY: I couldn't get her back.

TISH: No.

BOBBY: And her face. Geez. It was like someone had painted a different face and I wanted to wipe it all away, but I couldn't.

TISH: Me.

BOBBY: What?

TISH: Do it with me.

BOBBY: What?

TISH: Please. I need you to…Do it with me.

BOBBY: What?

TISH: Wipe it off. Please. *(He wipes off her face.)* My lids, my lashes, cheeks. Please.

BOBBY: Rose cinder.

TISH: Right. Rose cinder on my lips. I I uh. I want to touch you. Can I? Touch you? *(He nods. She touches his chest.)* I want to see you. Can I see you? *(He nods. She undoes his shirt. They stand there.)*

BOBBY: I don't know who did it.

TISH: No, we don't...

BOBBY: I miss her...

TISH: Yeah. The red of her hair.

BOBBY: I still loved her.

TISH: The mole on her back.

BOBBY: Yeah.

TISH: A kiss from God—

BOBBY: She said.

TISH: And I knew it was true.

BOBBY: I had to leave her the way she was.

TISH: Yeah.

BOBBY: And then—

TISH: What?

BOBBY: I saw her in you.

TISH: No. I think she's gone...Do you ever forget?

BOBBY: What?

TISH: How to play, do you ever—forget?

BOBBY: Every day.

TISH: Yeah?

BOBBY: Yeah.

TISH: Did she show you how to dance?'

BOBBY: What? No.

TISH: Something about being on the beach as a kid. I've been trying to remember, but I keep getting it mixed up.

BOBBY: Go ahead.

TISH: What?

BOBBY: Go ahead.

TISH: Oh. Um, Well, ok. It's the beach, and I'm right by the water, and I take off my dress, I take off my shoes and...and it's just me. *(She slowly starts to dance. Blackout)*

END OF PLAY

HOT 'N' THROBBING
by Paula Vogel

Biography

Playwright, screenwriter, and professor Paula Vogel has headed Brown's Playwriting Workshop since 1985. Vogel has taught playwriting at Cornell University, The University of Alaska, The Writer's Voice in New York, and Trinity Conservatory in Providence, Rhode Island.

Her most recent playwriting credits include productions of *Hot 'N' Throbbing*, originally produced at the American Repertory Theatre, and *The Baltimore Waltz*, originally produced at Circle Repertory, at the Tarragon Theatre in Toronto, the Yale Repertory Theatre, Portland Stage, and The Magic Theatre. *And Baby Makes Seven* was produced by the Circle Repertory Company in the Spring of 1993. Her other plays include *Desdemona, The Oldest Profession,* and *Meg.*

Vogel is a member of Circle Repertory Company and is on its Board of Directors. Among her most recent awards are the prestigious 1995 Senior Artist Residency Award from the Pew Foundation and a 1993 Fund for New American Plays for *Hot 'N' Throbbing*. Other recent awards include a 1991-92 Obie for Best Play for *The Baltimore Waltz*, which also won the AT&T New Play Award 1991-92; a Yaddo Fellow (May 1992); a Rockefeller Foundation Bellagio Fellow (Summer 1992); a McKnight Fellow (1991-92); a Radcliffe Bunting Fellowship; and a National Endowment for Arts Playwriting Fellowship (1980, 1990-91). Vogel was also the recipient of the Rhode Island Governor's Arts Award.

Author's Note

Some plays only daughters can write. *Hot 'N' Throbbing* was written on a National Endowment for the Arts fellowship — because obscenity begins at home.

Original Production

Hot 'N' Throbbing was originally produced at the American Repertory Theater under the direction of Ann Bogart. The cast was as follows:

Voice Over . . . . Alexandra Loria
Woman . . . . Diane D'Aquila
Girl . . . . Amy Louise Lammert
Voice . . . . Royal Miller
Boy . . . . Randall Jaynes
Man . . . . Jack Willis

CAST

GIRL, about fifteen

BOY, about fourteen

WOMAN, almost thirty-four. Wears Lina Wertmuller glasses. On-again, off-again member of Weight Watchers

MAN, over thirty-four. Holes in dungarees. Almost a beer-belly. *(Note to actor: you've got to go gang-busters on this role. The bigger the asshole you are, the more we'll love you; Trust me on this.)*

VOICE-OVER, Hard to tell her age under the blue lights. Voice-over narrates the script that the Woman is writing, her inner voice. She is a sex-worker: at times, bored with her job; at times, emphatically over-acting, trying to land a role in a legitimate film. Voice-over watches the stage action from her glass booth, where she dances. Her voice is amplified through a microphone. Her voice is sensual and husky.

THE VOICE, He is a presence, more than a person. At times he acts as a bouncer/owner in the erotic dance hall. His voice is also amplified through a microphone, and it is always theatrical, rich, baritone and commanding. The Voice breathes a lot through the mike. According to the quote, the Voice's dialect varies from German, French, Victorian British and Brooklynese. And it often sounds just like The Man. The Voice also acts like a live D.J., spinning the score of the piece, always impassive to the on-stage action. The Voice may wear head-sets and sun-glasses.

NOTE ON KRAFFT-EBING FOR THE VOICE: Krafft-Ebing has three sides in this piece: his lectures on sexuality to first-year medical students; his condescending talk to a Ladies' Club luncheon; and his impassive dictation during an autopsy for police.

SET

There are two play worlds in this piece. The stage lights and the blue lights—reality, constructed as we know it, and the erotic dance hall, as we fantasize about it.

MUSIC NOTES

I wrote this piece to several sound-tracks: Janet Jackson's "Control" (particularly "Nasty"), and Kaoma's "World Beat." After the Girl's last appearance, with the mention of horror movies, I wrote to the tape of Michael Jackson's "Thriller," and "Silence of the Lambs." Sound-tapes from horror movies, A.M.G. and other rap might be played under the action (Frank Sinatra is also a nice possibility). The main thing is that the music changes from erotic to terrorific.

Two more props. Blue light where indicated. And music. Music always helps to get it up.

Hot 'N' Throbbing

In a growing blue light, we see the Girl dressed in very tight pants and a halter top, making suggestive stripper or vogue-ing movements. At end of voice over, we see an older woman sitting at a computer screen, typing. Living room.

V.O.: Cut to: Interior. Night. Voice Over: "She was hot. She was throbbing. But she was in control. Control of her body. Control of her thoughts. Control of…him.

"He was hot. He was throbbing. And out of control. He needed to be restrained. Tied Down. And taught a Lesson.

"But not hurt. Not too much. Just enough. Enough to make the burning hotter, the throbbing hotter. Just…enough. She would make his flesh red all over. She would raise the blood with her loving discipline. And she would make him wait. Make him beg. Make them both wait…until she was ready."

Woman and Voice Over: And she would make him wait. Make him beg.

Woman: *(Types)* Sounds too male-bashing—"Make him ask?" Oh, fuck it. "Make him beg…Make them both beg…."

(Suddenly the bathroom door slams open in stage light; The Girl stands in front of the sink dressed as before. Screams)

Girl: MAAHM! WHERE'S YOUR EYELINER?

Woman: ON THE TOP SHELF! BY THE BEN GAY! *(Back to flat narrative tone at computer)* Until she was ready. Ready to release them both at the end of a long, hard night. Ready to heave herself to the other side of her love throes, ready to give it up—

GIRL: MAAHM! CAN I USE YOUR MASCARA!!

WOMAN: Sounds like upchucking. "Ready to pant, ready to scream, ready to die in each other's arms..." *(The Woman stops; call out:)* Leslie Ann! What are you doing?

GIRL: Puttin' on some pancake.

WOMAN: Why are you putting on make-up?

GIRL: I already told you.

WOMAN: No you did not tell me.

GIRL: I Did. So.

WOMAN: Why are you wearing make-up.

GIRL: I'm Going. Out.

WOMAN: Where?

GIRL: Out. To Lisa's. To spend the night.

WOMAN: This is the first time I've heard about it.

GIRL: I Told You!

WOMAN: I don't want you going to Lisa's.

GIRL: But Why?!

WOMAN: Because I. said. so.

GIRL: I'm goin'.

WOMAN: Her parents do not supervise that young lady. You are not going to Lisa's.

GIRL: But all the girls will be there!

WOMAN: You are not all the girls.

> *(The Girl slams bathroom door. We hear the water running. From offstage:)*

GIRL: *(Off)* I'MM GOING!

> *(The Woman sighs. Types.)*
>
> *(Blue Light. The Boy enters. The Girl emerges from bathroom in tight pants. Exaggerated movements of Boy humping Girl from behind with clothes on.)*

V.O.: Voice over continued: He wanted to enter her. Penetrate her secrets with his will. He wanted to gently pry open that sweet channel that leads to joy, and fill her with his passion until the dull pain faded into pleasure, until her hips locked into a rhythm to match his. Together they would rock each other, clinging to each other as the tempo got faster, faster, faster and faster, faster and faster and faster, faster...

> *(The Boy stops as lights go back to normal, and slumps on sofa; The Girl stands facing the Woman.)*

GIRL: You just don't care. You want me to stay in this boring house until I rot like you and four-eyes on the sofa over there.

WOMAN: Leslie Ann. I am behind my schedule. I've got to get out forty pages by the first mail tomorrow morning, and I'm on page twenty-six.

GIRL: Layla. I am not answering to a dumb-shit name like Leslie Ann.

BOY: *(Singing riff and:)* "LAY-LA!! YOU'VE GOT ME ON MY KNEES."

GIRL: MAH-HM.

WOMAN: I'm sorry, sweetie. Layla.

BOY: "LAY-LA! I'M BEGGING DARLIN', PLEASE."

GIRL: Shut up, creep!

BOY: Are you going out in those tight pants?

GIRL: What business is it of yours?

BOY: Those pants are so tight you can see your P.L.s.

GIRL: Shut up.

(The Woman looks up from typing with interest.)

WOMAN: What are P.L.s? *(No answer.)*

GIRL: Nothing'.

BOY: Hey, as long as I don't have to walk you up the aisle for some shot-gun wedding, you trouncing around with your p.l.s hanging out...

WOMAN: P.L.s?

GIRL: Why don't you just go beat-off in your room, you little pervo...

WOMAN: Those pants are too tight. Did you spray-paint them on?

GIRL: Betcha wish you had my thighs, huh, Ma?

WOMAN: We are not discussing the subject of my thighs. You are not leaving this house dressed like that.

GIRL: Huh. That's funny. Coming from you.

WOMAN: What's that supposed to mean?

GIRL: Nothin'.

WOMAN: I could kill your father for telling you kids a thing like that. I do not write *pornography*. There's a mile of difference between that and....*adult entertainment*. He wouldn't know the difference.

BOY: I think it's cool, Mom.

GIRL: Shut up, toady.

WOMAN: This is not about me. You will not fling...the *way* I make a living into my face every time I give. you. a. directive. The way I put food on the plate, and Reeboks on the feet. You are not leaving this house, period, young lady. I want you to go upstairs to your room and do some homework for a change. Your grades last quarter were a disgrace.

GIRL: Calvin gets to go out.

WOMAN: Calvin has a 3.5. Calvin can go out all he wants on a Friday night. You are staying home and opening up a book. You'll like it. SILAS MARNER. I loved that book.

BOY: Her book report's due Monday.

WOMAN: You children can read quietly in your room. I've got to get this section done. Go on upstairs and open up your books.

BOY: The only thing Leslie Ann wants to open is her p.l.s.

WOMAN: Calvin! Quit picking on your sister!

GIRL: Get your little tattle-tale nose out of my p.l.s, creep!

WOMAN: I'VE HAD IT! What are you talking about? Leslie Ann?

GIRL: Ask Calvin. Go ahead, little brother, tell Mom what you've been calling me.

WOMAN: Calvin? *(No response.)* I asked you a question.

BOY: P.L.s are a name for a girl's...you know.

GIRL: It's not very nice. You know, for an honor roll creep, you sure use some nice language.

WOMAN: When I was growing up, I didn't have a room of my own. And so I was determined that my children would each have their own privacy. Your mother sleeps on a convertible sofa that has to be made up each morning so you can have your own space. I want you both to go upstairs to your rooms, if you can't be quiet and act normal down here.

GIRL: Some privacy. The walls are paper-thin. How can I concentrate when all I can hear is four-eyes beating off?

BOY: I do not! You have the mouth of a slut, Leslie Ann!

GIRL: You beat off! In the catcher's mitt Daddy gave you for Christmas! I can feel the walls shaking!—

WOMAN: *(Suddenly interested, making notes.)* —Catcher's mitt. Open Window. Show Clipboard. Notes: Leather catcher's mitt—

BOY: Mind Your Own Business!

GIRL: That's not what Dad meant when he said practice. Catching pop-up-flies—

BOY: —Shut up!

GIRL: —That's why you wear glasses, Calvin. Nobody else in this family does, little brother. 'Cause you violate yourself.

BOY: Mom wears glasses!

(Startled, the two teenagers suddenly look at their mother with a horrified new idea; The Woman, oblivious, stares into her computer screen, typing with a vengeance. The siblings stop and erupt in laughter.)

GIRL: —Shut up, pervo!

BOY: —musta learned it from you. P.L.—

GIRL: Quit calling me that, and I might just learn you something interesting—

BOY: Yeah?

(They both look at their mother, deep into her typing.)

GIRL: Yeah. So you won't haveta hang in the bushes outside the house. You do, dontcha? *(The Boy is suddenly quiet, beet-red.)* Yeah. I thought that was you. Watching me undressing. In the bushes. Straight-A student. Yeah. I just might let you learn—
(Light change. Blue light: The Girl dances closer to The Boy; another Voice, a dark, rich, European baritone, whispers:)

THE VOICE[1]: "Lolita, light of my life, fire of my loins. My sin, my soul. Lo-lee-ta: the tip of the tongue taking a trip of three steps down the palate to tap, on the teeth. Lo. Lee. Ta." *(There is the sound of an automobile horn. Loud.)* "Lo. Lee. Ta." *(The horn imitates the voice. Three times. Lights change back abruptly.)*

GIRL: That's my ride! Mom! I've got to go.

WOMAN: You are not leaving this house. Young lady.

GIRL: You said I could!

WOMAN: When! When did I say that? *(Voice-over lights up a cigarette, bored, waiting. She puffs.)*

GIRL: Last night. I asked you. And you said you didn't care what I did. So I told Lisa yes.

WOMAN: Is that Lisa outside? I don't like you riding with her. Go out and tell her I said no.

GIRL: You said you need peace and quiet. I'm going to give you some. It's an overnight. A slumber party. I'll be back tomorrow.

WOMAN: You march upstairs. Right. this. minute. You are not leaving this house—
(Once more, the car horn trumpets: Lo-lee-ta.)

GIRL: I'll see you! *(The Girl rushes to the door, exits and slams it behind her. There is a pause. The Boy watches The Woman. She returns to her computer.)*

WOMAN: Oh, Jesus. I could use a cigarette.

BOY: You quit smoking.

WOMAN: I know. I miss it at times like this. Jesus Christ. Page... twenty-six.

BOY: Fourteen to go.

WOMAN: What's on your agenda for tonight?

BOY: I'm staying here with you, Mom.

WOMAN: You're not worried, are you, Cal?

BOY: Nope. Not me.

WOMAN: Because I can take care of myself. Nothing's going to happen.

BOY: I know.

WOMAN: Because if you want to go out, you should just go ahead—

BOY: I don't wannto. I'm just going to sit here, quietly, and read, all right?

WOMAN: All right. *(The Woman stares at the computer screen. The Boy stares at her. She looks up and sees him staring.)*

V.O.: "What are you looking at?"

THE VOICE: What are you—

V.O.: "looking—"

THE VOICE: —looking at?

(The Boy looks down at his book, quickly. The Woman goes back to the screen. The Boy stares at her again. The Woman tentatively starts to type. Stops. Starts again. Stops.)

V.O.: "What are you looking at?"

THE VOICE: What are you—

V.O.: "looking—"

THE VOICE: —looking at?

BOY: Writer's block, Mom?

WOMAN: I'm running out of words.

BOY: How about...

THE VOICE: *(Whispered.)* —throbbing—

BOY: —throbbing?

WOMAN: Don't make fun of me son. My writing puts food in your mouth.

BOY: I wasn't making fun! I was just trying to help!

WOMAN: I know. I'm sorry. Maybe after you go to college, you'll be able to be a real writer. I'd like that.

BOY: I'm not going to college.

WOMAN: We'll see.

Boy: To Allegheny Community? With all the geeks?

Woman: That's where I went, remember. But I meant maybe somewhere away from home. It would be good for you to get away.

Boy: Leslie Ann's the one who wants to go away.

Woman: I worry sometimes that she'll get as far as the backseat of a car.

Boy: I don't think so. I bet she's scared to death...

(Pause; The Voice breathes heavily twice.)

Woman: Why?

Boy: No reason.

(Pause)

Woman: Okay. *(Voice stops breathing.)* Page twenty-six. ...I need some words that pack a punch...

Boy: So how about throbbing?

Woman: I've got throbbing all over the page. There are only so many ways to say throbbing....

V.O.: —"pulsating"—

The Voice: —"beating"—

V.O.: —"heaving"—

The Voice: —"battering"—

V.O.: —"pulsing"—

Woman: —Wait a moment!—that's it, Charlene—when in doubt, cut to—cut to—

(Light change to blue. The Boy stands, like a somnambulist, with his catcher mitt, looking up, staring.)

V.O.: "Cut to: Exterior. In the bushes outside the house. Nighttime. We see a YOUNG BOY, not yet old enough to shave. He is peering up through the bushes at:

Cut to: Boy's Point of View. We see an attractive older Woman, full-hipped, through her bedroom window, looking at herself in the mirror. The Woman removes her glasses, and gazes at her image.

(The Woman removes her glasses at the computer. The Boy stares at her.)

Cut to: The Young Boy, standing now. He watches as she strokes her face. We see him raise his hand, which holds a baseball mitt. He strokes the leather with his free hand, softly feeling the texture."

(The Boy follows the instructions of The Voice Over.)

"Close up: on the mitt; The Boy fists it several times, then raises the glove to his face, breathing into the leather.

Cut To: The Woman, who begins to feel her own body.

Cut To: Young Boy, who begins to run the glove across his chest.

Cut To: The Woman who closes her eyes and runs her fingers over her rounded hips, and down into her waistline.

Cut To: Close up on leather mitt, rubbing up and down the Boy's blue-jeaned thighs—

Cut to:—"

(*Suddenly, an overlapping voice, deeper, darker, cuts in: The Boy stands frozen; The Woman halts at the computer. It is the voice of Krafft-Ebing, 19th century sexologist:*)

THE VOICE[2]: (*À la Krafft-Ebing*) "The pale complexion, the glassy gaze indicate the lunatic victim to this vice. Loss of memory, apathy and…impulsiveness of action are characteristic of chronic dementia resulting from—

V.O.: (*Simultaneously with Voice*) —"masturbation in young men."

THE VOICE: (*Simultaneously with V.O.:*) —"masturbation in young men."

(*Lights change back. The Boy sits on the sofa, fondling his catcher's mitt.*)

WOMAN: —What was that?! Shoot. Lost it. "Cut to—Cut to…cut to…." Fudge. Fiddlesticks.

BOY: Something wrong, Mom?

WOMAN: I don't know. I'm distracted, I guess. Other voices are coming in over the airwaves.

V.O.: (*Smoking*) "Cigarette. Lo-lee-ta. Cigarette."

WOMAN: Concentrate, Charlene. "Cut to—"

V.O.: "Do the dishes. Dishes. Dishes."

WOMAN: Oh, God. Time for a break. Power down. First—save; exit; close; quit. Ah. (*Pause*) Calvin?

BOY: Yeah, Mom?

WOMAN: Where does your sister go on weekends?

BOY: Ya know. Out.

WOMAN: Out where? Where does she go with Lisa?

(*Blue light strikes the area outside of the sliding doors. The Girl does a slow, expert teasing dance for an imaginary male clientele; The Boy parallels her movements.*)

BOY: Well…see, first they hitch into town with some suburban-father

308 * PAULA VOGEL

type in his Volvo station wagon. They then hop the cross-town bus, the M2, to the corner of Pike and 7th. They get off by the bus station, and walk two blocks east. They check to make sure they're not being followed. Then they duck into this joint, it's all red brick on the front, with the windows blacked out, except for the Budweiser sign. The door is solid metal. They nod to the bouncer, who always pats Leslie Ann on the fanny. They trot behind the curtains in back of the bar, quick, see, so the clientele won't see them in their street clothes. And backstage, Al who's the owner, yells at 'em for being late.

And they slip into this toilet of a dressing room, where they strip off their jeans and sweats in such a hurry, they're inside out, thrown in the corner. And they help each other into the scanty sequins and the two inch heels. And they slink out together in the blue light as the warm up act, and wrap their legs around the poles. And Al keeps an eye out on the guys, who haven't got a buzz on yet, so they're pretty docile, 'cause the girls are jail bait. And Leslie Ann and her best friend Lisa shake it up for only one set. And before you know it, the twenty minutes are up, just a few half-hearted grabs, and they're doing full splits to scoop up the dollar bills that will pay for the midnight double feature at the Mall and the burgers afterwards at Big Bob's.

(*Blue light out on The Girl. The Woman, who has been mesmerized, breaks out of the reverie.*)

WOMAN: Calvin!

BOY: Jesus, mom. Take a joke, will ya? She probably hangs out at Lisa's being dumb.

(*Pause*)

WOMAN: Don't you have a nice girl you can take to the movies tonight?

BOY: I don't know any nice girls.

WOMAN: Well, how about calling up some of your friends and doing something with them?

BOY: All the boys at school are creeps.

WOMAN: I know. But it's Friday night!

BOY: So.

WOMAN: Calvin, sweetie, it's not right for you to spend every weekend in the house.

BOY: Am I bothering you?

WOMAN: That's not the point. You're never going to meet someone slumped on the sofa.

BOY: I'm not slumping.

WOMAN: You are. Sit up straight; you're wearing the springs down that way—When I was your age—

BOY: *(Agonized)* —*What*. Do You *Want* From me?

WOMAN: I just want you to have some *Fun.*

BOY: I'm going.

WOMAN: Where?

BOY: What does it matter? I'm going Out. I can't even sit in the privacy of my own home—

WOMAN: Now wait; sweetie, I don't want you to take it like that—

BOY: —Jesus. I'm gone. *(The Boy stalks to the door, opens it and slams out.)*

WOMAN: *(Guiltily)* Have a nice time! Don't stay out. Too late.... *(The Woman pauses, then turns the computer back on.)* Boot up. Drive A. *(The Woman waits. Pauses. The Woman stealthily turns, opens up a desk drawer, takes out a pack of cigarettes. Waits. Carefully selects one. Fishes out matches from the drawer.)*

WOMAN AND VOICE OVER: Our little secret, Charlene. *(The Woman lights up. Starts to type.)*

V.O.: Cut to: Close-up: "She tentatively licked the tip, a gentle flick of the tongue, before perching it on her lips. Her head instinctively reared back, before its acid taste. She gently sucked, letting it linger in her mouth—she gently sucked—"

(The Woman pauses, reads what she wrote, inhales and exhales— the voice of Krafft-Ebing begins; Charlene, struck, listens:)

THE VOICE[3]: "—the married female—"

V.O.: "She...sucked...the tip...she..."

THE VOICE: "If the married female conceives every second year, during the nine months that follow conception she experiences no great sexual excitement."

WOMAN: Where is that coming from? *(The Woman begins to type.)*

THE VOICE[4]: "While women are suckling there is usually such a call on the vital force made by the organs secreting milk that sexual desire is almost annihilated. ...The best mothers, wives, and managers of households are not very much troubled with sexual feeling of any kind. Love of home, children, and domestic duties, are the only passions they feel."

WOMAN: Jesus. I can't use that crap. Erase. Cut to:

V.O.: "Cut to: Exterior. the boy, in the bushes, watches The Woman smoke. His tongue gently flicks his own lips in response."

(*We see The Man at the picture window, easing himself against the sliding glass window, watching The Woman.*)

"Cut to: Interior. The Woman, in front of the mirror, oblivious to being watched. She arches her throat and releases a jet of smoke."

(*The Man at the window disappears.*)

"Cut to: Exterior. Now we see The Boy begin to manipulate himself with the gloved hand, through the denim, his excitement growing. He closes his eyes, and begins to sway.

Cut to: Interior. The Woman hears a noise, and turns to the window. She gazes below and sees The Boy who—

Cut to: The Boy begins to grow urgent in his need, and begins to strike his limbs, softly at first, and then he begins pounding the cupped glove—"

(*There is a pounding at the door; The Woman is puzzled*)

"Pounding, pounding the cupped glove—"

(*The Pounding at the door grows louder—*)

WOMAN: (*With some fear*) Who is that?

MAN: (*Off-stage*) Special Delivery! I got a *package* for you, Charlene—

WOMAN: CLYDE?!! God damn you—I'm calling the police— (*The Woman races to her trimline on the desk; she dials 911 but we hear nothing but clicks.*) Shit! What did you do to the phone?

MAN: (*Off*) You don't need the *phone* baby. I'm here to reach out and *touch* someone—

WOMAN: God damn! You're drunk again, aren't you?! Get away from here, Clyde! I told that stupid-ass judge a restraining order wouldn't work—

MAN: (*Pounding; off*) Open the fuckin' door. Now. I wanta talk to you.

WOMAN: I'm working.

MAN: I asked! Nicely!

(*We hear the door being violently kicked. The Woman, with a grim calm, reaches into the desk drawer and pulls something out. We hear a click—possibly amplified. She sits back down at her computer, and waits. Starts to type.*)

V.O.: (*Urgently*) Cut to: Exterior. The Boy thrusts himself against the front door. His hands hold onto the frame of the door.

Cut to: Interior. The Woman, on the other side of the door, presses against it, moving her body gently against the wood—

MAN: *(Off)* I'm Coming! I'm Coming In— *(With another savage kick, the door flies open)* Shit!! *(The Man flies in disheveled, drunk. The Man grins, sings:)* "I hear You KNOCKIN' But You Can't Come In!"

WOMAN: Get out of here, Clyde. Your last chance. *(The Woman pretends to type.)*

MAN: I'm here to audition. To Give You. New Material. The E-Rot-icly UnEmployed. To get your undivided attention. Write this up, Baby. Oh my god! Is that a doorknob in my pocket or am I just happy to see you? Baby? Stop looking at that goddamn screen. Look. At. Me. *(Before The Woman can stop him, The Man pulls the computer plug from the outlet—)* Ta-DA!!—And Now! The Burlesque Theatre of Allegheny! Presentin'! SEX—ON—WELFARE! *(The Man begins to strip and grind, taking off his t-shirt, and unzipping his dungarees, while singing the trumpet stripper theme:)* "BWAH-BWAH-BWAH!!! BWAH-BWAH-BWAH-BWAHHH!!! BWAH-BWAH-BWAH!! BWAH-BWAH-BWAH-BWAH— bwah—BWAHH!!—bum-bum—BWAHH!!—bum-bum—BWAHH— bum-bum—BWAHH—bum-bum *(At this point, he has turned his back on The Woman, and has lowered his pants and underwear, mooning her—The Woman stands, calmly, with a gun in her hand.)*

WOMAN: I want. You. To stand. Very still. Don't move, Clyde. Don't. Move. *(The Man, seeing the gun, stops, still bent over, exposed)* I don't want to kill you. By accident. I'm just going to shoot you just enough to send you to the hospital— *(The Man, panicked, begins to rush for the door—*

MAN: Jesus-Christ-Char-LENE!!

(Blue Lights On. There is the sound of an amplified gun shot. Very slowly, in stylized motion, The Man grabs his behind, and writhes, a slow, sexual grind in agony. A male porn star voice dictates:)

THE VOICE: He was Hot. He was throbbing. He was Hot He was Throbbing. He was Hot He was throbbing He was hot and throbbing He was hot He was throbbing He was hot and throbbing He was hot He was throbbing He was hot and throbbing He was hot He was throbbing—

(When the regular lights come up, The Man is lying on his stomach on the sofa. The Woman, holding towels, stands over him. The Man is crying.)

MAN: —Jesus H. Jesus H. Christ. I can't believe it. My own wife. I can't believe—

WOMAN: Hold still. Calm down and quit wiggling like that. I can't see anything with you moving around—

MAN: Am I gonna haveta be in a wheelchair? For Life?

WOMAN: I said. hold. still. I don't want any blood on the carpeting. *(The Woman regards the wound. The Woman regards The Man's butt.)* Yup. I gotcha, all right. How does it feel?

MAN: How does it feel? How does it *feel?!* Like someone rammed a poker in my flesh! That's how it feels!

WOMAN: Don't move.

V.O.: —"Don't—"

THE VOICE: —"Don't Move—"

V.O.: *(Seductive whisper)* Cut To: Flashback: Five Years Ago.
(Blue light comes on. The Man turns on his back, and the Woman straddles him. They start to make out.)

THE VOICE[5]: *(As Krafft-Ebing; through the following, Voice Over breathes heavily.)* Case 103. Mr. C., aged thirty-six; an unemployed steel worker of hereditary taint, asymmetry of the skull and other signs of degeneration. Mr. C evidenced constant alteration of exaltation and depression. The subject, as a school boy faced disciplinary action due to hyperaesthesia sexualis— Masturbatio Coram Discipulis in Schola.
(Voice-Over giggles)

THE VOICE: Subject, as an adolescent, showed enormous development of the zygomae and inferior maxilla.
(Voice Over is impressed, erotically:)

V.O.: Ooooh. *(Back to her screenplay/dominatrix voice)* CUT TO:—
(Abrupt lighting change: back to bright stage lights. The Woman stands over The Man, now on his stomach again, with bandages, tape and antiseptic.)

WOMAN: I said Lie There! You're gonna mess up my sofa! Thank God for Scotch-guard...There. That's better. You might not need stitches.

THE VOICE[6]: *(In a thick Scottish dialect)* "Tha's got such a nice tail on thee. Tha's got the nicest arse of anybody."

WOMAN: I'm going to put some antiseptic on it now; it's gonna be cold—
(The Woman pours on liquid from the bottle; The Man roars.)

MAN: AAHHH!!

WOMAN: It's not supposed to sting like that—

MAN: Don't You Tell Me How It Feels! You Ain't My Butt!!

WOMAN: Compliments will get you nowhere. I can't do anything with you when you get in moods like this. *(The Woman efficiently bandages him; tears the tape with her teeth; she whiffs the air.)* Hooey! God, Clyde. You can't afford to buy yourself BVD's, but you can throw it away on alcohol.

MAN: It's my money.

WOMAN: I'm getting you some coffee before we go to the hospital. Sit up slowly. And sit on the towel.

(Like a man missing a limb, The Man tentatively feels his behind. Slowly, he pulls up his underwear. He tries to pull up his jeans, winces, and leaves himself undone. He sits up penitently, like a little boy, on the towel, favoring his good cheek.)

WOMAN: *(Off)* There's no milk in the house! So you haveta drink it black!

(Blue light. While The Voice narrates, The Man slowly reaches into the back of his pants, wetting his hand with the blood. Hypnotically, he stares at the red on his hand, either getting faint or aroused. The Man closes his eyes, bringing his hand closer to his face. He breathes in the scent of the blood, and then almost tastes his hand.)

THE VOICE: Case 103 continued. Although subject continued self-abuse through his adolescence, authorities noticed nothing unusual at the time. C. married early, a woman of his own age from the same village. At first, he fulfilled his marital duties in a typical if somewhat energetic manner, not yet exhibiting the traits of hysteria virillis that led to the breakdown of said marriage.

(In a change of voice from Krafft-Ebing to porno film director; the lights change back to stage lights.)

THE VOICE: Jump Cut!

(The Woman hands coffee to The Man.)

WOMAN: Jesus! How did you get blood all over?

MAN: I guess I sprayed a bit when...the shot...hit me.

WOMAN: Drink this. Slowly. Then we'll go.

MAN: Okay. *(The Man and Woman sit at opposite ends of the sofa, sipping their coffee.)* Good Coffee. *(The Woman looks suspiciously at him.)* You're looking good. Filling out a little bit?

WOMAN: I've quit smoking. Or I'm trying to.

MAN: —It looks good on you...really...So—this is like old times, huh?
Us sitting up, drinking coffee—

WOMAN: Forget it, Clyde. Whatever you're thinking, forget it.

THE VOICE: CUT! Take two.

MAN: So this is like old times, huh. Us sitting up, drinking coffee—

WOMAN: Forget it, Clyde. Whatever you're thinking, forget it. *(Pause)*
How does it feel?

MAN: The more coffee I drink, the more it throbs.

THE VOICE: I want you to—

WOMAN: "I want you to *feel* it. Maybe then you'll—"

THE VOICE: —*listen.*

(The Woman just hears what she has said.)

WOMAN: Jesus. That sounds like something you would say.
(Pause)

MAN: Say, uh, what happened to the—?

WOMAN: Don't worry about the gun. I know what I'm doing. Just
behave yourself, and it won't go off.

MAN: Call me old-fashioned, but I prefer the days when havin' protection in the house meant your supply of birth-control.

WOMAN: You're a laugh-riot tonight.

MAN: Seriously, Charlene, I don't like thinking about you havin' that
kind of shit in the house—

WOMAN: It's my house. *(The Man stands with some pain.)* Where are
you going?

MAN: I can't talk to you when you're like this.

THE VOICE: CUT! Take three.

MAN: I came to talk and you shut me out.

WOMAN: You're about ten years too late.

THE VOICE: Jump Cut!

MAN: So. How's work?

WOMAN: I was on page twenty-nine when you arrived. I'm behind
deadline. The shoot's scheduled on location for Monday morning.
I guess I can always fax it.

MAN: How are...the "gals?" At work?

WOMAN: The women?

MAN: Right. Are you starting to turn a profit at—? I don't remember
the name of your production company.

*(The Boy goes to the booth upstage where V.O. is caged and begins
to funnel quarters in. Voice-Over moves, obligatorily erotic, for ten*

seconds each time The Boy feeds the slot, abruptly stopping. Again, The V.O. moves, almost mockingly, and then stops. The Boy searches his pockets for change, and frustrated, starts to shake and kick the booth, in silent mime. V.O. laughs at him.)

WOMAN: Gyno Productions.

MAN: Right. I knew it rhymed with wino. I never can remember it.

WOMAN: It's the root for "woman". In Greek.

MAN: I can see that's important. But it's still hard to remember.

WOMAN: Yeah. It is. But we just designed a new logo, for our stationary and business cards—want to see it?

MAN: Sure. *(The Woman goes to her desk, opens the middle drawer, and takes out a business card—she gives it to The Man.)* Wow. Charlene Dwyer. Story Editor, Gyno Productions. They promoted you. That's really nice, Charlene.

WOMAN: No, not that—what do you think of our new mascot?

MAN: Well, I'm not sure—what is that thing on here? What is it doin'— it's dancing?

WOMAN: It's a Rhinoceros—"Rosie the Rhino." She's dancing.

MAN: Uh-huh. That's...cute. But, don't you think. Those pink...pasties...are goin' a bit far? *(The Man looks closer.)* And the G-String? A Rhino in a G-String does not inspire me. I mean, as well you know, I like my women with flesh on their bones, but this mascot looks a little like you—*before* Weight Watchers. But what do I know? Maybe I'm not your average guy on the street.

WOMAN: I like the G-String. It was my idea. And it's supposed to be...funny. For women.

MAN: I don't know. It looks like a stripper in a lesbo bar to me who's just taken off her flannel shirt.

WOMAN: Oh, forget it. Are you done with your coffee?

MAN: Look, do you want to talk? Talking involves disagreement. Or do you just want me to nod my head, yes, sure, that's great, Charlene—if I don't tell you what I'm thinking, even if it's ignorant, how can I learn anything about what you're doing when you say you're working.

WOMAN: Yeah? Like what do you want to know?

MAN: Well—do you ever think you're gonna run out of words when you're writing like that?

V.O.: She thinks about it all the time.

(The Woman stares at The Man.)

WOMAN: I think about it all the time.

(By this point, The Voice becomes a bouncer, crosses the stage and stops The Boy from beating up V.O.'s booth.)

WOMAN: Forty, fifty pages a day, seven days a week—it's a lot like the Victorian theory about masturbation and young boys.

THE VOICE: *(To The Boy.)* Ya gotta have money to be a player.

WOMAN: They believed that men only had so much semen; over the years, men could spend all the pennies they had in the bank.

(The Boy reluctantly digs in his pants for change. The Voice give him quarters; The Voice and Voice Over try not to laugh. The Voice leaves; The Boy slowly slips in another two-bits.)

MAN: Huh. That's funny.

WOMAN: Yes, it is. *(They giggle; The Woman a lot more than The Man, who looks a bit worried.)*

MAN: But it's not true. *(Quickly)* Is it?

WOMAN: No, of course not. *(Pause)* Can I have my business card back, please?

MAN: I'd like to keep it, if I may. As a…memento. I know it has…your work number on it—but I won't use it. Okay?

WOMAN: Right.

VOICE OVER: Shit, that was dumb, Charlene.

(The Woman sits tensely.)

MAN: Just relax, will ya? So where do all these words come from?

WOMAN: I don't know. When I really get going, it's like a trance—it's not me writing at all. It's as if I just listen to voices and I'm taking dictation.

THE VOICE: Case 103 continued. Subject however, experienced constant excitation, due to what the subject described as inner "voices" usually urging him to erotic arts.

MAN: Doesn't that spook you? I mean, whose voices are these? Who's in control?

V.O.: But she was in control.

WOMAN: Well, they're the characters speaking, or the script itself. I mean, I know it's me, but I have to get into it. At first it spooked me a little. But now I know when I hear them, it's a good sign. And I am in control.

MAN: I used to think that porno flicks were all pictures and no words—

WOMAN: Look, Clyde, I don't write *porno*. I didn't appreciate you telling Leslie Ann that.

(The Boy, out of pocket change now, starts to rattle the booth again. A silent figure erupts with Voice-Over.)

MAN: Well, what do you call it? What was the title of your last opus? *Moonfuck?!* So what is that—Bergman?

WOMAN: It was a critique and a satire of Moonstruck.

MAN: Uh-huh.

WOMAN: Gyno productions is a feminist film company dedicated to producing women's erotica.

MAN: Erotica is just a Swedish word for *porn*, Charlene. Just face what you're doing. Take pride in it.

WOMAN: What's the use. Are you through with your coffee?

(By this point, The Voice becomes a bouncer, crosses the stage and seizes The Boy. The Voice roughs up The Boy and throws him out.)

MAN: Look, this is what happens every time I challenge you. You just. shut. down. As if I'm bullying you. And it's just my way. Of showing interest. A burning interest, as it happens. It's the way men learn to argue through contact sports. As if words were body grease, so you gotta grab hard to pin your opponent. And I'm stuck here, feeling stupid and cut off, because you won't explain things in plain English. You speak in a code. A code designed for signals between members of the female sex. Well, pardon me, but I did. not. go. to college.

WOMAN: In plain English: I am not a pornographer. I write erotic entertainment designed for women.

MAN: Yeah. So to return to what I was askin': what's the big difference?

(Voice and Voice-Over begin to make orgiastic noises when the Woman says "aroused".)

WOMAN: For one thing, desire in female spectators is aroused by cinema in a much different way. Narrativity—that is, plot—is emphasized.

MAN: *(Stares at her)* Yeah. There are lots more words. So what else?

WOMAN: The "meat shots" and "money shots" of the trade flicks are not the be all and end all of Gyno Productions.—Why are you laughing?

MAN: I seen one of your movies—and it had tits and ass just like DEEP THROAT.

WOMAN: Physical expression is the culmination of relationships between characters. Most importantly, we try to create women as protagonists in their own dramas, rather than objects. And we try to appreciate the male body as an object of desire.

MAN: Now you're talking! *(In his enthusiasm, The Man moves too much and flinches.)* Oh, suffering Jesus on the cross!

WOMAN: Is it bad?

MAN: Yeah.

WOMAN: Come on, let's go.

MAN: —No, wait a minute, wait a second. I'm a…little woozy. Do you have anything in the house. For the pain?

WOMAN: Whatdya mean, for the pain?

MAN: I could use a shot of something.

WOMAN: You want me to give you a drink, Clyde? Are you insane?

MAN: One drink is not gonna hurt. In fact, it will dull the throbbing in my butt. And since it was your bullet that's in my butt, I think you owe me. One.

WOMAN: You get mean when you drink. I don't want to participate in enabling behavior.

MAN: Goddamn Oprah Winfrey! Just get me something, will ya, Charlene? My Butt is bitchin'…

WOMAN: One shot. That's all. I'll get some for me.

(The Woman exits. While she is out of the room, The Man quickly searches under the sofa pillows and cushions for the gun. She returns with a bottle and two shot glasses. The Woman pours them drinks and hands The Man his glass.)

MAN: Wow. That's nice.

WOMAN: It's Remy.

MAN: It's been a while…since I had Remy. Well—let's toast. To love and success and a long film career—to you.

WOMAN: To…to you. To you, Clyde. *(They sip. Pause.)*

THE VOICE: Jump Cut!

WOMAN: You've got to let go now.

MAN: I…kinda lost my head when I got that restraining order today, Charlene. Some things will never be *over*. Like everything you taught me.

WOMAN: What did I teach you?

MAN: You taught me all about desire. That's not over. I think about you all the time. I have since high school.

WOMAN: You're not thinking about me—you're obsessing. On me. It could have been anything, just as long as it kept your mind off of your job. And now that you've lost your job, you're obsessing about me to keep your mind off the fact that you don't have a job.

MAN: No—I think differently than you do. That's all....And because you can never understand what's going on inside a man's head, you imagine the worst.

THE VOICE: *(Krafft-Ebing)* Case 103 continued. However, in time the constant excitation of hysteria virillis leads in turn to paraesthesia sexualis. The subject became convinced in his mind that only violence done to his fetishized obsession could restore him to his former virility.

THE VOICE: Jumpcut!

MAN: I'm gonna put myself together—get retrained in something. Maybe go back to school like you did. It really changed you, Charlene, when you went back to school.

WOMAN: I think that would be wonderful.

MAN: I have to work out my "karma". Because I really fucked it up in this lifetime. And I have to pay for that by trying.

WOMAN: I don't believe in "karma".

MAN: I do. I believe in it. There's no other way to explain stuff like high school proms...

(The Woman laughs. The Man smiles.)

WOMAN: I forget sometimes how unique you are. When you're not drinking.

THE VOICE[7]: *(Brooklynese)* She will embrace me warmly, as if we had never embraced before. We will have only a couple of hours together and then she will leave—to go to the dance hall where she still works as a taxi girl. I will be sound asleep when she returns at three or four in the morning. ...I love her, heart and soul. She is everything to me.

MAN: You're everything to me.

THE VOICE: Jumpcut!

WOMAN: I...think about you. I try to figure it out. All the time. Why I stayed with it so long. And then one day, I realized that every dish in the house had been replaced with plastic ones. Part of me got off, living on the edge like that. But I was losing control.

THE VOICE: Jumpcut!

MAN: I never stop thinking about it. It's this tape loop. It's torturing me. I'm standing outside my body, watching this actor doing that to you. A stunt man who's got my face.

320 ✱ PAULA VOGEL

THE VOICE[8]: *(Krafft-Ebing; as lyrical as a German sexologist can get)* "Woman is a harp who only yields her secrets of melody to the master who knows how to hand her...the husband must study the harp and the art of music..."

WOMAN: Try to make the next woman in your life lucky. It will be better, the next time.

V.O.: "She can...smell...his sweat. So warm, she can smell"

THE VOICE: "So close, she can almost taste—"

V.O.: "Smell. His."

THE VOICE: "Sweat."

(A blue light fills the stage again. There is a rustling at the sliding glass window. We see The Boy against the glass, watching. He stretches his arms against the frame.)

MAN: It will never be as good as it is with you.

THE VOICE: "CUT TO: INTERIOR. THE WOMAN closes her eyes."

(The Woman closes her eyes.)

"Close up on her lips as she kisses The Man, hard, on the mouth." *(The Woman sits by The Man and gently kisses him. They look at each other. Then they kiss again, a long, hard kiss, breathing each other in.)*

V.O.: "VOICE-OVER: What are you doing, Charlene?"

THE VOICE: "THE MAN and THE WOMAN look at each other for a long time."

V.O.: "VOICE-OVER continued. This is not a movie, Charlene."

THE VOICE: "THE MAN and THE WOMAN move towards each other, lips parted"

V.O.: *(urgent)* "CUT TO: EXTERIOR. We see the door of the house burst open and—"

THE VOICE: *(cutting in)* "THE WOMAN begins to breathe, quicker; THE MAN moves closer and presses against her, urgent now—"

V.O.: *(trying harder)* "CUT TO—CUT TO: EXTERIOR! We see THE WOMAN run from the house—"

THE VOICE: —"THE WOMAN sighs; THE MAN reaches out and strokes her hair—"

V.O.: *(Insistent)* "—Get out of the house!"

THE VOICE: "Long shot. Exterior. THE BOY watches through the window." *(There is a freeze; The Man and Woman on the sofa; The Boy, stretched on the window. The blue light changes to the normal lights, and then dims; The Man starts unbuttoning Woman's top:)*

WOMAN: What about your—?—No, Wait—

MAN: Shh! Don't talk. Not now.

(*The Man and Woman resume. Just then the door flies open violently; the Boy flies into the room:*)

BOY: I AM. GONNA. *KILL* YOU!!!

MAN: What the fuck—? (*In a fury, The Boy throws himself on top of the couple; The Man and Boy roll onto the floor. The Man screams.*) SHIT! AAAAH!

WOMAN: CALVIN! NO! STOP! Watch out for his butt!

(*The Man and Boy wrestle; they stand. The Boy, from behind, gets The Man in a lock, one hand pinned and twisted; The Boy's arm is locked around The Man's throat, choking him.*)

MAN: (*In a squeezed voice:*) It's getting harder to...to be a...family man...these days.

BOY: You leave her alone. Understand?

WOMAN: Calvin. It's not. As it looks.

BOY: *You* don't live here anymore. Get it?

MAN: (*Appreciatively, in the same squeezed voice:*) You're getting...mighty big, son. (*And just as quickly, The Man slips around and out of The Boy's grip, quickly kneeing him in the groin. The Boy gasps and falls into a fetal position on the rug.*)

WOMAN: Jesus Christ, Clyde!

MAN: He's playing with the big boys now. (*The Boy says nothing. His face, beet red, presses into the rug.*)

WOMAN: Calvin—

MAN: Don't touch him. He'll be all right. (*Pause*) Son? You all right? (*The Man offers his hand to The Boy, who refuses it, and slowly gets up.*) I'm sorry. Reflex action. No man likes to injure the family jewels.

WOMAN: Calvin—

BOY: What's he doin' here?

WOMAN: Your father...just...

MAN: Dropped in. For a little adult conversation.

BOY: That's not what it looked like to me.

WOMAN: Honey, I can appreciate your concern, but he's still your father—

BOY: —What's he doin' here?

MAN: —Look, maybe I should just call it a night.

WOMAN: No, wait a minute, Clyde. No matter what's happened

between you and me, you and Calvin have to learn how to talk to one another. I will not be used as an excuse for getting in the middle of the two of you. Do you both hear me? I want you to both act civilized to each other in my living room for at least sixty seconds. *(Beat)* I'm putting on a fresh pot of coffee. *(The Woman exits.)*

MAN: Whatta night, huh? *(As The Man hobbles past The Boy to sit on the sofa.)*

BOY: Hey, what happened to your butt?

MAN: Your poor, defenseless mother shot me.

BOY: Mom? Mom? She shot you? *(The Boy starts to laugh.)*

MAN: I don't see anything particularly amusing about it. Men might hit you in the balls, but they do it to your face. Women—they shoot you in the butt.

BOY: You musta deserved it.

MAN: This is something private between your mother and me. *(Pause)* So—how's school.

BOY: Okay.

MAN: And life? In general.

BOY: Okay. *(Another Pause)*

MAN: Aren't you going to ask me how I'm doin'?

BOY: How are you, Dad?

MAN AND BOY TOGETHER: I'm warmer than shit and tighter than mud. *(Another Pause)*

MAN: So—how's your sister?

BOY: Okay, I guess.

MAN: You guess? You don't know? You gotta keep an eye on her, son. She's at...that age. Know what I mean? *(Man punches Boy in arm.)*

BOY: Yeah, sure I do.

MAN: That's right. You're the man of the house, now. Best thing to do is just lock her up for a couple of years. She's gonna cause a lot of men heartbreak. You gotta watch her, son.

BOY: I do. I watch her all the time.

MAN: I mean, it's not her fault, right? But that body of hers...you know what I mean?

BOY: Yeah.

MAN: The body of hers...your sister should be *licensed*.
(Blue light stage left of glass door. The Girl begins to work to the music. The Man and Boy stare appreciatively.)

MAN: Where is—your sister?

BOY: She said she was goin' to some sleepover.

MAN: And your mother believes that crap? We don't believe that crap, do we?

(*The two share a laugh, settle back and watch with glazed attention.*)

THE VOICE[9]: "One of the things that made Cleo's dance fascinating was the little pompon she wore in the center…it served to keep your eyes riveted to the spot. She could rotate it like a pinwheel or make it jump and quiver with little electric spasms. Sometimes it would subside with little gasps, like a swan coming to rest…It seemed to be part of her. Possibly she had acquired it in an Algerian whorehouse, from a French sailor. It was tantalizing, especially to the sixteen-year-old who had still to know what it feels like to make a grab for a woman's bush."

(*Blue Light out on The Girl. The Woman enters with a tray; a coffee pot, two mugs, a plate of cookies. And a tall glass of milk. The Woman pauses, watches them. She sets the tray down on the coffee table.*)

WOMAN: You two are just…chattering away like magpies.

MAN: We've been talking. Right?

BOY: Yup.

MAN: Man-talk.

BOY: You just caught us during the pause.

WOMAN: I've fixed us a late-night snack. A last cup of coffee before I drive your father to the hospital.

MAN: I don't think that's…necessary, Charlene.

WOMAN: This is nothing to fool around with, Clyde. Let me see how it's doing. Turn over.

MAN: Not in front of the boy, goddamn it.

WOMAN: For Christ's sake, he's your own flesh and blood. Turn over.

(*The Man turns his wounded cheek towards her. She carefully lowers his pants and examines the wound critically; The Boy peeks.*)

BOY: Wow.

WOMAN: It's still bleeding. Not as bad as before, though. It needs stitches and a fresh bandage.

(*Pause*)

BOY: Mom? Didja really shoot Dad?

WOMAN: Yes.

BOY: Cool. Mom?

WOMAN: Calvin, we're not going to discuss it.

MAN: Why don't you just drink up your milk and go to bed...

(*The Boy stares with disbelief and disgust at the glass of milk.*)

BOY: You have got to be shittin' me...

MAN: Lucky for you this is your mother's house. I'd turn the strap on ya for language like that...

BOY: Mom! MILK?!! MILK!?

WOMAN: Well, sweetie, it's too late for you to be drinking coffee, and I saved the last glass of milk to go with your cookies.

BOY: I'm not drinking that shit.

MAN: Growing boys need their milk? Right?

WOMAN: Let's just drop it, Clyde.

MAN: Only wusses are scared of milk. A real man can drink milk.

BOY: You drink it.

MAN: Okay, son—I'll show you how it's done. How a real man drinks milk—

WOMAN: —Stop it. Stop it. I hate this.

(*The Man abruptly grabs the milk, and guzzles half the glass. It dribbles down his chin and shirt.*)

MAN: Num, num. A man who can't drink milk can't love women. Is that a problem for you son? Are you that kind of man?

WOMAN: Why does everything turn into a nightmare around here?

MAN: Show your old man. Drink the milk. (*The Man presses the glass into The Boy's face. They freeze:*)

THE VOICE[10]: —"there's the mark of his teeth still where he tried to bite the nipple I had to scream out aren't they fearful trying to hurt you"— (*End freeze*)

MAN: Drink the milk.

BOY: No. Shit! Get out of my face.

MAN: It's just Milk. What are you scared of? Milk can't hurt you—

(*The two tussle with the milk; it splashes them both.*)

BOY: You're. An. Asshole! (*The Woman and The Boy instinctively flinch. A moment's pause.*)

MAN: (*quietly*) What. Did. You. Call. Me?

WOMAN: —Enough! (*The Boy goes to The Woman, scared*).

BOY: You don't scare me. This is not your house. You keep away from us. Stop thrusting yourself on Mom, You.Hear.Me?

MAN: I wasn't thrusting myself on your mother. Quite the opposite. Did I thrust myself on you on the sofa, Charlene? Did I?

WOMAN: I'm taking you to the hospital.now.

MAN: Your mother kissed me. First.

WOMAN AND BOY: *(Together) (Woman:)* This is getting ridiculous—
   (Boy:) —That's a lie! Isn't it, Mom?

WOMAN: We're ending this conversation. Now.

MAN: Tell him. You kissed me.

BOY: Don't be scared of him, Mom. I'm here.

MAN: I know it's hard to believe, Calvin. She's amazing when she kisses.

BOY: —Did.You.Kiss.Him? Mom? After all he's done?

THE VOICE[11]: —"and his heart was going like mad and yes I said yes
   I—"

WOMAN: Calvin—honey, it's hard to explain, at your age—it was
   just...for old time's sake!

BOY: I DON'T BELIEVE YOU!

MAN: Don't raise your voice like that to your mother—

WOMAN: —For God's sake, Calvin, I'm a human being, too—I have
   needs—

BOY: I'm Getting Out. Of. Here—

MAN: When your mother kisses a man, it's like your heart gets
   squeezed. Too bad she's your mother and you'll never know—

BOY: ARGHH!! *(Holding his head, The Boy rushes for the door, opens
   it, and runs out into the night, screaming:)* I AM SO FUCKED UP!
   (Door slam.)

THE VOICE[12]: "She kissed me. I was kissed. All yielding she tossed my
   hair. Kissed, she kissed me. Me. And me now."
   (The Man and Woman sit, weary and tense.)

WOMAN: Why do you always do that?

MAN: Do what?

WOMAN: Oh, you know. You know very well.

MAN: *(Getting angry)* Christ!
   (Man and Woman look at each other. Blue Light.)

V.O.: FLASH-BACK. THREE YEARS AGO.
   *(The Man strikes the Woman hard on the face; in slow motion, it
   almost looks like a caress. The Woman falls on the sofa. Man drags
   on cigarette and then moves it toward Woman's face.)*

THE VOICE: "Case 103 Continued. Subject increasingly resorted to violence against wife as an erotic stimulus for erec—"

V.O.: CUT TO:—
   *(Abrupt lighting change: back to bright stage lights. The Woman
   stands, scared.)*

WOMAN: *(Trying to be composed:)* Calm down.

MAN: Calm down—I don't have a job, I've got no fuckin' family, no wife—I've got shit for a life!

WOMAN: Maybe you should go now.

THE VOICE[13]: "We will have only a couple of hours together and then she will leave—to go to the dance hall where she still works as a taxi girl."

MAN: Christ, Charlene. I just wish—shit, I just wish we could go back, ya know? Before college, before I got fired, before everything started busting apart. I wish I could just close my eyes and you'd be coming home through the door in your uniform, after your night shift.

WOMAN: Oh, God. I hated that fucking uniform. It made my backside enormous. Made me into a tired, washed-out Cow in White.

MAN: You'd come in, tired but sweet. I'm under the covers. First you flip on the coffee in the kitchen, and the aroma comes up to me before you reach the bed. And then I feel your hands on my stubble, stroking it, and then I hear the sound of your shoes hitting the floor, one by one. And the zippers. The sound of the uniform sliding down your slip. And then the next thing I know, there's your warmth in bed. And your voice urging me up to work. Already slipping into sleep. And every morning, I went to work with a hard-on. It was great.

WOMAN: Great. *(The Woman stares into nothing as she slowly pours the coffee as a trickle into a cup)*

V.O.: "And every night, she would stand in the middle of the ward and think, 'I can't do this any longer.' Holding another bed pan, swimming with someone's fluids. Urine, excreta, blood, infection, vomit, mucus. Bodies and mess.

Mess and food. Cleaning up messes. Cleaning up messes. This is where a high school diploma gets you, Charlene. Other people's messes.

MAN: You're going to spill that coffee.

(The Woman speaks, far away, holding the coffee.)

WOMAN: I hated that fucking job. I hated how I had to see human flesh.

MAN: But then you came home. To me and the children.

(The Woman laughs, but decides not to say what she's thinking.)

(Pause)

WOMAN: This writing is…saving my sanity. I'll never go back.

(*Pause*)

MAN: So where's Leslie Ann at tonight?

WOMAN: She's spending the night with a friend.

MAN: A friend, huh.

WOMAN: Yes. A girlfriend. She asked my permission.

MAN: It's your house.

WOMAN: Don't you dare start implying—

MAN: What? Who? Who's implying—

WOMAN: I work very hard at being a good mother.

MAN: You're a great mother.

WOMAN: I try, that's all.

MAN: Leslie Ann's just at...that age, is all. You know.

WOMAN: No, I don't know. What age is that?

MAN: You can't be too careful. Look, I'm hardly the one to give you advice...seeing as how my back-seat activities got me into messes.

WOMAN: I know exactly where my children are. I know exactly where Leslie Ann is, right now.

V.O.: "CUT TO: INTERIOR: In the rec room of Lisa's house. Night."
(*On the ramp, The Girl, now in an oversized tee-shirt, huddles in her sleeping bag, addressing her best friend Lisa. The Girl and Voice Over speak to each other.*)

GIRL: You're my best friend, Lisa. You. *Know*. That. Since Seventh Grade. And you're gonna be my best friend long after I get married and have kids. If it wasn't for the fact.that.I.get to see you for homeroom and lunch, I woulda stopped goin' to that stupid school a long time ago.

V.O.: Uh huh. Is your sleeping bag warm enough?

GIRL: I feel like there's nothin' you couldn't tell me. You know? I would die before one'a your secrets would roll out. Of. My. Mouth.

V.O.: Me too. You could tell me—anything.

GIRL: That's good. Are the other girls...asleep?...Do you—do. You—

V.O.: What? Come on, you can tell me—anything—

GIRL: And you won't tell?

V.O.: I swear. I swear! Com'mon, what is it?

GIRL: I've never said this to anyone else before. I'll kill you if you—

V.O.: —You can tell me. Anything.

GIRL: Well. Do you...do you...think of boys a lot?

V.O.: (*Giggling*) All the time.

GIRL: I mean at night, when you turn the lights out?

V.O.: Especially at night. When the lights are out.

GIRL: But I mean do you think about…think about…

V.O.: What? What? About…doing it?

GIRL: Yeah, but not just that— *(in a rush)* I mean, I think of that, too, but sometimes…do you think of them, like, "hurting" you? Well, I don't mean like hurting you, but like, you're tied down and you can't stop them and they do things to you that hurt you, that make you scream but you can't and you wouldn't really want it to happen in real life, you would really get hurt, but when you close your eyes, you see it and it makes you get hot only it's 'cause it's not for real? *(Pause)* Lisa? Lisa? Are you asleep?

(Film slate clap. Lights back up on living room.)

WOMAN: Leslie Ann is still a child. And I want her to have every second of childhood that she can get.

MAN: A child, huh? Have you looked at your daughter lately?

WOMAN: I had a body like that when I was her age. Remember?

MAN: —Now we're talkin' ancient history—

WOMAN: There's too much pressure on her, already. Lectures on safe sex, birth control, condoms. The boys in the hall at school hitting on her, accusing her of being frigid. The married men on their way to work who leer and wink at her and her friends. I want her *left. Alone.*

MAN: Okay, okay. You're her mother. But have you walked out of your front door lately? Seen the world?

(Pause. Through the next beats, the tension escalates.)

WOMAN: It's not the world outside I'm worried about her seeing.

MAN: What's that supposed to mean?

(Pause)

WOMAN: I think we should go now. I'll drive you.

MAN: I can drive myself.

WOMAN: Let's go, then.

MAN: I'm not ready.

THE VOICE: Cut! Take two.

WOMAN: It's late. I want you out of here.

MAN: I just got here. I'm not ready to go.

WOMAN: Don't.

MAN: What am I doing? Having a cup of coffee?

WOMAN: You can't stay, Clyde. I need you out of here.

THE VOICE: Cut! Take three.

WOMAN: I want you out of here.

MAN: I'll leave when I'm ready. Or are you going to make me?

WOMAN: If I have to.

MAN: Oooh. I'm scared.

WOMAN: Don't mock me, goddamn you—

(*There is the sound of door keys, loud heavy metal music and door slam, and The Girl enters. They all blink at each other.*)

MAN: Hi, baby girl.

GIRL: Daddy! *(To Woman)* You didn't tell me he was gonna be here.

WOMAN: What are you doing here?

GIRL: I came back for somethin'—Lisa's waiting outside—

WOMAN: Why don't you just go back out to the car and Lisa—

GIRL: —Why didn't you tell me my father was coming tonight?

WOMAN: Did you notice the knob is off the door?

MAN: Don't I get a kiss anymore? *(The Girl runs to her father and hugs him.)* That's more like it.

GIRL: It's good to see you, Daddy.

MAN: My God, you're getting big. What are you doing tonight, princess?

GIRL: I'm doin' a sleep-over at Lisa's—she's my friend in the car. Do you want to meet her?

MAN: No—that's okay. What do you girls do together?

GIRL: We're watching movies, mostly. Friday the 13th, Halloween—

VOICE OVER: *(À la horror-movie.)* "Get out of the house! Get out of the—

WOMAN: I don't know how you can watch those.

GIRL: They're just movies, mom. *(To The Man:)* Are you coming back home?

WOMAN: No! He was just leaving—we were on our way out—

GIRL: I just got here!

WOMAN: Leslie Ann, your father and I are in the middle of something—

GIRL: —Lay-la. Where's Calvin?

MAN: He left after a little chat.

GIRL: Are you gonna be here when I get back?

WOMAN: No.

GIRL: You just came over for a visit? Daddy?

MAN: I wanted to try to talk to your mother, that's all. *(Man hands Girl $5.)*

GIRL: Good luck. She's hard to talk to.

WOMAN: Okay. That's enough. Go on with Lisa—

GIRL: Why don't you two just try to talk it out? Daddy, you've got to give up drinking, that's all. And get another job. It's no big deal. I don't see why you two can't work it out.

MAN: Well, I'd like that, Layla.

WOMAN: It's more complicated than that, honey.

GIRL: I don't want to be just another kid in a one-parent home. I don't see why I can't have two parents, like you're supposed to have. I hate being a latch-key kid, if anyone wants to ask about my feelings.

WOMAN: You're not a latch-key kid. I'm always home, working.

GIRL: Oh, great! I'm in a one-parent home, with a working mother, who types porno all day long on her butt in the living room! You can't even work a nine to five—

WOMAN: Listen, young lady. My nerves are just about. Shot. Don't push me. Not you, too—

GIRL: I'm gonna tell Lisa to go on without me.

WOMAN: No. You are going. With Lisa. And have a nice time.

GIRL: Everybody gets to talk to him but me!

(*There is the sound of a car horn. Three times... "Lo-lit-ta".*)

THE VOICE: Daddy's girl...

(*The Girl goes to the door and yells:*)

GIRL: Go on without me, okay?!

(*There is the sound of a car horn again, with The Voice echoing:*)

THE VOICE: Daddy's girl...

GIRL: I wanna stay here and talk.

WOMAN: Not tonight. I mean it.

GIRL: I can't even talk to my own father!! Why can't we be like other families? Don't I even get a chance? Where's my fucking 4-H club? When did we ever say grace at the dinner table! I'm a fucking statistic from a broken home! A goddamn teenage statistic without enough money for a fucking double-feature who has to lie that my mother's a secretary and that my father's a secret agent so no one finds out I've got a pervo for a mother, a drunk for a father and a four-eyed geek for a brother who beats off in his catcher mitt! FUCK! (*The Girl slams out of the house.*)

WOMAN: I'm not a mean woman. But I'm really going to enjoy watching her when she has children of her own.

MAN: I don't remember talking to my mother like that.

WOMAN: The only reason Leslie Ann thinks the sun shits out of your ass is 'cause I've lied to her all these many years. She thinks I'm just...clumsy.

MAN: Yeah, well you are.

WOMAN: I wasn't "clumsy" until after we got married.

MAN: Okay, Charlene. I've ruined your life. Okay? I'm fucked up as a husband and a father, and I've ruined whatever fucking chance at happiness you and my children have in this lifetime.

WOMAN: I'm not asking you for that, Clyde.

MAN: What do you want from me?

WOMAN: Why'd you come over?

MAN: I...wanted to see you.

WOMAN: Why? What is it you want?

MAN: I want...I want...what's the use. *(The Man gets up to go.)*

WOMAN: Just tell me the truth. Okay? I'm listening.

MAN: You...you'll hate me if you know...

WOMAN: I can't hate you more than I have for the past ten years.

MAN: Well. Okay, this is hard for me, all right? It's...it's a fuckin' Friday night. Right? And so what do we do, Friday night? Go out, drink some beer, and...ya know...cruise the strip. I mean, if you're a guy who's alone, that's what there is to do in this town on a Friday.

WOMAN: I'm with you so far.

MAN: Right. So I...take a shower, you know, spruce up a little bit. And I count out the change I have left. And it's not much. And that gets me a little depressed, but I think, okay, shit, I'll economize, I'll buy a six-pack for the truck, and I won't drink out, you know? So I go downtown, and hit the streets...and I go in to a few...places...but mostly there are minimums. So I think, fuck, I can't even watch the live action.

WOMAN: You gotta have money to be a player.

MAN: So—so—so I go into a corner bookstore, and it's packed. And I change a five into quarters, and slip into the booth—and I—

WOMAN: —You watch—

MAN: Right. And all it does is get me even more agitated. I'm thinking, this is not what I want, on A Friday Night, the feeling of my own fist in a booth—I'm like numb to that by now—and so I get back into my own truck, and I drink a few beers, to get my nerve up—and I empty out my pockets—I check the dash and under the seats, and I count—and I come up with a lousy 18 dollars and 37 cents.

WOMAN: Well, that's better than nothing.

MAN: Are you being...funny?

WOMAN: No. I'm not. I'm not making judgments. Go on.

MAN: Well, I think, you know, times are hard, maybe some working girl will consider it—you know? Maybe I'll get lucky, or I'll hit someone green on the street—so I crank up the engine, and start to drive it slow, down the side street—and I see them, it's warm out tonight, and they're there, in groups—laughing, wearing next to nothing, and they're so close, they're laughing at me, calling out to me—

WOMAN: —So why didn't you ask someone?

MAN: —I don't know. They were all together. I couldn't get one off by herself; I thought they'd laugh—I couldn't just call out, you know "how about $18.37?!" I just...just lost my nerve, I was so...down by then...then...and then I just kept driving and the truck kind of drove here by itself.

WOMAN: *(Quietly)* So you're telling me that you drove to your ex-wife's house because you couldn't afford a prostitute.

MAN: Jesus, Charlene, don't make it sound like that!

WOMAN: I'm not taking offense, Clyde. I'm telling it like it is. It's the truth. I'm a grown woman. I can take the truth. In fact, I prefer it.

MAN: I mean, the truth is...the truth is...that lately nothing really seems to do it for me. I don't know what...what's happening to me...but all the usual...uh...escapes...turn me on but they don't work anymore—I just get more and more depressed and anxious—like what if it just won't work at all, I mean, it happens, sometimes to men, and something's happening in...in my head—well, frankly, it scares the shit out of me. And it's building up into a big problem now.

WOMAN: I don't understand.

(The Man starts to shake, ever so slightly, trying not to cry.)

MAN: I mean like magazines, or girls in the booth, you know? I'll try to watch them, to use them, but...something's changed...I start thinking, she's young enough to be my daughter, or...I'll bet she's married, or she's someone's mother...the words I read in the books I buy, I start to wonder if some woman's writing them, the way you do, to pay the rent for her kids...and...I think I'm really, really fucked up. I'm sorry...I don't mean to do this to you, I know you've got problems of your own, but I just think I need to talk to a woman, you know... *(The Man is crying, quietly.)*

WOMAN: Sit down. Just…sit down. Okay? *(The Man does so.)* It's okay. It happens. I think you should find someone to talk to about this, okay, Clyde? I mean a professional. It's not anything…insoluble…Just take a second, now. *(Pause. They sit quietly beside each other on the sofa. The Woman makes a decision.)* How are you feeling? Does it still hurt?

MAN: Huh? Oh, that—no, I barely feel it. I think it's stopped bleeding.

WOMAN: Okay—listen. I'm just a woman on a Friday night, okay? I've come down on my price for you—just tonight—for $18.37. You've hit the jackpot, mister. I am not your wife—or anyone's mother right now. Just this once—Clyde—we've got to be quick, before the kids come back. Put the chain on the door, and make the sofa bed up, okay? The sheets are already on it, you've just got to take the cushions off and pull it out. I'm going…to change into something.

(The Man has a hard time talking.)

MAN: You don't have to…

WOMAN: I know I don't.

MAN: I'm not sure if I can…if I—

WOMAN: Then we'll just hold each other. All Right? Quick, now, before I change my mind. I'll be right back.

(The Woman exits into the bathroom. The Man, unable to believe his luck, sits for a few moments on the sofa. Then slowly, he gets up, in pain. He begins to take the cushions off the sofa. When he turns back to the audience, we can see that his jeans are soaked in blood. He sees that he has drenched the cushion, and quickly turns the bloody side to the wall. He stops and calls out:)

MAN: Charlene! Uh—Charlene—

WOMAN: *(Off)* What!

MAN: I don't have…anything on me…you know? In case—

WOMAN: *(Off)* That's okay. I've got some protection in the house. *(Laughs)* The other kind. A girl scout is always prepared…

(The Man stops, scowls. Blue light blends with stage lights, slowly.)

THE VOICE: She's got protection in the house.

V.O.: A girl scout is always…prepared…

THE VOICE: She's got plenty of protection. She's prepared.

V.O.: Always prepared.

THE VOICE: Case 103 continued. In June of this past year, authorities were notified by subject's wife and promptly charged Mr. C. with a restraining order. However, Mr. C. ignored said order, and managed to isolate his ex-wife in her home, where, unable to arouse himself by normal stimuli, he was overcome with a desire for what I term "lust-murder." Only after he had satisfied himself with violence on ex-wife's body was subject apprehended.

(Steadily angry, The Man begins to pull out the bed. He reaches his hand into the sofa frame, and stops again. He feels something. The Man slowly pulls out a gun. He stands there, thinking, holding the gun. He checks the ammunition. Then he tucks it into his waistband, and finishes making up the bed. Then he sits, brooding. The screenplay goes on while he waits:)

V.O.: *(Breathy)* "She was hot. She was throbbing. But she was in control. Control of her body. Control of her thought. Control of...him.

"He was hot. He was throbbing. And out of control. He needed to be restrained. Tied Down. And taught a lesson..."

"Okay. Now we separate the men from the little boys—"

THE VOICE: —Cut! Listen, there's been a change in the script—

V.O.: What change?

THE VOICE: Al says he wants the bondage in reverse. Okay?

V.O.: That's not what we rehearsed...

THE VOICE: Since when are movies made by screenwriters? Directors make the movies. Not some broad sitting on her ass. Improvise, can't you? Your dialogue has gotta be as good as the dumb ass writer...

V.O.: But I thought—

THE VOICE: Do we pay you to think? You're a professional, aren't you? Do you want the role or don't you—we're wasting overtime—

V.O.: Okay. The show...must go on.—Hey, guys, wait, these restraints are on awfully tight—

THE VOICE: Come on! Let's finish this take...Ready, camera, action—

V.O.: *(Bad acting:)* Please don't hurt me...

THE VOICE: I'm not gonna hurt you, baby...I'm just gonna teach you a little lesson...a lesson you'll remember... *(There is the sound of a large switch.)*

V.O.: *(Pain)* Shit! Wait a minute, guys—that really hurt. Larry—stop the camera—Larry? Where's Larry?

THE VOICE: We told Larry to take a walk.

V.O.: *(Scared)* I don't know any of you guys...are you guys with Gyno Productions?

THE VOICE: This is not your screenplay.

V.O.: I don't understand...

THE VOICE: Ever hear of snuff films?

(*Just then, the bathroom door opens, and The Woman, in a peignoir, reenters the room. With a well-developed animal instinct, she stands stock-still, smelling the change in the atmosphere. The Boy and Girl have appeared as well, pressed against the window glass. The Boy watching the action cries but the Girl watches as if filming.*)

THE VOICE: What are you—

MAN: What are you looking at?

WOMAN: *(Scared)* Nothing. Maybe this was a stupid idea.

VOICE: You look great.

MAN: You look...great.

VOICE: Really great.

MAN: Really great.

WOMAN: Really? Worth $18.37, huh?

THE VOICE: Ya gotta have money to be a player.

MAN: Let me...hold you. Come here.

THE VOICE: Lights, camera, action! (*The Woman goes to The Man, they embrace.*)

WOMAN: This feels good.

MAN: You smell good.

V.O.: Get out of the house.

MAN: I've been thinking—ya know, trying to figure out women. What turns them on and I think tonight I've found the answer.

WOMAN: Let's not talk.

MAN: Is it our smell? Our torso? Our butts?

WOMAN: Let's not bring that subject up. (*The Woman gently strokes his wounded half and stops at the wetness:*) Hey—wait a moment—

MAN: I think women really get turned on to men in pain. That's what they like—

(*The Woman breaks away; in fear she examines her hand, now bloodied.*)—

WOMAN: Oh my god—Clyde, you're—

MAN: Blood! Blood?! Does it excite you, baby? Get you hot? (*The Man reaches in to the back of his pants, and rubs her face with the blood—*)

WOMAN: Oh my god— (*The Woman starts to dash for the door, but he gets there first. The Man carefully draws out the gun.*)

MAN: You left your "protection" under the sofa.

WOMAN: Clyde—listen—

MAN: Shut, up, God. Damn. You! *(The Man savagely hits the woman.)*

THE VOICE: The woman is a harp.

MAN: Do you remember the last time? *(The Woman starts to cry.)* I asked you a question. Do. You. Remember. The last time.

WOMAN: When...we...made love?

MAN: No. When I beat you to within an inch of your life. You didn't learn then, did you?

WOMAN: No.

MAN: I. Can't. Hear. You.

WOMAN: No.

MAN: I'm going to have to teach you all over again.

(The Voice starts to play rap music)

WOMAN: Please—stop—

MAN: Shut. Up. ...Now—get on the bed like a good wife.

WOMAN: Please—

(The Man strikes her again.)

MAN: Stop crying or I'll give you something to cry about.

VOICE: The woman is a harp.

MAN: On. The. Bed! *(The Man backhands The Woman and she falls on the bed.)*

THE VOICE: *(Whispered under:)* Now. Don't. Move.

WOMAN: Don't.

MAN: Don't Move. *(V.O. starts to plead quietly—"please" and "don't" until the Voice plays James Joyce.)*

THE VOICE: I'm beating you to teach you a lesson. Understand? And I'll stop when I feel like it. Bitch. What makes you think, with your big fat butt and your cow thighs, that you're worth 18 bucks? Huh? What man would pay for that?

(The Man unbuckles his belt, draws it from the loops, as The Woman continues to cry. A cry erupts from The Man's throat)

MAN: *(Crying)* —You're the one making me do this, Charlene. You should of never—never gotten that restraining order—kicked me out of my own home! Jesus Christ, Charlene—why did you do that? Why?

WOMAN: —Don't cry—don't— *(The Woman embraces the Man.)*

MAN: A man's home is his Castle. His. Fucking. Castle. What we do in here is our business. It's our fucking sacred business...Not the goddamn judge's!

(*The Man punches the Woman in the stomach and loops his belt around her neck and begins to strangle her.*)

THE VOICE[14]: *(Whispered under/simultaneous with V.O.:)* "When I put the rose in my hair like the Andalusian girls used or shall I swear a red yes and how he kissed me under the Moorish wall and I thought well we well him as another and then I asked him with my eyes to ask again yes and then he asked me would I yes to say yes my mountain flower and first I put my arms around his yes"—

V.O.: *(Simultaneous with V.O. above)* Get to the door Charlene can you shit keep calm so you can get out of this one no keep fighting try to get under the strap no ask him with your eyes to no please ask him would he no there's no air left no for the kids stay calm you can make it stars put your arms around him squeeze don't stop stay calm keep eyes open ask oh god would I no to say no my god my god and no no air I can't no—

(*The Woman breaks free for a second—*)

WOMAN: —Why?!!

(*The Man strangles The Woman with his bare hands. He leaves. The Voice and Voice Over follow him and the Boy and Girl disappear from view. But a tape-recording of the Voice begins and then slows down, warped:*)

THE VOICE: *(Longer section of Ulysses:)* and drew him down to me so he could feel my breasts all perfume yes and his heart was going like mad and yes I said yes I will Yes.

(*There is a flash of light, and a blackout. When the lights come back on, the stage is empty, except for the body of the Woman, strewn across the bed. The door opens, and The Girl walks in.*

The Girl should see the body of The Woman. She stands still for a beat. The Girl walks quietly and quickly to the bed, and touches the body.

Then, The Girl steps into a spotlight, as the light dims on the body. "The Stripper" theme music plays. She does not bump or grind.

If this play were a film script, we would see The Girl age before our eyes, transformed over the years from what she has just seen. The Girl dresses to the music. She puts on knee-socks, and a long sleeve shirt. Then thick jeans, and finally, running shoes. She arranges her hair, tied back. Her body becomes a bit more worn, more protected from our gaze, her bones less light, her face more deter-

mined. She picks up the glasses The Woman wore and dons them. She walks over to the computer, turns it on, and as the theme music fades, she begins to type:)

GIRL: "Setting: In the midst of a dance-hall there is a living room, almost like an island floating in the deep blue light. Down stage left, we see a large white office desk, holding a computer. At the top of the Act One, the mother types a screenplay.

GIRL: "CUT TO: INTERIOR. NIGHT.—

(The Girl hears something; abruptly looks over her shoulder. Beat. Then she turns back to the computer.)

VOICE OVER: "She was hot. She was throbbing. But she was in control. Control of her body. Control of her thoughts."

END OF PLAY

NOTES

1 Nabokov, *Lolita*.

2 These words were actually written by William Acton, 19th century sexologist; but in this play, they should be delivered as if written by Krafft-Ebing.

3 William Acton.

4 William Acton.

5 I fabricated Case 103 quotes in the style of Krafft-Ebing's *Psychopathis Sexualis*.

6 D.H. Lawrence, *Lady Chatterly's Lover*.

7 Henry Miller, *Plexus*.

8 T.H. Van de Velde, *Ideal Marriage*.

9 Henry Miller, *Plexus*.

10 James Joyce, *Ulysses*.

11 *Ibid.*

12 *Ibid.*

13 Henry Miller, *Plexus*.

14 James Joyce, *Ulysses*.

COME TO LEAVE
by Allison Eve Zell

Dedicated to Max Ted and Carole Inez Zell.

BIOGRAPHY

Allison Eve Zell, a dual citizen of Canada and the United States, was born and raised in Montreal, Quebec. She started out in theatre as an actor, some of her past roles have been Death in Frederico Garcia Lorca's *Blood Wedding*; The Chorus Leader in Euripides' *The Medea*, the Succubus in Charles Busch's *Vampire Lesbians of Sodom*, and Freda Bridgestock in Harley Granville-Barker's *The Madras House* (directed by Mark Wing-Davey with the British American Dramatic Academy in London). It was at Vassar College where she realized that she loves to direct plays. Her first was Sam Shepard's and Joseph Chaikin's *Savage/Love*, followed by a trilogy of student work by Steven Mazzola's titled *kinfolk*, and then a mainstage production of Euripides' *The Bacchae*, which was a part of her senior thesis. As an Independent Major, combining Drama, Classics, and Anthropology, she explored how playwrights make rituals theatrical. Also at Vassar, she wrote the first draft of *Come To Leave*. After graduating, she spent a year at home teaching acting to children and teenagers, and working with Make Haste Productions, a critically-acclaimed company she co-founded with her partner Jennifer Engels. With Make Haste, Allison played Denise Savage in John Patrick Shanley's *Savage in Limbo*, co-directed and played Joyce in Caryl Churchill's *Top Girls*, and directed a bilingual production of Jean-Paul Sartre's *Huis clos/No Exit*. Summer 1994, The Drama League of New York chose her as one of the artistic directors of the Lab Company at Ithaca's Hangar Theatre, where she directed Carol Lashof's *Medusa's Tale*, Christopher Durang's *Naomi in the Living Room*, A.A. Milne's *The Ugly Duckling*, and performed *Come To Leave*. She is now in Chicago getting her Master's degree in Directing at The Theatre School of DePaul University. Her favorite Chicagoian theatrics to date have been co-directing and creating *Soviet Voices* (a reading at an exhibition of Dmitri Baltermants' photographs), assistant directing Jean-Paul Sartre's adaptation of Euripides' *The Trojan Women*, playing the Angel in José Rivera's *Marisol*, doing research for The Goodmans's Studio production of Gertrude Stein's *Melanctha*, titled *Each One as She May*, and working on her own writing. She is directing David Ives' *Speed-the-Play* and Don Nigro's *Specter* this spring at DePaul, and looks forward to ever so much moremuchmore blah-dee-blah… later.

AUTHOR'S NOTE

I first started telling this story when asked to talk about something that meant a lot to me as an acting exercise at The Body Politic Theatre in Chicago, during the summer of 1991. I was then inspired by Rachel Lampert during my senior year at Vassar College when I saw her perform a solo piece about the loss of someone very close to her. Soon after, she agreed to guide me through an independent study in which I wrote the first draft of *Come to Leave*. The following year, I revised and performed it at the Hangar Theatre in Ithaca, New York. It then became important to me that another actor could perform the piece. Autumn 1994, I worked on the final draft with the intention of making it as independent as possible. With the guidance of Dean Corrin, a professor of playwriting at DePaul University, I was able to make the piece what it is today.

ORIGINAL PRODUCTION

COME TO LEAVE was first produced August 1, 1994 in the Hangar Theatre's Lab Space, in Ithaca, New York, with Jonathan Silverstein and Noel Salzman directing.

Woman . . . . Allison Eve Zell

CAST

A woman who is graduating from college.

SETTING

A bare stage with the following elements strewn across it:

- an empty trunk big enough for the woman to fit in it.
- six books, they should have the following as visible as possible in their titles:
  1. "Nietzche"
  2. something problematic (*e.g.* "Middle Eastern Politics")
  3. something necessary (*e.g.* "Simple Cooking for Busy People")
  4. "Freud"
  5. something complex (*e.g.* "Advanced Harmonics")
  6. something logical (*e.g.* "Symbolic Logic")
- a framed photograph of a baby
- an International House of Pancakes pamphlet
- a peacock feather
- a toy sheep
- a jug of wine
- a jar of peanut butter
- a jar of "Goober" (brand name) = layers of peanut butter and grape jelly in one jar
- a toy ghost
- a candle and matches

COME TO LEAVE

A closed trunk is on stage. A woman wearing graduation garb appears out of the trunk, speaks and proceeds to pick up specific objects off the floor at designated times. These moments are marked with an "*" over the course of the monologue. After picking up the objects and using them to communicate, she packs them in the trunk. Sometimes she throws them, and other times she places them gently. When it is a book that is found, if a "Little-Bo-Peepism" follows, it is to be written as an inscription inside the cover. Everything should be packed, leaving a bare stage by the end of the piece. She is wearing two class rings, one on the right hand, and the other on the middle finger of her left hand.

(Whispers this line.) I haven't spoken a word...in years *(Pause.)*

Well, Golly Gee, I didn't think that "apathy" existed in my dictionary, until zzzzzzzzzzzzip! *(Pause.)* No more words. *(Pause.)* I just stopped talking. *(Pause.)* I didn't know who the hell I was talking to anymore... I couldn't tell anyone apart. Every damned sentiment spilled for everybody. Sentiment spilled, sentiment spilled sentimentspilledsentimentspilledsssssssssssspp. Spring, sophomore year something went "ding!" In a Philosophy of Art and Aesthetics class, I learned that * *(Find Nietzsche book.)* Nietzsche defines pain as the simultaneous feeling of repulsion and attraction. I'm not the only one who has felt like running across the country and nestling into my mother's lap at the same time! Christ! *(Places hand over eyes peeking through the second and third finger.)* Is that why people cover their eyes with one hand and peek through their second and third? "I can't look!

(Takes hand off face.) Pain! Everybody's experienced that! Pain...not psychosis! Is there a test for the kind of pain that you can't look at...that you can't see? Why did I spend all my time the last few weeks of my first year at college getting blood tests? *(Shows inside of elbows.)* I was making sure I was healthy...when all I really wanted to do was prove that I was sick.

* *(Finds framed picture of baby.)* 1989 was a year full of firsts and lasts. Even though I am the baby of the family, my leaving home to go to college was a first...so was a grandson...my sister had it. Firsts...and lasts. Everything implodedexplodedimploded explodedimplodedexplodedimplodedexploded baby leaving, baby arriving, that's a fair trade, right? July 7th, 1989, the first grandchild was born. A BABY! Sidney is a name that's so great because it's old enough to be unique without being a Mildred. He was named after my mother's father...who I never knew.

When faced with one more space on my S.A.T. form, I asked my brother, "what should I write here?" *(Says each letter rather than word.)* V-A-S-S-A-R. He heard it was kinda weird...he thought I would probably like it. Like usual, I took his word for it...when I got in to this interesting sounding place, I accepted before even seeing it. (Says *whole word, drawn out.)* V-V-V-A-A-A-S-S-S-S-A-A-A-R-R-R-Right, it's right, the word's just right—I wonder if it's alright there? I wonder if I'll be alright there?

I only realized its fame when I heard Lisa Simpson, after having to give away all her savings, say "there goes my childhood dreams of Vassar." Wow! The only television show I ever watch, and there it was! I hope she gets to go, just so there'll be an episode: *The Simpsons Drive Lisa to Vassar College.* The thought of Homer walking around Vassar is mindboggling...I guess he'd end up in the campus bar, Matthew's Mug. Matthew Vassar was a brewer by trade, who thought it was about time that America had an institution dedicated to the higher education of women...that was in the 1860s...in "the sixties", hey I never realized that! It seems like even in the nineteenth century "the sixties" were "groovy!" I so was lucky...out-of-control trees, beautiful architecture, lots of rabbits hopping around...no frats, no sororities, no football...just two and a half thousand interesting young women and men (they were allowed in in 1969)...and the classes...and the professors! I couldn't of hoped for better, especially from a blind date.

* *(Find IHOP pamphlet.)* August 24, on the way to Poughkeepsie, and poo-kip-see, my mom and dad and I went to the International House of Pancakes where I got one of those maps that has stars across the US on all their locations...Good Things Cookin'. Breakfast, Lunch, and Dinner. I asked them both to write something in it as a souvenir of my collegiate journey. Mom wrote "On the road to Vasar *(Say: "Vazar".)*, with one "s," Love you! MOM" across the top. * *(Find peacock feather and use it to imitate signature on the map.)* Dad signed just across the map. But his signature is like a spread peacock all over Louisiana, and up into Mississippi, Alabama, Tennessee, Kentucky, West Virginia and Pennsylvania. I know the cross-country boldness of my father's signature, I never realized how much...I see now that it makes me part all the Red Seas...sometimes his hand-me-down boldness works for me and other times it turns out to be the Mississippi pumping blood...red sound and fury signifying nothing...but everything else.

Did my father know that our arguments gave me the strength of Moses? How could he? * *(Finds toy sheep.)* I was his Little Bo-Peep.
Little Bo-Peep has lost her sheep
And doesn't know where to find them
Leave them alone and they'll come home
Wagging their tails behind them.

Come home? If we leave...if we leave them alone...then they'll come home? Where do they go? Why do they go? How do they come home? Do they really wag their tails? They don't really come home, do they Dad?

* *(Finds a "problematic" book.)* "No one said it was going to be easy, Little Bo-Peep."

I know, I know...no one said it was going to be easy...I know this. College confirmed my idea that life was a lot easier in class. As soon as I walked out of class, the beautiful campus and all the beautiful people mocked me... you have to trust me, how could I possibly prove it to you? Is there test for pain? *(Cynically offering inside of elbows as bogus "proof.")* Blood test pricks on the inside of my elbows? *(Pain comes back.)* My eyeballs are going to burst, a prick releases wetness and comfort. Pain in leaving...loss...never again...they won't come home...I can't go home. *(Bucks up and gets on soapbox.)* Pain in leaving? Only if you're leaving with nothing.

Who will leave here with only sexual satisfaction and a degree? Some intense hormonal purging and a contract. No blood bonds whatsoever...blood is thicker than water, thicker than anything! I made blood sisters and brothers. I'm so glad that...well, I guess "glad" is the wrong word. Dad, can we really make blood?

* *(Finds a "necessary" book.)* "Necessity is the mother of invention, Little Bo-Peep."

I definitely needed them. I was lucky to have had so many friends in my veins, they pumped me through the years. I still need...I will needIneedIneedIneedIneedIneedI...have Yay! Freshman year my friends began to ferment fast. * *(Opens and drinks wine.)* We weren't fresh for long...but we made wine...wondrous wine with willful wackies watering my weary W-W-W-H-H-H-I-I-I-N-N-N-E-E-E-S.

Did we really make blood between us? From water to blood in one uncontrollable swoop. I know you can make it out of cheap corn syrup and red food coloring, I made a lot of it for a Greek Tragedy once. It involved Bacchus, who I like to call "the fluid god", so we used water, honey, milk, and wine in aluminum turkey roasters and extra large Mrs. White's pickle jars, and made buckets of blood. I loved making it actually, just like the wine friends. *(Say the following while pouring the wine on head until "father"—stop pouring.)* I love my friends, I love my family, I love my father...he died on October 5th, 1989.

* *(Find Freud book.)* MEN! There are a lot of screwed up things about Freud, but I gotta admit that suddenly, every man, everywhere, all of a sudden, was my Dad. Family, friends, lovers, professors, doctors, postmen, bank tellers. MEN!

I met a boy my freshly fatherless year. He came into me, set up camp, then burned it down. I hate camp! I never went! I always came home wagging my tail in the summer (some people think they like camp, but actually they don't like their houses in the summertime). The boy lived in me...as I did in him...at least for awhile...before it became too much. Not enough too muchnot enough too muchnot enough...living inside another as an escape from living inside yourself inevitably becomes uncomfortable. Soon the other's skin becomes just as boring as your own and then what? Instinct sucks us back into ourselves, tails between our legs. He felt for me like something I've never experienced...sleep-away camp: utter immersion, always with the knowledge of the return home at the end of the summer.

Talking about summers...I remember the one after that freshly fatherless year as the worst three months of my entire life. I returned to my house in the suburbs, the one that my family had spent the last two decades in. Just my mother and I in our big empty home full of ghosts. Ghosts from the seventies and eighties. We also had the impending task of selling the empty fullemptyfull of ghosts to the highest bidder. The boy paid me a visit That Summer. He surprised me...I usually love surprises...he showed up unannounced with a buddy of his. I don't think he understood. Myself, my mother, my home, and...my lllllllllove? That would have been okay. But no...a selfish boy and a stranger friend. A couple of greedy guys. Myself, my mother, my home, and a couple of greedy guys. Which one of these things is not like the other? Which one of these things does not belong?

* *(Finds ghost and peanut butter.)* I think the boy and I remind each other of peanut butter and ghosts, they always seem to come up. "Poetry and peanut butter are sticky" sealed off the rawness of a poem he once wrote me. I once asked him if we were going to talk, or just smooth things over with peanut butter and move on. * *(Finds Goober.)* He then brought up the alternative of layering things next to each other, like one of those new fangled peanut butter and jelly combo jars. It's called "Goober"...(you may have seen it in grocery stores, especially if you shop for little P B & J fans). The ghosts came after. He turned into one. Around me he drifts...wide-eyed and clumsy...always floating further away. When I accuse him of disappearing, he claims he just HAD to become a ghost...out of necessity. Okay...I try to sympathize, necessity IS the mother of invention...but I have enough ghosts in my life, thank you! Goober and ghosts. That's all that's left, absurd symbols signifying nothing...but everything else. Goober and ghosts. Sticky and scary...well, the worst is apathy, right? Apathy! Am I kidding? Shhhhhhhhhhhhhhhhhhhhhhhhhhhhhhhhhhhh.

(Whispers.) No more words. *(Pause.)* I just stopped talking. *(Pause.)* I didn't know who the hell I was talking to anymore...I couldn't tell anyone apart. *(Pause. Continues at normal volume.)* I couldn't tell the difference between my longings for my father and my longings for others...especially the boy...Every damn sentiment spilled for everybody sentiment spilled, sentiment spilled sentimentspilled sentimentspilledsentimentspilledsssssssssssssssspp. I just couldn't take it anymore. Everyone had to become no one because I had no idea who I was.

* *(Finds a "complex" book.)* Nothing is black or white, Little Bo-Peep."

(Transition from "story telling" to "stream of consciousness." Make realizations as you speak, rather than before you speak.) No black and no white: GRAY. But black and white are so exciting. Determined. Exhilarating. Dramatic. Attractive. Simple. I'm wearing black...stark black...I've definitely felt black: black blood crust dried gone dead life open wounds bleeding bleeding water tears flowing wet damp dark moist...black. I like black and white, too muchnot enough, emptyfull, sticky and scary. I like tension, gray is too loose and blah. Blah blah blah, is the world blah? Blah blah? Gray glop. The whole world may have well been gray glop when I found out the person I lllllllloved, loved my weakness, not my strength. Was I ever strong then? Are we ever...when we are in love? Does losing a loved one take away strength...or give

it? (*Says the following lines while taking off graduation robe, revealing gray clothing, throwing robe in trunk after last question.*) Or both? What is love? What is strength? What is weak? What is gray?

(*With resentment.*) Everything boils down to gray. A grayish muck.

(*With pleasure.*) Everything boils down to gray. A grayish softness.

Is it weak to admit that you really love the colour gray? The comfort...the soothing ease. Or...hate it? The dull, compromising blend. A mixture of black and white. It takes the edges off black and white. Gray takes the sting out of black and white. Gray takes the falsity out of black and white. Gray is a balance...between black and white.

My father taught me the lesson he always wanted to teach me when he died. The lesson of gray.

(*Imitates clichéd Hollywood ending.*) EXIT: leaves walking into a gray sky. He left...he's not coming home...I left...I can't go home...leave them alone and they'll come homemmmmmmmmmm.

What does it mean to lose your sheep? Can it mean anything if we believe they'll always come home wagging their tails? Maybe they really do come home in a way we don't understand...maybe they don't. When it's over, it's really over. You never told that one to Little Bo-Peep! No profound epilogues...just nothing. (*Pauses and ponders the notion of nothingness.*)

Meaninglessness...what does that mean? Just because we die, things don't have meaning? If we lived forever in this world would then things have meaning? Or would it be the same mundane madness again and again andagainandagainandagainandagain would that be good? Would that be meaningful? Death GIVES meaning: we are mortal, being human MEANS being mortal. But can death be the ONLY thing that gives us our meaning?

* (*Finds "logical" book.*) "That's neither here nor there, Little Bo-Peep."

Look, you have to let me figure out where my sheep went! I can't leave them...or you...alone...okay? I know that you're not coming home...alright? Why can't sheep just stay home and wag their tails? Leave them alone and they'll come home...bullshit! When I left, you left too. Why leave them alone? Why leave?

(Return to "story telling" for as long as it lasts.) I certainly wouldn't want people to act if it was the very last time they were going to see me every time we parted company. Well...maybe just my closest friends...maybe just my family. I DON'T HAVE A CHOICE! Was I supposed to know that my Rosh Hashannah visit of 1989 was the LAST time I would EVER see my father? How can we know when people are just going to leave like that? What the hell are we supposed to think, say, feel, do in the meantime? LIVE?!?!?!?!? What does that mean? There's that fuckin' word again... "mean", what a measly meandering "me" word...maybe that's it! It's a "me" word, a word that people get caught up in when they get caught up *(Self-referential gesture.)* "me", in themselves. Is me...aning a self-centered word? Maybe the only way to live in the face of death is not to think about me...aning: dealing with death daily might get a little overwhelming. Dealing with death dailydealingwithdeathdailydealingwithdeathdailyhmmmmmmmmmmmmmm... "me...aning". Meaning the Me Word.

Memememememememememememememememewhen does it stop? Self absorption. Can we really get sucked up by ourselves? Are we like sponges slurping slurpingslurpingslurpingllllllllovingklickinglikinglaughing? When do we squeeze out? I hope it happens...it has to happen before we drooldemistifydelineatedigestdefydenydevastatedigdrydribble...die! Die...I'm going to die, you're going to die, you're going to die, and you're going to die. Can't argue that one just like chickens and eggs, apples and oranges, or ghosts and goobers...phew! That's a relief! Is it a relief? We all know that we are going to die...but how 'bout this: I'm dyING you're dyING, you're dyING, and you're dyING...we are all dying...well, in the process of dying...or wait! WAIT! I thought we were LIVING...hey! Are they the same thing? I couldn't have been the first one to figure that out! So what? That's great! We are all dying we are all living we are all dying we are all livingdyinglivingdyinglivingdyinglivingdying. We are all dying in the process of living and living in the process of dying...we're staying in the process of leaving.

Paradox, I love that word. I don't know why I should love it...it's the singular most frustrating infuriating disempowering word in the world, the universe. But it's not REALLY, I mean, let's see what do I ME...AN, MEMEMEMEMEMEMEMEME I mean that paradox is empowering, it is a word that makes me feel okay because it makes contradictions come together into one cool sounding word... *(Say "paradox" with a drawn out cool tone.)* paradoxxxxxxdo paradoxes stop? Or is it the nature of one never to stop? If our livesdeaths are paradoxes does that mean that we never stop? If my father is still in this class ring, that I wear on the middle finger of my left hand, even though he wore it on his pinky (thank God because otherwise it wouldn't fit—did somebody know that?) does diddoesdiddoesdiddoesdiddoesdiddoesdiddoes that mean he never stops?

(Looks at rings.) Berkeley 1951. He left, but he stayed.

Vassar 1993...I'm leaving, but I'm staying.

(Look around and in trunk.) What's coming with me?

What am I leaving here?

What's coming with you? What are you leaving here?

(Get into trunk.) We've all come to leave.

(Approach lighting candle—hesitate to light it according to following questions, which struggle to reconcile "the end" and continuing on.)

So why do we light candles for those who leave?

Who should I light a candle for?

Why should I light a candle?

Who should I light a candle for?

How can I choose?

Why should I light a candle?

Who should I light a candle for?

Him?

Her?

Them?

(Refer to people in audience.) You?

You?

You?

Me? *(Pause at prospect of staging one's own funeral.)*

(Resolved in thought that we're all in the same boat.) Everybody.

(Light candle.) Why should I light a candle?

Haven't we all come to leave...things behind?

(Close trunk over head.)

END OF PLAY

Smith and Kraus *Books For Actors*
THE MONOLOGUE SERIES
> The Best Men's / Women's Stage Monologues of 1994
> The Best Men's / Women's Stage Monologues of 1993
> The Best Men's / Women's Stage Monologues of 1992
> The Best Men's / Women's Stage Monologues of 1991
> The Best Men's / Women's Stage Monologues of 1990
> One Hundred Men's / Women's Stage Monologues from the 1980's
> 2 Minutes and Under: Original Character Monologues for Actors
> Street Talk: Original Character Monologues for Actors
> Uptown: Original Character Monologues for Actors
> Ice Babies in Oz: Original Character Monologues for Actors
> Monologues from Contemporary Literature: Volume I
> Monologues from Classic Plays
> 100 Great Monologues from the Renaissance Theatre
> 100 Great Monologues from the Neo-Classical Theatre
> 100 Great Monologues from the 19th C. Romantic and Realistic Theatres

YOUNG ACTORS SERIES
> Great Scenes and Monologues for Children
> New Plays from A.C.T.'s Young Conservatory
> Great Scenes for Young Actors from the Stage
> Great Monologues for Young Actors
> Multicultural Monologues for Young Actors
> Multicultural Scenes for Young Actors

SCENE STUDY SERIES
> Scenes From Classic Plays 468 B.C. to 1960 A.D.
> The Best Stage Scenes of 1994
> The Best Stage Scenes of 1993
> The Best Stage Scenes of 1992
> The Best Stage Scenes for Men / Women from the 1980's

CONTEMPORARY PLAYWRIGHTS SERIES
> Romulus Linney: 17 Short Plays
> Eric Overmyer: Collected Plays
> Lanford Wilson: 21 Short Plays
> William Mastrosimone: Collected Plays
> Horton Foote: 4 New Plays
> Israel Horovitz: 16 Short Plays
> Terrence McNally: 15 Short Plays
> Humana Festival '93: The Complete Plays
> Humana Festival '94: The Complete Plays
> Women Playwrights: The Best Plays of 1992
> Women Playwrights: The Best Plays of 1993
> EST Marathon '94: One-Act Plays

GREAT TRANSLATION FOR ACTORS SERIES
> The Wood Demon by Anton Chekhov, tr. by N. Saunders & F. Dwyer
> The Sea Gull by Anton Chekhov, tr. by N. Saunders & F. Dwyer
> Three Sisters by Anton Chekhov, tr. by Lanford Wilson
> Mercadet by Honoré de Balzac, tr. by Robert Cornthwaite
> Villeggiatura: The Trilogy by Carlo Goldoni, tr. by Robert Cornthwaite

CAREER DEVELOPMENT SERIES
> The Job Book: 100 Acting Jobs for Actors
> The Smith and Kraus Monologue Index
> What to Give Your Agent for Christmas and 100 Other Tips for the Working Actor
> The Camera Smart Actor
> The Sanford Meisner Approach
> Anne Bogart: Viewpoints
> The Actor's Chekhov
> Kiss and Tell: Restoration Scenes, Monologues, & History
> Cold Readings: Some Do's and Don'ts for Actors at Auditions

If you require pre-publication information about upcoming Smith and Kraus books, you may receive our semi-annual catalogue, free of charge, by sending your name and address to *Smith and Kraus Catalogue, P.O. Box 127, One Main Street, Lyme, NH 03768. Or call us at (800) 895-4331, fax (603) 795-4427.*